Sleeping with Strangers

What to wear? *Bringing Up Baby* (1938)—with Cary Grant,
Katharine Hepburn, May Robson, and a naked wire-haired terrier.
But everyone was wired in delicate situations like this.

Sleeping with Strangers

HOW THE MOVIES

SHAPED DESIRE

David Thomson

 ALFRED A. KNOPF · NEW YORK · 2019

THIS IS A BORZOI BOOK
PUBLISHED BY ALFRED A. KNOPF

www.aaknopf.com

Knopf, Borzoi Books, and the colophon
are registered trademarks of Penguin Random House LLC.

Library of Congress Cataloging-in-Publication Data
Names: Thomson, David., [date] author.
Title: Sleeping with strangers : how the movies shaped desire / David Thomson.
Description: First edition. | New York : Alfred A. Knopf, 2019.
Identifiers: LCCN 2018017604 | ISBN 9781101946992 (hardcover) |
ISBN 9781101947005 (ebook)
Subjects: LCSH: Men in motion pictures. | Machismo in motion pictures. |
Homosexuality in motion pictures. | Women in motion pictures.
Classification: LCC PN1995.9.M46 T57 2019 | DDC 791.43/65211—dc23
LC record available at https://lccn.loc.gov/2018017604

Front-of-jacket image: *Blue Velvet* © 1986 Orion Pictures Corporation. All Rights Reserved.
Courtesy of MGM Media Licensing. Print: Everett Collection
Jacket design by Carol Devine Carson

Manufactured in the United States of America
First Edition

33614080865503

For Kieran Hickey

The condition of memory, that painful place to which we return over and over because a fundamental question is still unresolved: something happened to us years ago which was important, yet we hardly know if an angel kissed us then, or a witch, whether we were brave or timid.

—NORMAN MAILER, "A Course in Filmmaking,"
Maidstone, 1971

Because I just went gay all of a sudden!

—DAVID HUXLEY (Cary Grant)
in *Bringing Up Baby,* 1938

This business, movies, is all about two things—power and sex. And guess what, they're the same thing.

—PETER GUBER, 1989

Psychologically I'm very confused, but personally I don't feel bad at all.

—KLARA NOVAK (Margaret Sullavan)
in *The Shop Around the Corner,* 1940

Contents

Sleeping with Strangers

Naked at the Window

Faye Dunaway and Warren Beatty set up as *Bonnie and Clyde* (1967).
It's a production still that knows what the movie is about, including
the uneasiness within the couple. Fifty-two years later, Bonnie's hurt look
is explained: she told *his* story—but what about hers? It's time.

THE MOVIE SCREEN IS A WINDOW, and the trick of the medium is to let us feel we can pass through it. I saw this film five times in a week in 1967 in London. Did it change my life? It ruined it. Made me a prisoner of desire.

The picture is set in a wild Southwest, some time ago. Two young animals meet and sniff each other out. They are so vivid, and their display is so emphatic, it has to be a movie. It says—*look*! The animals feel an urge to mate. That seems natural, biological, and cinematic, but then the male turns uneasy. This distresses her, and it saddens him. Still, their companionship prevails and they become fellow-raiders in their terrain. This makes them notorious and hunted, until she sings a song about their fame. That frees him. They fall in love. Then they do it, as so many have done. *It*. They really get it on—whatever *it* is. An idyll follows before vengeful guardians of order in the terrain find them and slaughter them. So the pair die together, a legend of outlaw sex and violence.

This is not the only way to describe *Bonnie and Clyde* (1967). You could say it's about two underprivileged kids finding attention and loot in Oklahoma and Texas in the early 1930s. It's a fable of Depression and self-expression such as we believe we deserve because the U.S. insists on the pursuit of happiness: that has been one of humanity's best daft ideas, though other cultures regard it as fatuous immaturity. That figures, because America, the movies, and *Bonnie and Clyde* are all resolutely youthful.

We are in a shabby bedroom in 1931 in the sketchy outlands of West Dallas. That year has been established with still photographs of Bonnie Parker and Clyde Barrow. Except that these pictures are sepia looka-likes for 1931 in which Faye Dunaway and Warren Beatty are pretending to be the two outlaws. Retrospective selfies. Photographs of the real Parker and Barrow do exist. They hint at poverty, hardship, the heat and dust of Texas, and its awesome distances in which it was easier to feel lost than found. The real Bonnie and Clyde might never have got past waiting tables in Midland or Odessa.

Bonnie looks sharp-faced and poverty pretty; she is narrow-eyed with a closed-mouth smile, and no makeup. She was certainly not the wide-eyed, drop-dead Faye Dunaway, the first person we see in that dusty bedroom.

Dunaway was twenty-six in 1967. She had gone to the University of Florida before graduating from Boston University. She had been in theater in the East for several years and Elia Kazan had cast her in a small part in his 1964 production of Arthur Miller's *After the Fall*. She was a unanimous knockout: that was in her physical being and her professional and cosmetic training. No one made movies in 1967 without a knockout as the female lead.

"Knockout" is an important word; it may even be disastrous. No matter that they were said to be lifelike, movies then were crowded with exceptional lookers. The culture quickly raised them to be the best-known people in the world. But a strange dysfunction came into being. The world at large was not populated with knockouts. Most of us looked ordinary or homely and felt some shame about that in the light of the screen. Though America was avowedly egalitarian, it had created a way of being seen that cut across any hope for humble human value with the flourish of a holdup.

This unnerving contract exists in the way Bonnie is discovered and Faye revealed. We are observing a fictionalized character and a real actress, but on first sight it is the actress we see. She is looking in a mirror, applying lipstick, so we see her face and its urge to be more beautiful. That mirror is a version of the flat screen we are looking at: its presence makes us more aware of our own watching. The mirror can be a character or a conscience in movies.

We realize this woman is naked. Her nudity dawns on us slowly, but then we want to see more. That is not out of line. We are at a movie where everything has been arranged for us: if we sit in the dark the brilliant life spills in our laps like a kitten or goodies. Watching is already sexual, yet slightly morbid; doing it from a secure dark suggests stealth and even the possibility that these live beings may be dead. Still, is it normal that a young woman in Texas in 1931 is putting on her lipstick while naked? The exhibitionism is as pointed as an aside in the script that says, "Her attitude and appraisal of herself here are touched with narcissism." Touched! It's what keeps her glowing in the dust.

That's a clue to things in a movie being as much show-offy as naturalistic. Our young woman goes to her window, which is another screen, both a way of parading and a kind of withholding. She looks through the glass and shouts out, "Hey, boy, what you doin' with my mamma's car?" It's a southern voice, but one that has been taught. It's lowdown but clear, and spread like jam. She's acting.

She directs her question at a young man in a dark suit who is nosing around the parked vehicle. He looks up and sees what we know: that she is naked at the window—though a screen and frosted glass give her some protection. But that makes his gazing as ardent as ours. And he *is* a good-looking guy—Warren Beatty did nothing to chase that idea out of our heads, or his own. He stares at her and she knows why he's staring: narcissism and being on show have their reward. As the script says, "She doesn't move or make any attempt to cover herself."

The movie has not conveyed the enervated souls customary in West Dallas in 1931 (average summer high temperature 96 degrees, without air-conditioning).

The two of them meet up on the street after she has thrown on a flimsy summer dress. (Underwear is not indicated.) They talk in a mixture of flirt and challenge. He says he's been in prison for armed robbery. She thinks he's boasting. He shows her his gun, a revolver; he holds it in his lap and she touches it in a gesture that was wacky even in 1967. But the equation of sex and violence was more than most films dared. As if to enact that mating dance, he then pulls a modest armed robbery, and Dunaway makes it clear that this outlawry has driven Bonnie horny to the edge of orgasm.

Then the unexpected happens. They race off in a stolen car and she is ready to have him and to be had. Right there in the car, *please.* She is demanding enough to be more aggressive than he is. He backs off, flustered and embarrassed, and tells her he "ain't much of a lover boy." She is frustrated and humiliated, for Clyde doesn't seem quite capable of getting it up—perhaps he doesn't do it on the first holdup? "Your advertising is just dandy," she tells him bitterly. "Folks'd just never guess you don't have a thing to sell."

A dramatic arc is set up in this thwarted relationship. The coitus interruptus will pay off later in a conventional love scene out in the fields when Clyde realizes that Bonnie has "told his story" by sending her ballad about them to the newspapers. They kiss fully, or as if for the first time, and then "They begin to make love," as the script advises, and the camera shot fades away. In the final shootout their shattered bodies rock and roll like lovers at last fulfilled. Censorship (in its dying days) stood by, helpless.

This seems a delayed enactment of classic courtship and union, with just a quick hint that Clyde might be impotent, or a suggestion that one day sex, our *it,* might not always be so compelling. After all, a film knows in its bones that, despite all our watching, we can't make love with the screen. Or not until the technology advances.

This famous movie might have worked differently. In the original screenplay, by Robert Benton and David Newman, when Bonnie and Clyde picked up C. W. Moss (Michael J. Pollard) for their gang, a ménage à trois came into being. Moss, a sweet, aimless boy, was to have sex with both Bonnie and Clyde. The supposition was that Bonnie needed to get sex somewhere, while Clyde had homosexual tendencies possibly acquired during his time in prison. He had killed a man there who, it's implied, had been assaulting him sexually.

Was Clyde gay, or just disgusted by any homosexual attempt upon him? Mart Crowley, himself gay, author of *The Boys in the Band,* had once worked on a film script about gangsters from the 1930s. He thought he recalled a suggestion in his reading about Clyde Barrow's sexual habits and he mentioned it to producer Warren Beatty in passing as *Bonnie and Clyde* was being prepared. I asked Crowley what he was sure he knew about Clyde, and he admitted he could not recall the exact history or its reliability.

This is common in a culture with mixed feelings over education and dreaming. Legends and gossip exist about gayness, and firm evidence slips away in a community of gossips and storytellers. So much sexual reputation blooms in the hothouse of half-knowing. What actually happened when *we* made love with *so-and-so* (remember?) is a haze of recollection or reconstruction—so-and-so may wonder if he or she was even there when they hear our version.

Benton and Newman clung to the threesome; they said it was non-negotiable; and Warren Beatty had seemed to go along with that. They should have known, though, that their star and producer didn't do "non-negotiable." Well before shooting started, Beatty made it clear that a threesome would be going too far. He was not prepared to have his male authenticity put in doubt. It was also required that the female love interest not be romantically compromised. Censorship was breaking down in the 1960s (a woman at her window could be half-naked), but there were few films where a heroine made the "mistake" of finding love and sex with anyone other than the hero, or her costar. She could not look forward to several men. Cross that line and the icon became fast and loose, and suddenly undesirable. Most movies still conform to that scheme of women as sexual property.

There was another, more potent reason: *Bonnie and Clyde* was intended as a mainstream success, a film to excite a large audience. (Eventually, after early doubts, it did turn out that way.) But in 1967, it was impossible for a film to show a bisexual hero and have him cherished (and desired) at the end of the picture. So Beatty and director Arthur Penn agreed that any bisexuality would distract from the dynamic of Bonnie and Clyde getting it on, when the *it* was a grail-like satisfaction that we had been waiting for since the first scenes.

In the rush of *Bonnie and Clyde,* it is curious that Clyde doesn't initially give Bonnie what she wants. It is odder still that the film doesn't explain this reluctance. Has Clyde had an injury, like the one that left Jake lacking in Hemingway's *The Sun Also Rises*? Is his wounded foot a clue? He can't find Bonnie less than appealing—that is fanciful in view of Faye Dunaway's look. Is he being perverse—rather like Beatty himself—as if to say, "You're going to have to want me a lot more before I come across?" Is he as magical as women can be in the movies? Or is Clyde gay in a film that can't admit it? If they're in a movie, why aren't they *doing it*?

Human beings had sex before photography: that statement may seem naive, but it is a reminder that our understanding of life is guided by the resources we have for depicting it. People had sex with people they knew then in the dark or unseen ages; that sounds obvious, but then consider how far the photograph permits the thought of sex with people you *don't* know (and how far that reappraises sex as an imaginary experience). Sleeping with strangers.

Once upon a time, princes and princesses, or bakers and their wives, slept with available neighbors, or they forced their will on people they captured or owned. Those rapist events might turn into marriage, and even "happy" marriage, for marriages have been more susceptible to arrangement than the code of true love cares to believe. Humans have not always trusted sincerity and chance in getting together. Incest occurred more often than we want to imagine now: family was the chief pool of availability. The human species knew that sex, or intercourse, could lead to pregnancy, and they pursued that imperative out of some longing for eternity and parenting, and because they knew that so many infants died young that reproduction needed to be repeated. This blunt accounting doesn't mean there wasn't pleasure in sex—you can feel it in literature and painting and in the swoon of music.

When photography arrived, earnest justifications were offered that said, Well, this is what Queen Victoria looks like, or George Eliot, or Eleonora Duse. But there were also "dirty" postcards of some nymph from Brooklyn or Balham who'd dropped her clothes for a plate of Irish stew and then gone around the world as masturbatory solace for lonely men.

Desire was being democratized and commodified: we have not found a way to have one without the other. As movies began, the attempt to be artistic could not shrug off this erotic undercurrent. And you know which urge excited the business. Movies told uplifting stories, but they did sex and violence in the back room. That tension was everywhere and made dynamic by the medium's voyeuristic pressure. Whatever we were looking at, *we* were in the dark, and furtive.

We customers were peeping toms not known about by the people on the screen. Schemes of censorship were swiftly enlisted to keep the business respectable, but that only made the illicit or forbidden more tempting. Some moviemakers tried to say their business was art, but we the people knew we were peeping at wonders of desire we were not usually allowed to see. So movie offered the Pyramids and coronation parades. D. W. Griffith said he was showing us the Civil War and the Ford's Theater where Lincoln was shot. But in *The Birth of a Nation* the melodrama cloaked the steady threat of rape for white women.

That was deplorable but enticing. To see the forbidden is to gaze on things we cannot own up to. In the movies, as well as life, desire is contingent on things we cannot quite have. As you may have noticed, satisfaction can kill desire just as desire can make you forget your status quo. That's how *Bonnie and Clyde* shook my life to pieces.

But there was another strain at work, something never offered until moving photography. Behold, here is the lifelike breathing of lovely living creatures, like wild animals in a zoo—I was not speaking casually of Bonnie and Clyde as creatures on show. And just as the movies seemed to say, here are men and women, take your pick, think of the screen as twin bathrooms, gentlemen and ladies, so the screen actually offered both. For a man, it said, you want to see pretty women? Very well. But perhaps you would like to see great guys, too; after all, desire is a limitless energy, and just as you might want to have Bonnie you can think of being Clyde (even if you look like C.W.).

There's a scene soon after the first holdup and Clyde's reluctance to be a lover boy in which he diverts Bonnie's frustration by telling her she deserves more because, "You may be the best damn girl in Texas." As proof, he takes her to a dejected diner. A waitress comes by, "a cheap, gaudy dame," the script notes, nearly middle-aged and desperate to look younger. Bonnie has already told him she is a waiter, too. Clyde sees a stupid kiss curl on this waitress and he realizes Bonnie has one like it, too. He tells her, "Change that, I don't like it": he has become her producer and a director—he is making the movie (and while Arthur Penn directed it, and did it very well, Beatty was in charge of the picture).

Notice the schizoid tendency: the movie plays with the idea that Bonnie Parker could remain a waitress until the day she drops, reliant on tips, grease, and furtive groping. Bonnie is also Faye Dunaway, ignoring the preposterousness of a woman so ravishing being confined to Texas diners. She is a movie star, acting coy. And so is he. They are fake, daring us to notice.

In life, Clyde Barrow had a long, oval face, ears bigger than Clark Gable's, and a rather oppressed look. He was like a man who had been in prison, and maybe he had been raped there enough to nurture a bitter edge of violence. In a line of male stars that goes from Richard Barthelmess, John Gilbert, and Rudolph Valentino to Robert Taylor, Tyrone Power, Marlon Brando, and Montgomery Clift, Beatty was desirable, egotistical, shy but vain, declaratory yet unusually secretive— it was his way of being smart. He looked and felt like a star capable of running residual percentages in his head, not a hapless Texas wastrel on the loose. And we accept that, because desire is the area of life or private illusion where even slaves are unrestricted. We cannot be deprived of what we dream of, no matter if we're homeless, sick and out of work, or in a cancer ward. And for the bulk of human beings in the age of movie and democracy, sex was their one unmitigated freedom. Millions of people will die treasuring the two or three great lays of their life.

A man watching the film may desire Bonnie, but he could also be attracted to Clyde in a spirit of emulation. There's a raffish nonchalance in the way Beatty's Barrow tells his brother Buck how he hated prison so much one day he chopped off a couple of his own toes just to escape work detail. Then—you know what?—a few days later he got paroled. Beatty sighs and grins, and murmurs, "Ain't life grand," a dreamy fatalism that lifts his mundane life and carries it on angel's wings up to the poetry of stardom.

Beatty on screen never had a purer moment—cocksure, smartass, stupid, and weirdly lucky. It's the bravado of an insouciant outlaw, the male charm that sustained this film through violence, bank robbery, and getting it on so that the actor playing the lead robber ended up very wealthy.

Warren Beatty isn't gay. A folkloric industry stressed that for decades and idealized his private life to the point of making it axiomatic. Nor do you in your dark have to be gay to enjoy the film. But there's a gayness in this medium that we're never going to shrug off, an attitude that says you can make do with sex—it's great—but don't fall for the whole construct of romance, marriage, being happy, and buying the package. It's the point at which narcissism makes us envious, and it's there in Beatty the earnest producer whispering past the toothpick in his mouth, "Are you looking at me? Aren't movies crazy?"

I'm suggesting a way in which the heroism and the romancing of movies became tongue-in-cheek as the decades slipped by. This leaves a tension in our picture show between belief and what some people begin to call camp. With *Bonnie and Clyde,* it was the conjunction of trying to believe we were in 1931, while knowing it was 1967. The design of that film had an instinct for translating gangster energies and antibanking pieties into the resistance welling up in privileged kids in America in the late sixties.

That slight look askance is close to disbelief. It's a reason why half the country—no meager 11 percent or whatever—began to slip toward gay irony by the millennium. And that is how the movies have exerted such a gravitational pull on the spirit of gay liberation, or same-sex marriage. Reactionary homophobes sometimes disapprove of gayness because of its apparent promiscuity. But the new feeling had an instinct for a deeper ruefulness over how our precious, sacred love lives could turn into the same old same thing. So why be so solemn over it, why insist on Molly Bloom's ecstatic "Yes" or Connie Chatterley's oceanic stirring, when the big show of sex can leave intelligent people sighing, "Well, was that it?" before dropping off to sleep?

In 1967, some viewers were disconcerted by the laughter in *Bonnie and Clyde.* Were we really chuckling as faces were split open? Looking on the bright side, hero-worshippers explained this away as the creative juxtaposition of contrary moods. But a deeper amusement was directed at ourselves for taking movies so gravely, instead of seeing that they were games or myths. Why be surprised if movies were at the dawn of a daring proposition: that they were dreamlike, not to be trusted as reality, hardly a model for real life? Yet perhaps it was the silliness that let our fantasies go free.

A vital part of that was the creation of sexual attitudes that offset old codes of male supremacy, or humorless authority. In our time, we have seen great advances in gay liberation, but we still need to be let out of the prison that believes power and leadership, guns, godliness, and virtue are the right of tough guys. The American idea will not survive those narrow-minded zealots.

Going to movies had been a courtship rite. Boyfriends and girl-friends went to the pictures, held hands in the dark, and sometimes more than hands. The movies they watched were laden with romantic meetings and sexual longing. It's a wonder more couples weren't married in chapels named Odeon, Granada, or Rialto. Not long after the couples got home, romance and sex fell in line with What's for dinner? and Would you make your bed for once? (Romantics like to leave the sheets in chaos as if some great photographer will capture the sexual glory.)

At the movies, however, the ordinary state of marriage was seldom explored. That substantial temporal experience was neglected once the arousal of wooing had been handled. "Domesticity" can be a depressing word, no matter that all people who are afraid—like all of us—cling to the comfort of "home" as a retreat or a place of safety. Moreover, it was around 1967 that movies became bolder about showing intercourse and nakedness. This seemed sensational at first, but it proved a feeble distraction that sucked much of the imagining from eroticism.

As soon as our beauties, Bonnie and Clyde, have got it on, they're gone. No time for boredom, stale habit, or taking out the garbage. Instead, they get one of the greatest orgasms ever put on screen. Their bodies writhe in ecstatic immolation, and they're still rocking fifty years later. The characters are dead and the two elderly players seemed confused when handing out Best Picture at the Oscars in February 2017. But their 1967 movie guessed that sexual climax and death could make a binding marriage.

A hundred years ago, movies were the industrialization of desire, a way of introducing the masses to sex as pleasure. So sleeping with strangers—with ghosts on the screen—was a new element in Romanticism as well as romance. It gave us such fun and it transformed our sense of self and possibility.

The material of this book is beauty on screen, desire in our heads, and the alchemy they make in the dark. But the book also sees these topics becoming a crisis in America's cultural development, and a struggle between delusions of male supremacy and a spirit of gay resistance. That's not all, for the advance of feminine significance and power is another air being inhaled. *Sleeping with Strangers* traces the interweaving of macho confidence, feminine personality, and gay wit, and it knows the struggle is not done yet. America is in the balance.

1

The Iceman Cometh

Kieran Hickey on Streatham High Road in London
some night in the early 1960s

IN CHILDHOOD, I had to be taken out of cinemas in tears, because the show overwhelmed me.

Long before education and temperament taught me to be a critic, judging whether Hamlet, a Doris Day song or *The Third Man* had been "well done" or not, I had been plunged into the alternative reality on the screen. I longed to be there. This was fantasy, not criticism. And still is.

I was told I was too "involved" with the lives on screen. Loving them so much, I could not endure their peril. But perhaps I was just empty, anxious to be filled. I wanted heroes, and I preferred them handsome, gentle, and wise, like Lassie, or Montgomery Clift in *Red River*. I waited for movie women who didn't know they were being watched. I tried to be there with them, but I could not get *into* the screen.

One of the few things to trust about the movies is that pictures seen at an impressionable age mean the most. Let us say this span usually lasts from about five to twenty. But the charm can linger past seventy-five. The children of the dark do not easily give up their secret love. Or the fear.

If you have been moved and formed by movies, don't let an educated historical-critical approach to them tame the mad experience. If you have been moved, respect that; for the experiment suggests that you exist and are of value. Going to the movies did not permit objectivity or critical intelligence. It was like meeting a stranger and feeling affinity.

Kieran Hickey was tall, gaunt, and rather forbidding. His close-cut black hair already had salt in it. He looked at me and demanded, "Well, what do *you* want to say?" There was an edge of hostility, so I retaliated. His surname was Hickey, and I called him "Iceman," because I had just seen Eugene O'Neill's *The Iceman Cometh* in London in 1958 where the character Theodore Hickman is called "Hickey." I had sat through the five hours of that play, carried along on its roaming speeches.

We met in early 1960. It was an exciting time and it seemed to be ours. The air felt fresh with starting. Some of us were determined to be entering a new world, no longer weighed on by the mistakes of sad elders. That was a vanity, of course, but young generations need that much gasoline vapor to see if they have an engine. There was a feeling in 1960 that change was coming: it was like a panther of the future coiled and ready to spring. It might be an apocalypse of nuclear testing or the verdict in the *Lady Chatterley's Lover* trial; it might be the erotic slashing in *Psycho* (which opened in London in August of that year) or that young, flirty Kennedy who was elected president in November.

In London, people wondered if the burden of winning the Second World War was over at last. This is not being snide about that war. No one doubted that it was a necessity and the last clear call in history, perhaps. Every war since then has brought disaster and undermined our faith in battle.

Why am I giving you history and memoir? Because you cannot get close to movies without grasping the mindset in which they were received. When you go to the movies, you take your history with you. The fantasy is about *you*.

Britain had been depleted by the war, and it recovered with invalid slowness. During my childhood there were untended bombed houses all over London and rationing of many foodstuffs that only ceased in the mid-1950s. By then, an awed relaxation was stretching in Britain. The prime minister from 1957 onward, Harold Macmillan, made a mocking point of telling his people, the proles, we had never had it so good. For my family and so many others that was probably true. We were getting used to our National Health Service and the 1944 Education Act. I went to a school, Dulwich College, my parents could not have afforded, so the London County Council paid for me to be there.

At eighteen I was educated—better than I knew at the time. I was horny and had lost my virginity to a smart, difficult, appealing girl in south London—we got rid of hers at the same time. It was self-help. The sex was pressing, but we were more moved by being in love. We were high-minded about sex and love being "integrated." I was hooked on this girl, crazy about movies, and tired of school. I also dreamed of fabulous screen goddesses, from Yvonne De Carlo to Rhonda Fleming.

Hickey jerked me out of a daydream: "You look as if you think you have something to say." He was tough about it, but I detected a tease or a challenge. We were standing on the steps outside the National Film Theatre on London's South Bank. I love that place more than I ever could Dulwich College or Oxford.

In my teens, I had spent increasing time watching movies. Knowing so little, I saw whatever my local cinemas chose to play—those flashy palaces on the high street, more lively than the churches. That automatic moviegoing had taken me to decisive events in my upbringing, movies that set me up emotionally for the big show of life. That list would include *A Place in the Sun, From Here to Eternity, Rear Window, East of Eden, Rebel Without a Cause, Funny Face, The Searchers,* Stanley Kubrick's *The Killing,* Anthony Mann's *Men in War,* and Orson Welles's *Touch of Evil.*

Already, my life was a conflict between sensationalism and reflection. But the profound emotional experiences of my life were ignored by school. At Dulwich, the boys were taught to respect the tradition of the polar explorer Ernest Shackleton and Trevor Bailey, a great cricketer. But in all my time there, no one mentioned or knew that the director Michael Powell had been to our school.

To get into Oxford—the Dulwich plan that I loyally went along with—I was reading Shakespeare, Milton, Pope, Wordsworth, and Gerard Manley Hopkins, as well as assessing Lewis Namier's reconstruction of English politics in the eighteenth century. I read Latin—Tacitus and Virgil. (The school didn't risk giving us Ovid. We did "sexual reproduction" at school, but only as practiced by rats. No teacher dared take on human desire.) That education had no room for research papers on Orson Welles. So I wrote in the school magazine, *The Alleynian,* about James Dean, Alfred Hitchcock, and Ingmar Bergman.

I was getting that school workload done as quickly as possible to leave time for the swansong of mainstream films in the late 1950s. You have to be lucky in life, and being movie-mad then was to be blessed. In my A-level years (adequate passes would make me Oxford-bound) along came *Vertigo, Bonjour Tristesse, Man of the West, North by Northwest, Rio Bravo, Anatomy of a Murder,* and *Some Like It Hot.* Namier never had a chance.

In the course of 1959, I told Dulwich and Oxford no thanks. My teachers at Dulwich were horrified; they said I was tossing away the opportunity of my life. What else will you do? they demanded. I told them I had seen an advertisement for the London School of Film Technique, a place where you learned how to make films. Where is that? they sneered. Just down the road, I said, in Brixton. I had hardly been out of London in my life then. What was the need?

Brixton? they groaned. Even by south London standards, Brixton was reckoned a dump, and dangerous. It had become home to immigrants from the West Indies, and that prospect of racial ghetto was seized upon by Oswald Mosley as a site for provocative meetings of his Union Movement (the label "fascist" had gone out of fashion, but that's what it was).

"Well, speak up," said Kieran, "or I shall become very bored." Somehow I didn't want to bore him. You must have had occasions in your life when all of a sudden—with a man or a woman—you've met someone and known you had to hold their interest.

Kieran was from Dublin and five years older than me. He had been born in 1936, on February 29. He made a sour joke out of that bad luck because three years out of four he missed his birthday.

We were in love with film and the dream of making our own movies. But we had Gerard Manley Hopkins in common, too. I had been taught about his sprung rhythm, his unexpected words, his yearning energy for nature. But I had learned little about the man. Our teachers never discussed the authors as beings who had been alive once. Kieran knew Hopkins's history and he felt for it. The poet had died at forty-four, in Dublin, buried in Glasnevin Cemetery, crushed by the work of being a priest. Kieran admitted that earlier in life he had thought of being a priest. In my learned, critic's voice I said of Hopkins, "Sounds to me as if he might have been a little queer." That was the word then in robust circles. Kieran nodded, wistful and unsurprised.

When I met Kieran I had done two months at the London School of Film Technique on Electric Avenue in Brixton (that address was the most exciting thing about it). The school then was not far from a racket: it had more students from overseas than from Britain—I met the first American I had known there. It had minimum production equipment and uncertain teaching, so there was a hum of grievance and paranoia as some alert students "appropriated" the cameras and taught themselves. That was proper preparation for the jungle called the film business. Still, I was having to mask the letdown on Electric Avenue. Then I noticed this aloof Irishman who came in some evenings to edit a film he had begun at the school. In a cheap suit and tie he looked like a bank clerk, rejecting the student air of the place. He was famously aloof, an Iceman, discouraging anyone who tried to talk to him let alone look at his film on the Moviola.

I learned his name on the steps of the National Film Theatre, where we were introduced. I was at the NFT because I had guessed that seeing old films was the best education I could find. Kieran was there, too, with the same habit, and that's when he looked at me so sternly and said, "Well, what do *you* want to say?"

It was a penetrating question, for I was still living with a stammer that left me timid about uttering the lofty and searching thoughts I hoped I had. Did Kieran know that just by looking? Film is about looking and the hunch that a face can tell you as much as a volume of letters. He didn't realize I stammered; he was not being unkind. Though he hardly softened toward me when he understood my pathos over speaking.

By our second meeting we recognized that an important friendship was at hand. Neither of us had been to university—we doubted it deserved us. He had a job, wrapping parcels at Selfridge's, the department store on Oxford Street. Some evenings he went back to Brixton to work on cutting his first film. It would be called *Faithful Departed,* a portrait of James Joyce's Dublin based on the historic photographs by Robert French that Kieran had found in the National Library of Ireland. I was doing my time at the school, but the education there was soon surpassed by the schedule we got into.

We believed in seeing as many films as possible. In part that appetite was satisfied by the National Film Theatre, which had come under the innovative programming direction of Richard Roud. London was still a mass of suburban cinemas that played double features of old films and changed their programs twice a week. We waited for the Wednesday arrival of the magazine *What's On* and planned the films to see—often a dozen in a week—going all over London thanks to the fluency of the Tube. We would race to make connections, eating sausage rolls and cakes as we went. This lasted more than three years. It was our university.

Kieran was not just older; he was also better read, and he knew classical music. He was a ferment on Irish history and derisive about the country that had sunk its claws into him. He rejoiced in Swift, Sterne, Wilde, Shaw, Joyce, and Flann O'Brien. He taught me the glory of *At Swim-Two-Birds* and the poker-faced comedy of Swift's *A Modest Proposal*. This eloquence enchanted Kieran. Years ahead of Ireland's joining the European Community and being subject to the international court of rights at The Hague, he believed Ireland had to be European, not nativist, Catholic, or "charming" in the dire way indicated in films like John Ford's *The Quiet Man*.

He had a brother in Dublin he disliked, and a mother who he said disliked him. He wasn't going back, he warned, no more than Joyce had any intention of returning after finding Trieste, Paris, and Zurich, and journeying in printed pages. Once away, Joyce re-created his own lost city in *Ulysses*. Kieran was departed, but he was bitterly faithful, and tortured by it. He never made a film that was not soaked in Irish regret.

He taught me to read most of an author's work: he proposed a schedule of Conrad and in return I recommended Faulkner. He made me listen to Mozart and I responded with Charlie Parker and Miles Davis. We went to see Miles live: he played two numbers, then turned his back and walked off the stage. I felt that Miles's hauteur impressed Kieran more than his kind of blues.

We were such snobs over our passions that girlfriends faded in the intensity. They came to some films and tried to talk about them. They must have known our hearts were given over to Jean Seberg. But Kieran was my teacher and he was insisting that I speak up. That pressure left me knowing I had to find something to say. It took me a while to realize that his nagging wasn't just for my sake: he needed someone to talk to.

It grew clear that despite his cinematic urgings, Kieran lacked the aggression or the confidence to sell himself in the movie business. Did he think I could supply that? Or were we both in love with a medium whose manners horrified us? Decades later I found this quote from Peter Guber, producer on *Rain Man, Batman* (1989), and many other films. He was talking to Tina Brown, the editor of *Vanity Fair:*

> Tina, what you have to understand is, Hollywood is ruled by its dick. Men are ruled by their dicks. Mine against yours. Excuse me, I know you're a woman, but you understand what I'm saying. This business, movies, is all about two things—power and sex. And guess what, they're the same thing.

That was said in 1989. A moment ago.

I know what Guber means, and I hear his gunslinger homage to dicking. Kieran and I were fearful of our chances in "the business" because we were not naturals at dominating a room, lying your head off, leaving a big tip and going off with the pretty receptionist. Guber is exultant about a habit that waited a century to be exposed. The gangster pride in the boys' club of movies has been a cultural failure that has misled the whole of America.

So we did nearly everything together, day after day, week after week. At the National Film Theatre we had complete seasons of Fritz Lang, Howard Hawks, and Jean Renoir, as well as an extended survey of French cinema. This made for a magical coincidence in education, for it was in the early 1960s that revolutions occurred—the films of the French New Wave: *The 400 Blows, Shoot the Piano Player, Jules and Jim, Les Cousins, Paris Belongs to Us,* as well as *Breathless* and *Vivre Sa Vie.* It was not just that these were wildly exciting movies. They were made by young men we knew from the yellow-covered *Cahiers du Cinéma* where they had for years been reveling in Hollywood cinema. They adored Howard Hawks, Hitchcock, Fritz Lang, Preminger, Vincente Minnelli, Sam Fuller, Anthony Mann, and Nick Ray. In *Sight & Sound* (the prim English film quarterly we deplored), there had been an article by the editor, "Ray or Ray?," in which the humanist compassion of Satyajit Ray was preferred to the desperate cinematics of Nicholas Ray. We admired Satyajit Ray, but we adored Nick Ray because his films were closer to our world. His *Rebel Without a Cause* was a knowing title, getting at the existential uncertainty in modern opportunities. Kieran and I collaborated on the most complete Nick Ray filmography yet done for the insurrectionary magazine *Movie* in 1963.

There was an occasion, at the London Film Festival, when François Truffaut came to introduce *Shoot the Piano Player*. I was late to the screening, but I caught up with Kieran and asked him, breathlessly, "What's the film like? What's *he* like?"

Kieran looked at me as if the realization had only just sunk in. "Truffaut?" he said. "He looks like us."

Truffaut was four years older than Kieran and nine years older than me. But there was some generous truth in the comparison, for Truffaut had that pale, wide-eyed face, and the shabby appearance of a kid who had spent too long in the movie dark to know how to look respectable—or to live a "normal" life. His outcast panache was what we sought as filmmakers in the new age.

It turned out that Kieran would be gay—is that the right way to say it? When we first met, I don't believe he knew he was gay. But maybe he sensed that I had the scorn for homosexuals, or queers, that an English public school relied on. It was a scheme for overlooking all the gay flirtations among youths who needed relief. We talked about girls and getting married. He had a girlfriend who was witty, attractive, and who stood up to him in conversation. It was plain they were good for each other. There was a shining in their eyes when they talked and Kieran had a sly grin for her. He asked this woman to marry him—they both told me that—but she declined.

He was hurt and at a loss, though he never talked about what might have been the reasons. I had no inkling then that he was gay, but had I known anyone who was? Never mind our new confidence, there were deep inhibitions about candor. (Britain was emotionally secretive—that was its richest asset for cinema; you can feel it all through Hitchcock.) Boys at Dulwich did mutual masturbation—during a class, even—but that was hormonal pressure that had to be relieved. Being homosexual was not just against the law, it was alien to the self-conscious liberty-seeking kids who were ready to shrug off archaic habits but who remained ignorant, stupid, and terrified of so much true novelty. We knew how rats copulated, but our own desire was not explored.

We were trying to make small movies of our own. Kieran had a project with one of the most beautiful women I had ever seen. Did she work in the perfume department at Selfridge's, or was he making that up? I don't think anything happened between them, but it was not for want of his yearning. I set up a film about a bass player in love with an older woman, a refugee from the war in Europe, Jewish and Polish. For me, that project was part of a longing to be the lover of an older woman I had met and who I cast in the film. She was fond about it and let me kiss her once or twice, but really, she said, it was not on. Still, I realized she was interested in seeing herself on film, or how I saw her. She was not seductive, yet I felt her rather austere self was led on by the chance to see her face on film. Photographing people is sometimes a bud for sexual flowering.

To put a woman in your film was like a declaration of love or desire, and some women were stirred by that offer. We felt that veiled drive in so much cinema: in Griffith, Josef von Sternberg, Hawks, and Hitchcock, and in the early 1960s it was there in the way Truffaut gazed at Jeanne Moreau, and Antonioni reverenced Monica Vitti, not to mention Ingmar Bergman's concentration on all his women.

My 16 mm project crashed when the bass we had borrowed for the film had an accident on the streets of Streatham one night. I had to reimburse the owner and that was our budget gone in one mishap.

Time moved on. Kieran did go back to Dublin, because a film job opened up. I met a magical woman, Anne, who had a daughter, Kate. I think I married both of them. I desired Anne, but I guessed I loved her when I saw photographs of her I had taken. I called Kieran to tell him about this and asked him to be my best man. He declined. I could not think why. Filmmakers have to act very knowing, but that often masks stupidity. I got a job in publishing, and he carried on his struggle to be a filmmaker. With him in Dublin we saw less of each other, but we began to correspond intensely. We made a documentary film together on Jonathan Swift (born and died in Dublin). I wrote it and he directed, and it played on the BBC, not because of us but because we got a startling cast of voices for it: Alan Badel, Cyril Cusack, Siobhán McKenna, and Patrick Magee. To hear Magee's liquid growl speaking for you was to smell wizardry.

It wasn't until the late 1970s that Kieran let me realize he was gay. Not long after that, he became a spokesman for gay rights in Dublin. He is esteemed in that city for his brave part in the liberation of sexual ideas made possible by Ireland's entry into the European Economic Community in 1973. It was still difficult to be gay in that world, let alone shape a career as a maker of film. We never discussed his decision as we had once talked about girls and marriage. We were as close as ever, perhaps closer in that we expanded in letter-writing. I had a wife and three children. I was writing and getting published. He was making films and he had lovers in Ireland. But he kept that secret when he visited London.

Kieran was an "uncle" to my children, talking to them, teasing and nagging, caring and educating them in gentler ways than he had used on me, but still in the same slightly caustic spirit. (He told children to forget childishness; their task was to grow up quickly.) There were other children in his life whom he watched over in a similar way. Anyone who knew Kieran said that he should have been a dad, and he must have had that feeling. Had he come along thirty years later he could have had a gay marriage with adopted kids. We are at the mercy of our moment, though.

As I look back on our years "together," I wonder about the atmosphere of our friendship. We would have been so much less without the companionship and challenge; we fashioned critical thinking, humor, and a scheme of values from it. In trying to identify the "best" films, we were fussing over how one might live life. And we both had half an understanding of how cinema turned on a level of desire that could never quite be fulfilled. We gazed at the screen with longing, but we could never get there. Desire was vital and beautiful, but it was as silly and playful as a game. That's how I loved soccer: I thought of being Montgomery Clift *or* Jimmy McIlroy, the superb, shy inside right who played for Burnley.

Kieran's favorite film, his childhood treasure-house, was Vincente Minnelli's *Meet Me in St. Louis,* and he helped me see that it was not simply a pretty, reassuring MGM musical but an intimation of family ambiguity and erroneous coziness. He was an illuminating critic and he opened my eyes and ears to the anguish with which Judy Garland sings "Have Yourself a Merry Little Christmas" to her kid sister (Margaret O'Brien) as if a pulse of lament beat within the festive promise of "a Christmas song."

He also told me to study the films of Robert Bresson until I appreciated them better. In particular, that meant *Diary of a Country Priest, A Man Escaped,* and *Pickpocket.* I think these are still the great films by Bresson, and examples of his austerity or restraint in a medium that so often clamors to be expressive and excessive. They are also studies of men alone: the dying priest, the Resistance fighter imprisoned by the Nazis, and a petty thief. As I worked with these films, they struck me as Catholic allegories, and I was averse to that. I had had a girlfriend who dumped me because she was Catholic and her parents had instructed her not to be involved with a boy who was Protestant. It wasn't that I was Protestant; it was more that I disagreed with people on principle. I never attempted to break it to her that I was an atheist. Devout necking had its boundaries.

But in time, I began to feel that Bresson might be gay, too. This was never addressed in plot terms, but his films dwell on the soulful isolation of men, and Bresson liked to cast saintly and attractive men in the roles. There was no gay action in Bresson, but I felt the moodiness, above all in *Pickpocket* (the one film of the three where the man has a girlfriend).

Is that insight or speculation? I don't know. But the thought grew retrospectively with Kieran. (He died, too young, in 1993.) I think he only found his sexuality in Ireland. That's where we made another film together, *A Child's Voice,* a ghost story about a writer (T. P. McKenna) haunted by a child (June Tobin) he has invented for a story he reads on the radio.

I wondered later about Kieran's feelings for me, though I was shy not just of asking him the question but of asking it of myself. The movies seem bright and open, but their devotees so often act like spies. He made good films about hateful male bullies—*Exposure* and *Criminal Conversation.* It was only with him dead that I understood how much I had loved him. He had a heart operation coming up and he said it was a formality. I went to stay with him in Dublin for the weekend before hospital. The operation was a success, but then a friend called to say he had died, suddenly, from an aneurysm. Two days later, I got a postcard in Kieran's fierce black handwriting saying he was doing well.

I could not have had sex with Kieran. But you don't have to have sex to know about love. We all of us sleep with strangers in our heads. I have long consented to the folly in wanting to make love with so many women out of reach, and settling for making some of them laugh instead. Having women laugh at you is a start to being civilized, and less tiring than the other way. But Kieran affected my sense of what a man could be more than anyone.

What does that man want to be? Let me list some qualities: cool or detached—a player in the game but a little apart from it, like an author; a tease, a flirt, full of sex in the head; timid yet reckless, and scathing about "traditional" manliness. Are these the roots of bipolarity, torn between vanity and alarm? Alert to gracefulness, preferring Astaire to Gene Kelly, gripped by disabling doubts and risky hopes, capable of kindness without being ingratiating. Full of feeling but dreading sentimentality. Forbidding, eloquent, difficult. Fond of surreal connections, as in the word "screwball." Nostalgic for or anticipating sex but sometimes perplexed with it here and now. Grave yet frivolous. Debonair in his own mind, untidy in the eyes of others. And aware that when falling in love you should preserve a small margin of otherness in case familiarity goes stale. The falling is ecstatic, but have a parachute.

You can imagine sleeping with many people; you must. But stay awake. Remind yourself of Cary Grant in *His Girl Friday* and the exhilarating dance in his wooing of an ex-wife. If our culture is to survive, or deserve survival, then "straight" people need to accommodate and learn from gay experience. The two ways need to become more alike. Which is not sweet or easy, or anything like a tidy, happy ending. How could it be? Desire so often contains the seed of tragedy.

As I was finishing this book, a new movie opened with the outline figure of the male I have tried to describe: Reynolds Woodcock (Daniel Day-Lewis), a London couturier in the early 1950s in Paul Thomas Anderson's *Phantom Thread*. He is some kind of genius but he is also impossible. He desires perfection, yet he can turn ugly. He is as beautiful and as intricate as a line of close stitching. His is a face that we have to watch; it is a beast wondering whether to eat us. He wants women, and in the nature of his work lovely women come to him, begging for the chance of a job. He's not unlike the classic movie moguls perched on the ends of their casting couches. *Phantom Thread* is a love story for an era that seems to have given up on that genre.

Woodcock is a kind of Bluebeard—or is it Harvey Weinstein? It is not that he is gay but he is thoroughly closeted. He wants everything secret, or sewn into the clothes. He moves through a film that does not dare show sexual behavior, yet it is addicted to the sexiness of clothes, skin, the small movements of a mouth, smiles, and shoulders. Let's say appearance. He creates life while staying detached—that is the leverage of his control. He could have been a filmmaker.

2

A Powder Puff?

Rudolph Valentino and Beatrice Dominguez in the tango scene
from *The Four Horsemen of the Apocalypse* (1921)—an iconic moment,
or two kids on their way to early deaths

REYNOLDS WOODCOCK poses a lot in *Phantom Thread,* hesitating over austerity and sensuality and disdainful. He's a little like Rudolph Valentino. Now, think of the history.

Between 1815 and 1918, there were official self-important revolutions in the grind of world action. Bismarck laid down the shape of modern Germany; South America was so torn by revolutions that its insurrections became a joke for "settled" societies. Slaves were "freed"—in principle at least—and the notion of black equality became an appealing white lie.

In Russia, though modestly and locally in 1917, there was what became *the* Revolution. Meanwhile, the revolutions that had occurred in the United States and France had become models for progress. It was beginning to be thought possible that women could have rights. This would be a magnanimous gift from men.

But there were other revolutions: in the circling mechanisms of combustion engines, aircraft propellers, the whir of generated electricity, and the conversion of external reality into a set of pretty images in the motion picture camera. One consequence not much noted was that something called the "lifelike" had come into being. This could seem like riches for storytelling, but there was more to it. Reality (or nature) could be handled. Cinema did it first, and while it took seventy years—until CGI (computer-generated imagery)—we had reassessed nature as a plaything or a theory.

There was much to marvel at in the new thing called movie. It was a technological giddiness, reproducing movement and the passage of time as observed in life. The machine recorded duration, just as a photograph had become trusted as a means of identity. The photograph was rashly treasured for its apparent "accuracy." But those snaps were half-hearted and imperfect compared with the way film presented a persuasive imitation of appearance or performance in a context of passing time.

This became a new way of telling stories: we were eager to know what happened next, and serials rubbed that desire raw, so that we wanted it to be next week now. Movie was also, evidently, a business:

we were charged admission, and anyone could see that it cost significant money to build a version of historic Babylon (*Intolerance,* 1916) or a city from the future (*Metropolis,* 1927).

As the truth spread of how much money might be involved, so Hollywood represented absurd, transforming wealth in the naive imagination. This helped chase religious merit away in the rush of gambling. Moreover, this was money falling to hitherto impoverished, uneducated, and powerless people. That was another revolution after centuries of privileged ownership.

These lifelike images played with what we could only call fantasy or desire. Participating in the lifelike enabled dreaming, just because we were not quite *there,* in the picture: Freud published *The Interpretation of Dreams* in 1899, four years after the Lumière brothers showed fragments of time and motion to an audience in Paris. Movies created a shining place we might like to occupy when the one we lived in was compromised or too dull. People in these movies were icons or demons, and we were their slaves or adherents. A fundless youth out of Italy became world-famous in a few years, so talked about that the man himself wilted under the attention, until the pale moon of his face was emptied out of personality.

When Rudolph Valentino died, in August 1926, the funeral crowds in New York and Los Angeles were unprecedented. Reports claimed 100,000 on the streets of New York. At only thirty-one, "Rudy" had gained utter fame in just five years; so many adults had heard of him and recognized his empty "look."

Campbell's Funeral Chapel in New York was just beginning to appreciate the power of public mourning; so it was interested in a new kind of funerary show—having the dead lie in state managed like a tableau for great crowds. Valentino's was an early dramatic death in the age of movies, and he had been not simply a star but a vindication of being young, beautiful, . . . and different, ahead of the pulse of the moment. He had been a surprise, before the shock of his death, and proof of how a nobody and an alien could become iconic and even subversive. He was a guy, you had to agree, but he was more and less than that. He was a photographed spirit. In the old sense of the word, honored by children, he was a fairy.

Valentino seemed bemused by the stir he caused. A month before his death, an editorial ran in the *Chicago Tribune* which claimed horror over a ballroom in that rugged city having recently installed machines dispensing pink powder in the men's washroom:

A powder vending machine! In a men's washroom! Homo Americanus! Why didn't someone quietly drown Rudolph Guglielmo, alias Valentino, years ago? . . .

It is time for a matriarchy if the male species allows such a thing to persist. Better a rule by masculine women than by effeminate men. Man began to slip when he discarded the straight razor for the safety pattern. We shall not be surprised when we hear that the safety razor has given way to the depilatory.

There it was, unease over the way a male actor was presented on screen. Homo Americanus was ready to take umbrage or to retaliate. Hitherto, D. W. Griffith had chosen handsome young men, vigorous and honest but sometimes monotonous; it seemed that idols like William S. Hart and Douglas Fairbanks were really capable of their onscreen heroics. Chaplin's tramp was small, wistful, and often a loser, but he was a charmer who adored girls. Most male stars seemed strong and manly; they wowed the women as reliably as they dispatched bad guys, and without alarming male viewers who could watch Hart, Doug, John Gilbert, and Charlie and believe they might be like them. Now came the suggestion that Rudy was something else.

The *Chicago Tribune* editorial was aggressive as well as ugly. A wiser man would have ignored it and let the innuendo perish with the newsprint in the garbage. But Rudy was not as smart or as assured as his screen authority promised. So he chose to be insulted. He wrote back, saying, "You slur my Italian ancestry; you cast ridicule upon my Italian name; you cast doubt upon my manhood." That's what he wrote, though it sounds like an intertitle in one of his movies.

Then, as if to prove how out of touch he was, he challenged the unknown author of the editorial to a duel. He conceded that deadly weapons would be against the law in 1926, so he called for a boxing contest, to be held in private, to avoid any hint that he was courting publicity. Then he asked heavyweight champion Jack Dempsey to serve as his trainer. No response ever came to the challenge—the editorial writer was dying of tuberculosis.

Neither man could have made that fight. On August 14, Rudy went to see *George White's Scandals* in New York and then moved on to a late-night party. At about 1:30 in the morning he became violently ill. He was in such pain that he was rushed to a hospital where it was found that he needed to be operated on for acute appendicitis and perforated gastric ulcers. That operation was not performed until 4:30 in the afternoon. It's not clear what caused the delay, but it was a summer Sunday, so perhaps doctors were at the beach. Or was Rudy afraid of the operation, or of seeming afraid? He was a country kid, with more fame than education. Some said he hoped to keep his sleek body free from scars. He *was* that body. Or what people felt when they beheld it.

When he came around from the operation, Valentino asked his business partner, George Ullman, "Did I behave like a pink powder puff or like a man?"

Word got out as peritonitis spread in the star's body. The *New York Evening Graphic* ran a fake photograph of Rudy supposedly on the operating table, bare-chested, with a headline: "Rudy Brave in the Face of Death." His fever never abated, least of all in the press. Rudolph Valentino, once Rodolfo Alfonso Raffaello Pierre Filibert Guglielmi di Valentina d'Antonguella, died shortly after noon on August 26.

The oddity about this brief career is that the Rudy often depicted as a threat to women was actually more alarming to some men. There was a lesson that would take time to settle in: that great figures on the movie screen might seem to conform with their obvious gender identity, yet in truth they affected the nervous systems and the hormonal condition of all sexes, of everyone. Women looked at men and were stirred; they saw beautiful women and wanted to be them. Men lusted after the girls, but they looked at men and felt strange new emotional tremors that involved worship and envy. People were falling in love with strangers they could not touch. Valentino had been marketed as a dangerous thrill for women, but you could not offer that to the women without edging into the emotional insecurity of Homo Americanus.

The story of gayness in Hollywood and our movies has as much to do with the insecurity of American heterosexuals as with the liberation of homosexuals. We may free gayness in America, but what happens to the old imprisoning state of manhood?

The Valentino story was a muddle in which so many people had conflicting hands that sometimes Rudy felt he was being pushed around like a piece in a board game. Great stars seem elemental, heavenly, and untouchable, but that is the trick of a business that regards the stooges as money machines.

From "powder puff" to "adagio dancer" (that was Dos Passos's view in his novel *USA*), Valentino was a hapless typo. It wasn't only mocking editorial writers who got his name wrong. Show business tried many name changes for him before the kid from Castellaneta (in Apulia, at the southern end of Italy) emerged as Rudolph Valentino. Having done very little in school, and living briefly in Paris, he arrived in America in 1913, aged eighteen. He worked as a laborer and a taxi dancer for hire, expert in the new craze, the tango.

Then he was caught up in a society scandal: he had become friendly with Blanca de Saulles, a Chilean heiress, and when her businessman husband elected to divorce Blanca there were rumors that she and Rudy had had an affair. The husband pulled strings to have Rudy arrested (in turn, Valentino was ready to testify to the husband's liaison with another dancer). Blanca won legal custody of their son, but de Saulles insisted on keeping the boy to himself. She called on him, with a gun, demanded the child, and shot and killed de Saulles in a scuffle. No one doubted those facts, yet she was acquitted of murder in a 1917 trial during which the accused had sentimental support from the press and some suffragettes. It's a sleazy case, uncertain in detail, but enough to get Rudy written off as a wop and a gigolo. It feels like a movie melodrama with beautiful, foolish people striking poses and speaking in captions.

Meanwhile Rudy was drifting toward show business and small movie parts. There was little to suggest he had unusual talent or instincts. Biographers have concluded that Valentino was gorgeous yet dull, a package that prospered in silent cinema which often flattered attitude, stance, pure movement, and superficial iconography. Valentino's English was so poor he could not have made it in talkies, but in precious silence his phantom grace and serenity were personality enough.

In 1919, he married a minor actress named Jean Acker, from New Jersey, who had found herself in small movie roles, going nowhere, until she became lover to the illustrious Russian actress Alla Nazimova. Born in Yalta in 1879, Nazimova had trained with the Moscow Arts Theatre and when she came to America in 1906 she did major productions of Chekhov and Ibsen—her *Hedda Gabler* was especially revered.

She moved to Hollywood in 1916 for the film of *War Brides,* one of her stage successes. She took up residence on Sunset Boulevard, in a property that would be known as the Garden of Allah. She behaved, without shyness or guile, as a lesbian, with a club of lovers who tried to follow her codes of artistic behavior that included not just acting on camera or stage, but carrying yourself in life. Nazimova was tiny, and not the most beautiful of women, but she wore exotic costume in commanding poses that seemed ready to break into narrative. She was a little like the Bette Davis still to come—striking looking, with burning eyes that dared you to dismiss her as a beauty. Nazimova knew what she wanted and how to get most of it. That included a supply of young women lovers who never questioned her.

She is an early indicator that lesbians would have more self-confidence in Hollywood than homosexual men. And if some American men were disconcerted by Rudy, lesbians read him in one glance or photograph. Again, that reflects on the unease of straight manhood. Aren't women more relaxed about lesbians than men with stories of a gay next door?

So the generally subservient Jean Acker married Rudolph Valentino. Some said Nazimova had arranged or even ordered this, to assert her power. Others thought Acker had acted to spite Nazimova for favoring another woman. In no scenario does Rudy seem decisive. As quoted in Gavin Lambert's *Nazimova,* the great lady wrote to a friend with a disparaging sense of the groom: "Perhaps you've heard of Jean Acker's marriage? It was the worst thing she had done on top of all the other worst things she had done from the day she arrived here. You remember how I warned her that I would absolutely break with her if she did not behave? Well . . . she married a professional 'lounge lizard'—that's how she herself called him only a week before her marriage!"

"Professional lounge lizard" didn't speak well of Rudy, but what would have helped him except a story that he and Jean were wildly in love and incapable of behaving sensibly, or obediently? Was theirs a true love affair? Alas, that story jumps tracks: the couple were married, but Jean never let Rudy into the bedroom. The marriage, as is sometimes said, was "not consummated." Well, why would an "actress" go with a "lounge lizard"? How could they embrace without the quotation marks banging together? Why were they there in the first place except out of muddled story lines? Rudy filed for divorce, but then seems to have forgotten what he was doing. There are times when this great lover hardly seems safe out on his own.

So he waited to be picked up by another, more influential woman. June Hughes had been born in Leadville, Colorado, in 1887; she took the name "Mathis" as a child, when her mother remarried after the husband had gone away. Leadville was in the mining part of the Rockies, remote and tough, and 10,000 feet high. A place for Homo Americanus.

June Mathis was a sickly child, but in the process of surviving she developed unusual willpower and a spiritualist faith in herself. God was generally being given up at this time, especially when lives could be transformed by the chance of finding gold in the ground. But some souls clung to larger or more irrational beliefs. June went on the stage, initially in San Francisco. She was not beautiful; she was small, plump, rather homely, and apparently cheerful about those limits but all the more interested in learning how to make movies work. Free from any notion of being in movies herself, she realized how they might be in her. She came to feel she could see movies in advance, picturing them, writing them, casting them, all in her mind's eye. I doubt a man would have promoted Rudy in the way Mathis did. Or been so loyal: Mathis died a year after Rudy, but they are together in side-by-side crypts in the Hollywood Forever Cemetery, close to the Paramount lot.

The terminology did not exist yet, but June Mathis was storyboarding pictures as a kind of writer-producer, a visionary who foresaw what might be. She was so skilled that at Metro she had been put in charge of scripts, the most powerful creative position a woman had held in the movie business. It was this scruffy dynamo who seized on Valentino and turned "lounge lizard" into "great lover." She had guessed something, and she made us see it.

June Mathis had seen enough film footage of him to believe he could play in the big picture she was setting up, *The Four Horsemen of the Apocalypse.* For $300 a week, he was hired to fill the role of Julio Desnoyers, the playboy son of an Argentinian rancher and patriarch who will go to Europe and die in the Great War. This was only one element in the sprawling Blasco Ibáñez novel, but Mathis saw a way to make the role memorable. Julio would dance the tango.

This wasn't a story scene, despite Mathis's skill. It was a glimpse of sensation, like John Travolta getting ready to hit the street and the dance floor in *Saturday Night Fever,* or even John Wayne turning to go back into the desert at the end of *The Searchers.* In those moments, ordinary human movement can be shot and edited on film so that it becomes a rapture. The scenes are romantic affirmations of the old movie attitude, "a guy alone."

There is no preparation in *The Four Horsemen of the Apocalypse* for Julio's "arrival." He's pushed into our faces, early in the picture. We are in a rowdy Spanish cantina with a merry crowd. Julio Desnoyers appears, like an escapee from a society costume ball, as perfectly dressed as everyone else is rough-and-ready. We don't know who he is, or what he's doing. In a moment, we don't care; we just want more. We have no other task except to look at him and to be with him in the immediacy and intimacy of the medium. He commands attention, like a costumed attitude. He seems less natural than dressed up. He is a signal to how much clothes mean in movies. He is an empty god waiting for us.

His swag pantaloons are tucked at the ankles; he has riding boots and spurs *indoors;* a tight cummerbund; a loose blouse done up at the neck; and then a flat-brimmed gaucho sombrero, with a chin cord that shapes his bleak, possessive stare. In effect, that face is costume, too, for someone has made Rudy baleful, dominating, sinister, a dictator—and yet, half-dead, too, or ghostlike. Who did that? The director, Rex

Ingram, who didn't much like Rudy? June Mathis, who believed in the new actor? John Seitz, the film's talented cinematographer? The audience saw him alone, and they were changed. There was no doubt about it: the guy looked beautiful and flawless—but were real men meant to be so abstract or angelic?

Julio dispatches a rival dancer with one blow from his whip stock, and then engages with a very Spanish dancer, voluptuous but coarse, with violent lipstick and a kiss curl like an upside-down question mark. She is as raw as he is smooth. He leads her in a tango, bending her backward and then pulling her to him. In silent theaters the scene would have had the roll and hesitation of a rough piano accompaniment. The tango then was as new as jazz, a creation from the end of the nineteenth century that had arrived in New York just before 1914. It was a sexual novelty, alluring and male-dominated but with insolence, stealth, and intimations of violence.

The dance is handled in full shot and unbroken takes, recording the sinuous coiling of the whole body. Valentino was a sensational dancer for those few minutes, with low-slung hips and sinister grace. He is like a killer moving in, a cobra or a panther. People had danced in films before 1921, but there were no musicals and few instances of a man dancing for the sake of movement or seductiveness. There was only one comparison—on stage—in Fred Astaire; and Fred needed a partner, his sister, Adele. His sexuality was kept carefully wrapped, until he was able to sing in his films and then that blithe voice told us he was safe, more intent on dance than being predatory. Whereas, in *Four Horsemen,* Julio consumed his partner. She was Beatrice Dominguez, uncredited on the film, and dead within months of its opening—she died of peritonitis, the fate that awaited Rudy.

Emily Leider, the best biographer of Valentino, reports that this tango scene took three days to rehearse and shoot. She also points out that there had been no tango in the Ibáñez novel. In translating a novel to the screen, you can transcend it with one addition (equally, a novel can upend a movie with a single introspective paragraph). Ibáñez was literary; he did not think of wonders that didn't fit a story. But June Mathis had identified the potential of the tango and its way of delivering Valentino. He is never again that striking, in a picture that is often spectacular and archaically impressive but seldom makes you notice *now.*

Valentino's career took off. He was wooed away by Paramount when Metro was slow to realize what they had on their hands. He would have thirteen more films and another marriage, but he made a mess of that, too. The divorce from Jean Acker had not gone through properly (it was Mexican) when he married Natacha Rambova. She was another disciple, or protégée of Nazimova, and in her name she was trying to take on the arty thrall of Russian-ness.

"Rambova" was actually the remake of Winifred Kimball Shaughnessy, born in Salt Lake City in 1897, a young woman attracted to Nazimova's circle because of its taste for dressing up. Somehow she met Rudy, and they were married in 1923. Alas, chaos struck: Rudy was charged with bigamy—with one marriage unconsummated and the other on hold.

These women toyed with Rudy. He made a version of *Camille,* with Nazimova as the older woman, written by June Mathis again, and with Rambova doing the costumes (this was at the end of Valentino's Metro stint). When she first saw Rudy, Rambova thought him "fat and swarthy," but she agreed to take him on if he would diet and let her pluck his eyebrows. That head would be sculpted as if by Brancusi. But Paramount was suspicious of her influence. Rambova was not hired for *The Sheik* (1921), the film that brought Rudy the stardom touched on in *Four Horsemen.* He played Ahmed Ben Hassan, wooing the English Lady Diana Mayo (Agnes Ayres) and wearing Arab costume.

The Sheik feels silly now but potent (there are prospects of rape, and Lady Diana is ordered to dress like an Arab). Imagine the furore today if a Leonardo DiCaprio masqueraded as an Arab chieftain who seduced Natalie Portman or Jennifer Lawrence lost in the dunes. Arabs were not the flashpoint they are now in our naive imaginations, but 1921 was in the aftermath of the Sykes-Picot Agreement in which the world powers carved up the boundaries of "Arabia," to say nothing of the reputation of Lawrence of Arabia (who sometimes dressed in robes). As *The Sheik*'s plot collapses, we discover that Ahmed Ben Hassan is a lost Englishman raised in the desert—like Tarzan in the jungle—so Lady Diana can yield to him with ethnic safety.

With its mixture of surface folly and underground unease, *The Sheik* was a hit, returning more than seven times what it had cost. But the film placed Rudy in an imbalance of awe and hostility that determined his future. Many women adored him, or were thrilled by troubling thoughts about him; that left men hostile to the novel preciousness in his demeanor. So he tried too hard to be arresting, or "masculine." His own insecurity drove him into posing. If he had been more casual he might have had genius.

Rambova's influence on Rudy was disapproved of by Paramount. As Julio, he had played a domineering man; a male viewer could watch *Four Horsemen* with approval—perhaps some tried the tango. But as time passed, the actor became an exotic and a meek clotheshorse. After *The Sheik,* he was a matador in *Blood and Sand,* one of his best films, and then came *The Young Rajah,* made under Rambova's strongest sway. That was a more flagrant costume piece in which Rudy was often left looking like the epicene stooge wearing fanciful clothes. In that film, he was clearly prettier than the lead actress, Wanda Hawley. He had been swathed in art direction. This was a clue to the interaction of gayness and production design that would play such a role in Hollywood history.

Rambova dressed Rudy and posed him in photographs as a Nijinsky-like faun. In *The Young Rajah,* she sometimes adorned him with little more than costume jewelry and an impassive gaze. In *Monsieur Beaucaire* he was a French dandy, a fop—until he turned into a prince. But the public were shifting. The *San Francisco Chronicle* ran a poll in July 1922 in which men and women were asked what they felt about Valentino. Women often said that his screen lovemaking put their real guys to shame. One man replied: "Never did a professional beauty dress with more care to display his charms than does Rudolph Valentino. . . . Many men desire to be another Douglas Fairbanks—but Valentino? I wonder?"

"Doug" was a universal hero, and a reliable American. Hadn't he married Mary Pickford, "America's sweetheart," in 1920? No doubt they were in love (for a time), though the marriage was also propelled by the emotional thrust of publicity. Onscreen, Doug played laughing adventurers—Zorro, d'Artagnan, Robin Hood, the Black Pirate—and he enjoyed wearing costume. He was never an exotic, though, and he made the clothes seem as if he really wore them while doing his stunts. Doug had a terrific grin—while Rudy was best at staring, as if hypnotized or partaking in one of the spiritualist séances that he and Rambova enjoyed. Long before the powder puff debacle, Rudy was being made fun of. His mouth was closed and his black hair might have been painted on. A taunt sprang up about "Vaselinos."

At home, Rudy did the cooking; Natacha designed the house. He wanted children; she didn't. She was being ousted by Paramount and, before the end, she and Rudy were divorced, after which he spent most of his time with a gang of male friends. They swam; they did gymnastics and fencing, riding and sparring; they had parties with girls around. It was a male club, full of camaraderie, busy spending Rudy's money. There wasn't too much of that left in the end. After the divorce, Rambova went on to a career as a fashionable designer in Manhattan. Her significance in movies is as someone who espoused design for its own sake and who had married her ideal model.

Surely that marriage was consummated, if only in some radiant photographic portraits she did of them. Was Rudy gay—was he a practicing homosexual? Emily Leider decides that there is insufficient evidence of it. So Rudy's place in gay history is that of a question mark, and he will not be the last. For decades, enigma (or secrecy) was close to gay glamour. We may never be sure about Cary Grant.

There's reason to think Rudy was lucky to get into movies and have a few eager women trying to design him. He was a country boy, easily misled. It didn't matter: the thought of him, that name, and, above all, the look defined a new sexual possibility in the early 1920s just as he inadvertently revealed what could happen in a new mass medium where you could gaze upon people of your own sex, as well as the opposite, and feel excited and confused. Men had never had such a chance before. Some felt attraction, but far more were disconcerted by the odd pang of desire.

Rudy's screen character was notably alone—it would have been intriguing to see him with buddies or the male entourages he favored in life, and hard to see him in family situations. Yet his huntsman concentration on pretty women only provoked reliable male viewers.

There has always been a happy escape into male camaraderie in films for guys—you can see it in so many military films, in Robin and the merry men in Sherwood, and in the mutual admiration groups of the *Ocean's* films. In mainstream cinema, when does one man first look at another with romantic suspense?

Young people today have probably not seen Valentino. They may regard the name as camp, though the question that haunted him still preoccupies many guys: was he a powder puff or an authentic Homo Americanus? Could he be both? The box office is still insecure over that question.

We were left wondering what would have become of Rudy. Which makes it worth asking: what *did* happen to Ramón?

Ramón Novarro was born José Ramón Gil Samaniego in Durango City, Mexico, in 1899. He was from a good, settled family, doctors for several generations, who came to Los Angeles to avoid the Mexican revolution that we associate with Pancho Villa. Ramón was beautiful, but without the ghostliness or the recklessness of Valentino. He passed as handsome and as a wholesome gentleman, and though he was discreet about his homosexuality he was far more devoted to it than Rudy was to his identity. Novarro had had a bit part in *The Four Horsemen of the Apocalypse.* He became a star in the 1920s—aping Valentino, he was a Bedouin in *The Arab* (1924); he was the original Ben-Hur (1925); he played *The Student Prince in Old Heidelberg* for Ernst Lubitsch; and he was the lead in *Scaramouche* (1923), a lavish costume film by Rex Ingram, costarring Ingram's lovely wife, Alice Terry. Ramón hardly ever played an American: "Latin lovers" were not homegrown or trustworthy.

Ingram had directed *The Four Horsemen of the Apocalypse* and *The Arab,* though he seems to have disliked Valentino personally. Novarro was easier company: the Mexican actor often escorted Alice Terry to events when Ingram was away on foreign travels and foreign locations, and because Ingram was himself quietly bisexual. When he made *The Arab,* in North Africa, Ingram gave up Hollywood for the Mediterranean and a less inhibited life. He and Alice adopted an Arab boy. Ramón was an arrangement of convenience, without sexual relations with Terry—or with Ingram. Indeed, Novarro (who was socially sophisticated) took pains to keep his romantic life private; he never dreamed of finding lovers who were famous in the picture business. It was safer to choose extras or outsiders.

He did have a lengthy affair with Herbert Howe, a publicist and journalist. When that relationship ended, around 1931, Howe wrote a scathing but discerning portrait of Novarro that speaks to the way Hollywood homosexuals could slip into being actors without lives of their own. Howe wrote in regret and pique. He complained that all Novarro really wanted in life was an audience:

> All of his emotions are adolescent. He never hates because he never loves too much. He is not a particularly good companion. As he often said: "I have so little to give." His life is expressed in acting, not in thought or conversation. You get the essence of him seeing him on the screen. Off the screen he is . . . a theater with the lights out.

That is a pointer to the notion that actors, and those employed in pretense, may come close to the masquerade of gay people in situations where they need to be as discreet as Novarro.

Compared with Rudy, Ramón got away with it. He was a true star of silent cinema. He was well-off, and he lived for decades as a secure bachelor, interested in the arts and social gatherings. His career carried on into the sound era (he played opposite Garbo in *Mata Hari* in 1931), though he was soon confined to smaller character parts—Mexicans. He was no longer widely known, except to the community who knew where aging queers lived up in the Hollywood Hills in whatever grace they could afford.

In 1968, Novarro lived in his immaculate home on Laurel Canyon Boulevard, a house of concrete, glass, and oxidized copper designed by Lloyd Wright (the son of Frank). It was there on the night before Halloween that he was murdered by two hustlers (brothers, aged twenty-two and seventeen). They had invited themselves in. Novarro read their palms and he told one of them that he looked like Burt Lancaster and might have a movie career. When the brothers left the premises Novarro was dead, after extensive torture and beating. By 1968, the murder of a gay star in his own home was more urgent in a culture where gay behavior was becoming open but still being brutally resisted and assiduously concealed in some quarters. Filmmaker and author Kenneth Anger said that Novarro's murder had been hastened by an Art Deco dildo being thrust down his throat. That present had been given to him decades earlier by Rudolph Valentino, and it was believed that Rudy had modeled for the souvenir.

In the trial that followed, the older brother was asked to define a hustler. He said, "A hustler is someone who can talk—not just to men, to women, too. Who can cook. Can keep company. Wash a car. Lots of things make up a hustler. There are a lot of lonely people in this town."

"Lonely" there is a pregnant concept. It means more now, as "privacy" is ground away between manic public image and the pathology of isolation. Once the movies were a satisfying public occasion: we sat in crowds, hundreds or thousands, of likeable strangers and felt together. But movies now increasingly reach us at home or in the solitude that strokes that word. They do not tell stories for that old communal illusion.

But movie theaters were complicated havens. They were warm in winter, cool in summer; they had comfortable seats (more or less) and perfumed air (as if to quell germs); they were a shelter for voyeurs and their dreams. You could sit there from noon to midnight undisturbed. They seemed safe and expansive. But they were perilous, too: they sometimes caught fire from nitrate film stock; some strangers could be menacing and predatory; and the image could turn from calm to horror on a cut. So we could be trapped.

The screen was a room we might enter at our peril. There is a pervasive motif in films about a house and its invaders. In the year of Novarro's death, 1968, it was there in *Rosemary's Baby,* where the safe home (and the body itself) are betrayed, and in *Night of the Living Dead,* where a refuge can become a prison (and the body turns to rot). So Vera Miles is determined to enter the looming house in *Psycho,* but we are unsure about going with her. In *Blue Velvet,* the virginal Jeffrey is so curious about desire that he sneaks into Dorothy Vallens's apartment. When she appears unexpectedly he hides in a closet. But she drags him out at knifepoint and elects to fellate him. He is powerless because of his desire. And she might bite. "Home" comes under old-fashioned threat in a simplistic fabrication like *The Desperate Hours* (1955), and it is a site of conflicted urges in the chaotic (but endlessly intriguing) *mother!* (2017).

We want to get into the forbidden house. We are torn with indecision. Our loyalty to "reality" and all its assets is being nagged at by the perilous alternative of fantasy.

3

Is This Allowed?

On the occasion of their 1932 marriage, Paul Bern and Jean Harlow
pose for a picture. She often looked less than her best. But this was
as good as he would get. She was twenty-one! As if reality was involved.
She could be fifty in Florida today.

IN *BLUE VELVET*, Jeffrey, hiding in the closet, is fearful that Dorothy will guess he is there. Every Peeping Tom is on edge. Yet he is also ready to be found by this femme fatale, and amazed to discover how her willingness fits his dream. A rare allegory of power and compliance is being played out. In the movies that turned on the insistence that men controlled women by watching them.

One thrill in voyeur delight at the movies is the fear that male secret vantage might be revealed. Peeping Tom gets off on what he manages to see, but that is accompanied by the delicious dread of being exposed—thus the idea that movies are "dirty," when we yearn for the dirt. The movies have a perilous gift for us: the detached study of sex and violence that would be out of bounds in life. That liberty of desire quickly gets into perverse or irrational deals with itself. Suppose the apparatus of cinema reversed direction, so projection's beam came out of the screen to identify a figure in the crowd, demanding, "*You!* Who are you? Why are you watching?"

To which you could only whisper back, "Because I *shouldn't* be watching." But Peeping Tom is a willful outlaw. He wants to be recognized, to have his own visibility. He longs to get up on the screen. So Jeffrey in *Blue Velvet* goes from his dark and his safety to brave the terrifying Frank (Dennis Hopper, rampant with roars of "fuck"), to solve the crime, and to settle the lives of his women (Laura Dern and Isabella Rossellini). He wants to show that a good boy, a nice boy, can be in charge and trusted—that old American dream.

We are being allowed to see something that ought to be forbidden. Instead, it captivates us. Movies are the industrialization of murder and orgy as regular human fantasies. There has always been a shadow of censorship or control, and it adds to the air of an illicit thrill coming our way. Though lifelike, the medium is a ticket to transcend our humble circumstances. We say we believe in fidelity in our life, but on screens for decades we enjoyed different men and women, week after week. Faithfulness and promiscuity rattled in the same head, like dice being shaken.

· · ·

At the beginning, going to California was an escaping road trip where old rules and restrictions could be dumped along with winter clothing. There are still archaic strongholds in the East that reckon California is flaky, underdressed, or irresponsible. Recollect the arresting, insolent splash in David Hockney's first pool pictures and the sheer light of the movies. Winter territories can resent the West's benign weather and its casual liberalism and believe it should be punished.

But California is more than ever the cultural center of the U.S., leaving earnest institutions of the East like forsaken monuments. The West was an escape from the sentimental remake of Europe that had monopolized the East Coast. And if the West was a mechanism for desire and transformation, a far place of new prospects, so it made a medium out of screens where those hopes could come to life. There was no more comic image of this than a drive-in movie screen presiding over the desert. It's as if that screen was queering the idea of solid landscape and live entertainment. While the desert may prove the site of new industries, it also hints at an end to the world. The West had new weather, yet one day the revenge of weather will be recognized as our apocalyptic genre. There's a fusion of weather and miracle at Burning Man, in Nevada, a weekend illumination of desert.

In the time of Rudolph Valentino, the West was still a four-day journey from the self-conscious citadel of the United States—New York, New England, and Washington, business and government, the Church, the Ivy League, justice, and organized sports. Movie people rode horses to work, crossing fields and orchards. A romance of discovery and wildness coexisted with the charm of the "frontier" and its narrative of new ways of running things. That meant cinema screens at first, which turned into the multitude of social/personal screens, the brightness in our hands.

In 1850, there were fewer than 100,000 people in all of California when the country's population stood at 23 million. By 1900, it was 1.4 million in a total of 76 million. Today, there are about 40 million Californians in a nation of a mere 325 million.

The movie business had gone west for about three hundred days of sunshine a year, the gold in the air. Beyond that, California had an unsurpassed range of locations. It had space, the living sky behind so much story and imagery in early movies. It was also a place where enterprise, nerve, and shame-free strength could determine the law for itself. There was liberty in the West, which meant the chance to impose your own new controls. That aspect of the movie business is too often overlooked.

Making a movie in the first twenty years of the medium meant overcoming a series of technical difficulties. These involved the consistent functioning of cameras and projectors. Every second, a fresh frame of film had to be drawn into place, held steady, and then moved forward, sixteen or twenty-four times. In each split second, that pull-through ratio worked best if the amount of stillness exceeded the motion by three or four times. That revolutionary finesse was tricky, and the problems were intensified if the sprocket holes in the film were not exact and uniform.

The sophisticated inventions were so important that outlaws stole them. To safeguard those inventions, the Motion Picture Patents Company (an Eastern organization) came into being, well-funded, well-lawyered, and with strongarm gangs ready to smash the machines of upstarts. That's another reason why outlaws or independents headed west. But in that flight, the independents found the sunlit splendor of the West: every kind of location, from dunes to mountaintops; the honeyed land to build on; the winning example that outlaws could rewrite local law; and the new realization that, once established in the West, the independents needed to get organized in a Southern California so open to entrepreneurship or the freelance instinct, that the picture business might as well look after the law itself or turn it in for rewrites.

On the morning of September 5, 1932, Labor Day, the butler and the cook arrived at the marital home of Paul Bern and Jean Harlow on Easton Drive, off Benedict Canyon Drive, in Beverly Hills. They found the naked corpse of Bern, shot in the head. He was twice the age of Harlow, and a friend to important industry people like Irving Thalberg, the head of production at MGM. Bern was a producer who had cared for Harlow and advised her on her career.

She was only twenty-one, and though they had been married just two months she had apparently spent that night at her mother's house on Club View Drive, maybe a mile away. Some said that was because Bern hated the mother and Marino Bello, Mother Jean's second husband. Or maybe it was more complicated.

On finding the corpse, the servants called Harlow's mother, then informed personnel at Metro-Goldwyn-Mayer, the studio that had Harlow under contract. Mother did not tell Jean—that's the story. Maybe Jean knew already? Is that why she wasn't at home? Several MGM people came to Easton Drive: Thalberg, Louis B. Mayer, David O. Selznick, Whitey Hendry (chief of studio security), and Howard Strickling (the head of publicity). They studied the scene and settled on a story; they made a kind of movie of it: Bern must have committed suicide. There was a dominating wish to put Harlow in the clear, and so a theory was worked out—that the marriage had failed.

Why was Bern's corpse naked? Had he thought to undress before he shot himself, in a spirit of confession? Had a state of nakedness revealed his deficiencies? Had Jean been there to see that? Or had he been skinny-dipping in the pre-Hockney pool? What did the suicide note mean, the one that said,

> Dearest dear,
> Unfortunaely [*sic*] this is the only way to make good the frightful wrong I have done you and to wipe out my abject humiliation. I love you.
>
> Paul
>
> You understand last night was only a comedy.

Neighbors said another woman had been at the house who had driven away in haste. But their evidence was treated as a rumor. History is now more confident that Bern had been visited and murdered by a prior common-law wife, Dorothy Millette. Paul and Dorothy had been a New York couple for close to ten years (they lived at the Algonquin). The drowned body of Millette was found a few days later upstate, in a slew off the Sacramento River. The story goes that MGM paid for her burial in Sacramento. There are even those who think the event was arranged by MGM—after all, melodrama was in their nature and business was their imperative. Conspiracy theory is a natural child of celebrity, storytelling, and our being hypnotized by screens. Was that suicide note written by studio people? Could that "Unfortunaely" be a touch of genius, worthy of Nabokov?

The Bern story was arranged or presented. But it was 2:30 in the afternoon before Thalberg decided to call the police and report the death. The cops did not make an issue of that. They knew their place as walk-ons with no lines.

An hour later, Thalberg went to the mother's house and told Jean. "Isn't this too horrible, isn't this too terrible," she cried, before a doctor sedated her.

An interpretation sprang up that Bern, a famously smart and sensitive man, was not quite right or manly; that he had let Jean down sexually or romantically. So many coded words are in that sentence, not least the thought that to be "sensitive" means missing out on manliness. It might be that Paul Bern was gay and unluckily married to legend's sexiest reputation of the moment. That doesn't mean sweet Jean had an especially creative mind in the sack, or that she could live up to wild expectations. She had striven to look like a creamed pastry, a balloon inviting our pinprick. But that duty can be as tough on a girl as on Rudy Valentino. Suppose most of us are not very good at sex—I know, that's an un-American notion and one that movies have labored to erase. But let the idea breathe.

So the tragedy needed to enhance the commercial desirability of the "blonde bombshell." She was back at work a week after Bern's death. We'll never know exactly what happened with Bern, Harlow, and Millette, and that's a testament to how far publicity could transcend police procedure in Los Angeles. Don't write that off as quaint history: in 1995, with a trial that lasted nearly a year, a jury acquitted O. J. Simpson after four hours of deliberation. In 1992, another jury had found no crime in the beating of Rodney King. Those verdicts stood up for something irrational or fictional, and overrode evidence, even that prolonged home video of King being savaged.

The wanting was remarkable in a country still pledged to puritan principles and inhabited by people who had come to America because they had so little in their native country. That desire was a process and a technology that worked in ways we are still discovering. The technology was the catalyst.

You required a dark place, sufficient to focus the artificial light that would play on a screen. It was a plain process of architecture to make that place large enough for two hundred or two thousand people seated in rows. They would be charged money to be there. When it worked, the money was delirious, and that became an essential component of the narrative process. A picture might work for you, in your private mind and fantasy, but you knew it was doing the same for millions. You were part of that vast family called audience and that applies to Chaplin shorts, *The Jazz Singer, Gone With the Wind, Casablanca, From Here to Eternity* . . . or *Titanic.* These are not necessarily "great" films, but they were universal. Their entertainment value and dream appeal were so far-reaching there was no need to talk about "art."

What the light threw up on the screen seemed to be life, though it was recessed or safe. On a real cliff, if you saw a child in danger of falling off, you would leap forward to save her. On screen, you wait to see what will happen as in an action arranged for your suspense. If you saw a woman undressing in life, you might avert your gaze so as not to intrude on her privacy—or you could approach her and kiss her. At the movies there was no need to be so active or to stop the voyeur's pleasure, because the bright life was actually removed: this was witness without responsibility, and virtual reality long before that phrase became common. The woman would never feel your presence or your interest. For every suggestion that you were being put "in touch" with life through lively imagery on a screen, you were also being denied participation and excused from consequence.

You were just watching—and we have discovered how far we like to watch; it may be as sexy as sex itself. This allowed a feeling of privilege, but it was also a threshold to detachment. You could seemingly have your heart's desire but only with a gradual loss of the sentimentality that had once given primacy to the heart. The coolness of that could go cold, but desire seemed not to care.

If reality tries to be straight, then could movie be gay?—not just particular movies, but all of them and their gradual distancing of reality.

Let me unpack that. To be gay is natural and a right; it is so intrinsic in humans that the right does not need to be stressed. But stress did follow for this reason: that for the vast mass of dutiful straightness, to be gay seemed like a critique or a commentary. It was the threat of degrees of sensitivity or satire or weakness that threatened the orthodoxy that America needed tough, brave men who could shoot on the frontier and have pretty women fall asleep, satisfied and unquestioning, pregnant with the future.

It's over.

That is a principle in considering why so many same-sex people were drawn to the community of moviemakers and to a medium that assumed a bold improvement on reality and the stereotype of romantic happiness. It's because we now appreciate the intense commercial fabrication of Hollywood, the business, that we recognize the camp innuendo in its works, and the way reality was reduced to an hypothesis.

Eighty-five years after the death of Paul Bern, the world has forgotten who he was. Even film buffs at Turner Classic Movies get-togethers have to admit that its empire is an antiques road show. Jean Harlow, who died eighty years ago, is not exactly known. Young people may have heard she was a movie star once. Or was that Norma Desmond? But for a few years, in the 1930s, some people wanted to have sex with her. She was aphrodisia. In her scripts, the way she was photographed and publicized, Jean Harlow seemed on offer. Even her name was a veiled promise.

Bern is more interesting. He was born Paul Levy, in Hamburg, Germany, in 1889. His family moved to the U.S. ten years later and lived in New York. It was there that Paul met Edward Bernays, a nephew of Sigmund Freud, and an eventual genius in the history of advertising, someone with rare insights into human motivation and mind control. Paul was so impressed with Bernays that he changed his name to Bern. In America, names can be roles or acts.

In New York, Bern tried to become an actor, and that's when he lived with Dorothy Millette. We don't know what they did together, or who she was, really, but there may have been warmth enough to inspire Dorothy to kill Paul. So be wary of the legend that Bern's penis was pinkie size. Most men worry that their penis is not big enough. Most women reckon that most penises are about the same size, and that they wilt with the same rapidity.

Bern came to California, and his instinct for the ways minds work helped him find a place. He became friendly with Irving Thalberg, he began to write scripts, to function as a producer and an insider. He would have recognized how in Hollywood importance had to do with access and secret knowledge. To be inside you wanted to be needed by more important people—so Bern was said to have a gay bond with someone high up at Metro. For female stars, that cover can be supplied by a man who doesn't harass them sexually. The predatoriness of Harlow's time was more automatic than in the age of Harvey Weinstein. Thus the efficacy of the beard, a stable, loyal familiar who knows your secrets and does not interfere in them. Bern had that role in the hectic life of Jean Harlow.

Harlean Harlow Carpenter had been born in Kansas City, Missouri, in 1911. Her mother, "Mother Jean," was pretty enough to long to be in movies, but she failed in that ambition and thrust it on her daughter. They moved to Hollywood in 1923. Harlean was briefly at the Hollywood School for Girls, and there is a picture of her there in which she looks unnaturally blonde and bouffant, or vamping the staid school photograph. Aged fourteen, she quit school.

In 1927, at age sixteen, she married a handsome heir and dumped him after two years and an abortion. By then she had a contract with Hal Roach that got her into a number of Laurel and Hardy shorts. In one of them, for a lark, she scandalized the studio by coming on to do a scene half-dressed. She was casual with her lush kid's body; she had great breasts so she abandoned brassieres in a free-enterprise attitude unimpressed by "the future" or gravity. She posed for open-air shots in Griffith Park where she wears only a gauzy wrap. She is a knockout in those pictures, when in L.A. there were only another ten thousand knockouts her age. But what does "great breasts" mean? Is it another vague superstition, like the big penis? As most babies know, most breasts are home. Reviewing Harlow's last film, *Saratoga,* Graham Greene said, "She totes a breast like a man totes a gun."

Men liked her, which probably means she went to bed with them. There was no point in going to Hollywood at nineteen unless you felt that ease. It wasn't that moguls and directors were always predatory, but the system was a slavery deal. Howard Hughes put her in *Hell's Angels,* but she is barely noticeable in it because Hughes loved the aircraft so much more. She had a supporting part in *The Public Enemy,* with James Cagney, and there is a story about how on the Warners lot one day the cheeky Cagney noticed her and her breasts and asked her how she kept them so high. "I ice 'em," she snapped back; she was a sweetheart of early sound who learned to do wisecracks. Did she even write that line in advance? At twenty?

To push *Hell's Angels,* Hughes paid Columbia to change the name of a new film in which Harlow had a supporting role from *Gallagher* (the lead character played by Loretta Young) to *Platinum Blonde.* Harlow was a blonde, more or less, if she undertook a dyeing process with toxic chemicals that threatened her health.

People and promoters were crowding in on her. There was her mother and her mother's second husband, Marino Bello, a sinister dandy who promoted Harlow's affair with gangster Longy Zwillman. There was Hughes, as well as Thalberg and Louis B. Mayer, who ran her home studio, MGM. And there was Paul Bern. He was Jean's confidant—he was known as the Father Confessor at MGM. He married her in 1932. He may have slept with her once or twice, like taking photos at Niagara Falls, but Jean was having her sex with the camera. That exposure envelops so many movie people. Boxer Max Baer said that once you'd slept with Jean, she turned boring. She may have felt the same about him. The movies were always striving to erase that despondent realism.

Audiences wanted to look at Harlow. In *Red Dust,* shot in 1932 before and after Bern's death, there is a scene where she bathes in a large barrel with Clark Gable looking down on her. His face tells us what he sees, and after "cut" was called she stood up, topless, for the benefit of the crew. She was a good-natured twenty-one-year-old. She had had a "breakdown" at Bern's death but she got over it. She married a third time, to Harold Rosson, a cameraman—reports said MGM arranged that to avoid the scandal of her being named in Max Baer's divorce. She had at least two abortions as she made over twenty films in five years. She was manipulated like a commercial property or a figure in an Edward Bernays advertisement.

Her health had been shaky for years. She was a heavy drinker. There were often dark rings beneath her eyes—they offset her blonde hair. It was said she was suffering from gall bladder infection. Her mother was reluctant to let doctors challenge her own control over Jean. She was misdiagnosed—it was really nephritis. She developed uremia so that she smelled bad; Clark Gable visited her and was pained by the stink. Her body swelled, her skin turned gray. She became a grotesque version of the knockout. She died at twenty-six and the public said it was devastated. Her last film was not quite finished, so the studio found a body double and a voice imitator—the fakery had no tact, and in time the audience would have to come to terms with this endless contrivance. We no longer believed that the camera simply recorded reality. It deserved a fake reality.

Jean Harlow was hot for a few years at the halcyon moment of movie romance. The sex lives and the romantic dreams of audiences were being deeply affected by the movies. Indeed, they were instrumental in that rapture in which we realized that sex was available and might be the greatest delight—or the chief mercy—in our humdrum lives.

Harlow faded before she died. In her later films she looks older than she really was. Even in her heyday a suspicion was spreading that movie romance was bogus, or a veil trying to hide unscrupulous exploitation. F. Scott Fitzgerald's *The Last Tycoon* believed, romantically, in the aura of movies. But Nathanael West's *The Day of the Locust,* written a year earlier, loathed the lies and the systemic manipulation of the crowd. For a moment in bourgeois culture sex was reckoned essential to falling in love. We still tell our children to look forward to it, when we may be seeking divorce. We became—according to your taste—cynical, disillusioned, ironic, sadder, wiser, grown-up. That's why Jean Harlow is not a knockout now but an emblem for nostalgia, one of those female stars imitated at gay parties. Mae West is the godmother of that family line, but almost unwittingly Kardashiana has inherited it. Most stars pass into such a twilight condition—it's their best chance of being remembered. But that loss of faith (sometimes before thirty) has turned Hollywood into a waxworks for its own mockery.

In the 1960s, Jean Harlow biopics made forlorn attempts to mimic the real star of the 1930s. Carol Lynley and Carroll Baker played her—whoever they were. Fifty years later, the role would have to be grotesque—it requires a big blow-up blonde, like John Waters's Divine, or Donald Trump, a hideous odalisque. The idea of a sex goddess has grown outlandish. Narcissus can wipe out humanistic intercourse. So when we make love, we may be getting it on with our secret fantasies. Even idyllic couples may have strangers in bed with them.

America is reeling in the shock waves from this cultural quake. Our dreams can seem as hackneyed as video games. Sincerity has turned hypothetical. So men cling to desperate *masculinity* as if it was a gun, with hostiles on the prairie outside—that exploded backyard where our environmental crimes have betrayed us.

4

Hideaway

In *The Big Sleep,* the book, the hideaway cottage was on the fictional
Laverne Terrace, off Laurel Canyon Boulevard. That's where Marlowe finds
Carmen Sternwood in an incriminating setup: "She was wearing a pair of long
jade earrings. . . . She wasn't wearing anything else." But books tend to be vulgar.
In Howard Hawks's movie version (1946), Martha Vickers kids decency.
The guy on the floor is a prop.

AS MOVIES BEGAN, Southern California seemed far away and unpromising: it could get fiercely hot; there was a water problem; it was desolate, except for some Native American tribes, dispossessed Mexicans, and stoic Spanish missions. When the wind came from the east it could fan fires into ruinous yet unnoticed sensations. The Modoc, the Serrano, and the Paiute told tales of earthquakes. The desert felt ready to close in. It is still poised. There were poisonous snakes, and mountain lions—and then came strange animals named Donald, Mickey, Pluto, and Bugs Bunny. It's not quite safe in those hills, or comfortable. But managed peril can help you feel blessed. At the movies, we thought we were safe in the dark. So the Easton Drive home that Paul Bern and Jean Harlow had shared so briefly seemed a small secured palace on a twisting road into the hills. A hideaway home.

Realtors became scenarists in the West. They saw some hills were gentler than others; the land was folded in on itself, with canyons, recesses, backtracks, and what they could call lanes, glens, or drives. Brush clearance and tactful landscaping might provide attractive properties if someday there was enough population in the flatlands beneath the hills, and if a town could be constructed there. Then the hills could be a retreat for the rich, the bosses, and the owners. The air is better there, the views are inspiring. There would be a chance in those intricate hills for privacy. Build those sinuous roads, plant bougainvillea and azaleas, make streams and arbors, orchards and pools. Apply art direction to nature.

This was the making of a rare ecology, so unusual it helped the residents feel special. So many of the people who made movies lived in a city yet felt they were in a rural retreat. The hills in the north of Los Angeles can look and feel like a residential colony for artists. Thus the hideaway cottages (or mansions) help people believe they are artists.

A lyricist in real estate might sell the cottages, villas in a Spanish style, or casual French chateaux, where the residents could treasure their fragrant enclosure without seeing or being seen by "neighbors." There are houses below Mulholland on trails that sink into forest or undergrowth—the décor of love nests. They seem natural, but they are designed: this is a movie trick. In those locations people can count their money, worship obscure gods, make love with whomever pleases them, or simply gaze into the mirror, studying loveliness. They call it a city of angels, with reverence.

Within the confines of one of the world's largest modern cities, the powerful can live in nature plus air-conditioning, with anonymity and secrecy. I have resided briefly in such homes and felt the melodrama of a culture that hoped to reach bereft villages all over the world where there was so little security or comfort. There is a thrill there—to have it made—alongside the trembling that knows the venture could end in half an hour.

There is a sociopolitical aspect to this hideaway topography. It's like a couple in the same bed: one of them at rest and dreaming, the other aghast and past taking an Ambien. In the extended moment of the riots that followed the Rodney King verdict in 1992, "rough" parts of Los Angeles like South Central were abandoned by the police for several days and nights. There was a fear in the genteel hills that anger might invade Bel Air and take revenge. That has never happened, not yet.

But secrecy in the hills has risks. In 1922, the body of a top director, William Desmond Taylor, was found in his bungalow on South Alvarado Street in Westlake. That murder has never been solved. The Angelenos cherish stories that stay open to speculation—like the Black Dahlia killing, or the murder of O.J.'s wife. Suspicion over South Alvarado fell on many people, including the young stars Mary Miles Minter and Mabel Normand, nymphs Taylor had ravished in that bungalow. Ms. Minter's mother was a suspect, too, as part of the ivy of betrayal and intrigue that enveloped the house. Over the decades, the Taylor murder has been a basis for books and conspiracy theories, with reports of mysterious figures hurrying away from the site of the crime.

A similar uncertainty arose in 1932 with the discovery of Paul Bern's corpse. This sense of hideaway sites of violent tragedy reached its climax in 1969 when members of the Manson gang invaded 10050 Cielo Drive (off Benedict Canyon Drive, not far from Easton) and slaughtered five people, one of them the pregnant Sharon Tate. In all these cases, there was a superstition that the hideaway had assisted the crime. There was also a screenwriters' instinct—half irony, half hysteria—that such crimes might have been done with eventual movies in mind. That was absurd but much believed in: L.A. is the spectator to its own disasters. As Joan Didion observed about Cielo Drive, people were horrified at the news but not surprised.

Didion never explored why she was not surprised. That went with her morbid gaze that saw L.A. as a suave hell in *Play It as It Lays,* when she lived there in ice cream heaven. But the absence of surprise came from a hushed guilt that understood a Cielo Drive was a script consideration. Don't misunderstand me. Nothing excuses the savagery of that night. But a Didion or a Polanski guessed the hideaway spirit foresaw outrage. It knew its privilege was not just. Didn't the hideaway look down on rank L.A. and say, "I dare you to come and get us"? That insolence bred panic attacks. Whatever transpired, just say it was Chinatown.

This once wild place promised to become Eden, with water and the other necessary services. Expensive, architect properties were esteemed in a business eager to be part of American respectability. The stars and the bosses might gamble the night away, drink and do drugs, and engage in what the rest of the nation were ready to think were orgies. The word "orgy" is often a flight of publicity: it means more to people who have never attended than to those who have labored through them, but the Eden could touch on Babylon. Pornographic movies were sometimes shot on weekends, exceeding the carnal limits of the official screen. Young people of all known gender decisions were persuaded to do exotic, transporting things for the sake of novelty and the secret library of pornography.

Once, people had been famous through verbal report—for wealth, power, victory in battle, exceptional piety, and outrage. Reputation consisted of repeated stories, word of mouth, and print for those who could read. Then, suddenly, fame turned into a medium. Being in movies was as significant as running the world, and less tiring. By going to motion pictures we mainlined fame in a connection close to worship. This renewed the spiritual aspiration that had been declining at the churches because of reason, material progress, science, realistic dismay . . . and boredom. Movies reanimated our need for irrational belief. No belief would be more irrational than the faith in sex.

In movies, the young, the uneducated, and the underprivileged (Americans!) were studied with awe and envy just because they were beautiful or attractive or charismatic. Scandal acquired a streak of egalitarianism: the most surprising thing about Valentino and Harlow was how uneducated nobodies had gained the eye of the world because the camera liked them, even if you could guess they were impossible in life.

Hideaway secrecy laid down a new basis for community and politics in which pretty unknowns could be conveyed to the masses as models or temptations. In a decade, the nature of modern media was established as a new city altered our understanding of understanding. Los Angeles became a new center of inspiration and emulation without most of the slowly evolving growth that had attended Athens, Rome, Paris, London, or even New York.

People bought firearms for protection and they hired discreet bodyguards or minders. As if to goad this insecurity they shipped expensive art into their homes—Monets, Picassos—that only the invited few could contemplate. Another subindustry furnished those pictures, as well as fakes the illustrious idiots would not discern. Shrinks found premises below the foothills or even in recessed houses and curlicued lanes that resembled neurotic twists and suppressed memories. These places existed in a buzz of blossom fragrance and cicadas.

The way west had always been a playground of bigamy erasing prior and unhappy eastern ties. Some people tried sexual intercourse with members of any sex they could find. There were also the formal straight orgies. These practices piled up together so that bright young knockouts were dying at twenty-six or twenty-seven looking as if they had done several laps on the circuit of satisfaction and abuse.

In the press, from the pulpit, this new fun was condemned. Much of America was horrified to think that these young beauties were screwing their eyes out and nearly bathing in banknotes while addicted to opium, cocaine, or Johnnie Walker Red. But some of that thrilled public wondered if they might get a bit of depravity and a hideaway in the hills for themselves. Fidelity in America waned as desire was enshrined. At a practical, professional level, one legacy of the movies was divorce.

Another was sexual speculation, the power of wonder or dreaming about celebrities. Sometimes you could see that Jean Harlow had "forgotten" her bra. But how did the legend swell that she seldom bothered with underwear? Was that true of Barbara Stanwyck or Carole Lombard, Myrna Loy or Margaret Sullavan? It helped that the women were so slim and their 1930s clothes so sheer. The best guys were beauties, too. Johnny Weissmuller, an Olympic swimmer (five gold medals), was jungle-ready masculine: one of his five wives was Lupe Vélez, who had lately been with Gary Cooper and wearing him out. When Weissmuller first appeared as Tarzan, in 1932, no man had been so close to naked on screen, or so suggestive. Bare-chestedness was not yet a given for men. Some comic books eliminated male nipples. Suddenly Tarzan was there, in a gestural loincloth—of course, he was a savage, until he was explained as a lost aristocrat.

Gary Cooper functioned within a framework of realism. His roles might be exotic and romantic, but he looked like life and spoke in as unactorly a way as possible. Thus he earned the dignity of being believed. Weissmuller was different. His Tarzan was far-fetched, but Johnny was cherished, like a pet; he is still the Tarzan the world thinks of first. His physique was pluperfect. In their first Tarzan films he and his Jane (Maureen O'Sullivan) made a brazenly erotic couple in sketchy loincloths that must have been glued on (they were pre-Code, given some excuse by jungle heat and the company of wildlife). Then as time passed, and Tarzan became a little paunchy, the fantasy of the role was hard to ignore. He became camp in his own time, before that term was current.

The fondness remained, but Tarzan helped us realize that movies as a whole were ridiculous—even Gary Cooper pretending to be Wild Bill Hickok. As early as the 1930s some viewers knew that the movies were a travesty of reality. The plausible stories were as fake as advertisements. We wanted to believe in the screen, but we had seen that it was a trick, less a window on the world than a spyhole for voyeurism and escapism.

White women couldn't go bare-chested yet, so suggestiveness and rumor had to be employed in silk clothes ready to slide off and in reputations edging into shadiness. A paradox emerged: highly sexualized people were ashamed of their nakedness, so they dressed in profound or spiritual ways, and that costume was an inducement to the sex being covered. In *Phantom Thread,* Daniel Day-Lewis's dress designer is torn between dressing to hide something and wanting that grail to distraction.

Clothes have loomed in this book already—as things Bonnie Parker, Valentino, and Harlow abandoned or made a sport of. The erotic promise of movies lives on clothes or costume, for the essence of nakedness is always being alluded to. Clothing in life is practical; we put something on to keep us warm and secure and presentable—often without thinking. Clothes guard us against the naked state that is not just natural but also an object of desire *and* of guilt. Once filmed, the practical becomes a metaphor. The clothes people wear in movies *suit* them; they reveal them. *Phantom Thread* alerts us to the way filmed clothing is another layer of skin. So clothes make a proclaimed hideaway of the body itself.

Fan magazines and movie stills nursed this fascination. They said, You gotta have this secret, but you can't, or you shouldn't. Advertising works in the same confusion. *Conversations with Joan Crawford,* compiled by Roy Newquist, is an uncommonly good book on the conflicted experience of a movie star. It was published in 1980 from interviews done in the 1960s and 1970s (Crawford died in 1977). At one point, Newquist asks Joan, "I've heard—repeatedly—that in 1929 you made a porno movie in Pasadena,* and that MGM paid $100,000 in 1933 to buy up the negative, and that a dupe negative exists and that you're being blackmailed to keep it out of circulation."

In the 1970s, I'd heard about these rumors from Maurice Rapf, son of Harry Rapf who, as an executive at MGM, had helped discover the Lucille Faye LeSueur who became Joan Crawford. Maurie said there were pornographic movies then, made with studio equipment and top-class cameramen. He said the Hollywood he beheld as a youth (he was born in 1914) was a deer park of sexuality. He thought a Crawford stag movie could have been made around 1925–26, when her career was on the cusp.

---

* Pasadena is acute, for it is the old, respectable side of L.A.

Crawford answered Newquist's impertinent question, and fed uncertainty: "No comment beyond 'bullshit.' " That's a Crawford line. She wouldn't have done it, she said; she didn't need to. It's boasting enigma as self-defense. But nothing stills the rumor. It became a part of her career that Lucille had come from the wrong side of the tracks (San Antonio, Texas), and had fought and talked her way to get her close-up. She was typed as a working woman making her way in society, and not too scrupulous about how she did it. This character she played was inseparable from her actual status anxieties at MGM.

In the same book, she laughs at the way no one in life ever walked on her white carpets after a magazine story declared they were sacred. Sometimes life does all it can to live up to the legend. The culture of movie begs to suggest there is a hot secret in a photographed body and its cold, narcissistic stare. If "everyone" wanted to sleep with Joan Crawford, maybe there was no more need for her to be physically involved than in an onscreen close-up.

The confidentiality Hollywood craved was being slyly offered as an inducement. The secrecy of the star cult assumes an inner life, and in time that reached way beyond sexual indiscretion or some behavior that might have been recorded on film. It included liquor (Prohibition existed throughout the 1920s), implausible religious cults, drug dens, séance groups, spiritualist connection clubs, even to the point of Satanism or black-magic charades. Gambling became a favored obsession in the industry as well as a model of what they were trying to do with pictures. Movies might qualify as a business, but their every angle was passionately unbusinesslike. Hunches and hope had overwhelmed economic science and reason.

Another hideaway hobby was socialism, or Communism, or un-American activity—thus the spectacle of black limousines lining the verdant lanes for meetings where wealthy practitioners of movie arts could plot the liberation of the Western world from capitalism and tell itself that motion pictures were the hope of a radical future.

In time, that "Red" hideaway became a source of contention and persecution. There had been spies on those lanes who noted the license-plate numbers of the limousines and took photographs of the people using them. The standard Hollywood contract had always had warnings about "moral turpitude," which meant whatever the studios wanted it to mean. It was—and is still—a trawling net used in immigration law to protect the nation from "an act or behavior that gravely violates the sentiment or accepted standard of the community." This principle should have been used against racism, poverty, and the denial of women's rights, but in practice it has been a crude lever against difference or a tool to hurt those who have upset community sentiment in the land of the free.

Being Red came under that umbrella, though it was trumped up as being "un-American." The possibility of sinful or deviant behavior hung over the community, and it could lead to blackmail and extortion, but it was seldom used to victimize the most distinguished of the hideaway cliques—the gays—or if not *the* gays, then those who thought beyond the conventions on how humans had sex or love. Some gays were especially eloquent in disputing and teasing the orthodoxy of straight romance dictated in films. That voice reaches from Oscar Wilde to Noël Coward. Some heterosexuals had sensed this fakery in film feeling: in 1936, Graham Greene, then a film critic, lamented that "emotion on the screen is nearly always false emotion." That critique turned out more educational than the self-conscious gestures over going Red. Think pink, instead, if you recall Kay Thompson's number from the movie *Funny Face* (1957), and one of the wittiest political statements from an American film of the 1950s.

Then consider: Kay Thompson was gay. The producer of *Funny Face*, Roger Edens, emerged as gay as he carried on a successful career—his companion was Leonard Gershe, who wrote *Funny Face*. That movie was designed by Hal Pereira, gay, who also did art direction on *Double Indemnity* (rich in its feeling for hideaway houses), *Shane, Rear Window,* and *The Rose Tattoo,* among hundreds of others. The costumes for *Funny Face* (a film about fashion) were done by Edith Head, who had a gay side to her life.

On the other hand, director Stanley Donen was not gay, nor were the Gershwins who wrote the songs, nor was Audrey Hepburn. I'm sure there were other gay people working on the film as well as other heterosexuals. The same estimate of mixed origins could be made for any Hollywood film, so the mixture was nothing to get alarmed about. In 1957, there were still fierce disqualifications against Reds, but the pinks did their job and went home afterward to cook their gay steaks, watch their gay television, walk their gay dogs, and look forward to gay rest. (You see, the adjective can be dropped.) There was a decent normality, or what Joan Didion called "discretion." In 1973, she reckoned that in Hollywood "heterosexual adultery is less easily tolerated than respectably settled homosexual marriages or well-managed liaisons between middle-aged women."

Even today, there is a confident assumption that the people who did décor, costume, and hair were probably gay—Paul Schrader remarked on this to me in conversation, with a knowing smile. That is part of our understanding of a gay enclave in the factory system. That attitude knows for sure that not everyone involved in those arts and crafts is gay or lesbian. But it assumes that gay talent has congregated in those areas and has been inclined to hire other younger people of the same persuasion. Why not? Are we going to cavil at John Ford or Sam Peckinpah for hiring and rehiring their buddies—their collaborative family—over the years?

Again, those enclave arts—décor, clothes, hair—are not just decoration in film. They are essential elements on which the light falls. Movies are about their stars and the stories, of course, but light makes clothes and décor alive. Consider the case of Travis Banton and Josef von Sternberg.

They were not lovers, but they made a stunning marriage on film. Banton (1894–1958) was born in Waco, Texas, and taken to New York as a child. He studied at Columbia and the Art Students League and he entered the world of fashion design just after the Great War when clothes were having their own revolution. Yards of fabric and dignity were discarded. Bodies acquired shape and skin glowed. Would that have occurred without movies? Banton was thrust forward in the profession when he designed a wedding dress for Mary Pickford in her 1920 marriage to Douglas Fairbanks. By 1924 he was in Hollywood.

He then embarked on a career that inspired so many costumiers. Banton could misbehave. He was a notorious drunk and depressive who would disappear for days when supposedly engaged on major productions at Paramount. His young assistant, Edith Head, covered for him, rescuing him from drunken binges and easing him out of paranoia and rage so that he could draw beautiful dresses. Banton was gay, though he hardly had time for exploring that. For sheer difficulty and unreliability, he was an example of how talent meant more than any trace of moral turpitude or unreliability. As Edith Head saw it, "He was a god at Paramount."

Several studios seemed to defy the severity of the 1930s by dressing its people like swells and socialites. Few spectators were offended. Audiences rose to the challenge of desire, and women in the audience looked at Kay Francis, Claudette Colbert, and Carole Lombard (all mannequins for Banton) and said: I want that. Their first target was the clothes, and economically that was impossible. So they aspired to the slim bodies, the hair, and the glamour in these women.

The "look" of the filmed world was as important as the story, the characters, and the thing called acting. "Movie" was a place people longed to be, and glamour made all things and surfaces subject to desire. There is an innate modernity in saying, "Look at this look—it means more than what the characters are saying or doing." And what they were doing sexually was tauntingly withheld—it was another hideaway. For there was an imagined orgy, over the rainbow or beyond the next fade-out, in which clothes might slip to the floor along with tuxedos and top hats. We love the money shot of discarded clothes on a moonlit floor.

The movie screen opened up this spectacle for millions, but the revolution was larger. Throughout the hollow propriety of polite society, there was mounting discord between desire and decorum. You felt it in Freud's scenario of wild intimacies jostling bourgeois composure. It's in the new perception of atomic agitation beneath settled surfaces, and in the way cinema was revealing spasms of uncertainty in our alleged fluency. You can see it in Gustav Klimt (1862–1918). He painted bravura society portraits where the color and pattern of clothes became frenzies of decoration. He also made ghostly pencil drawings of unknown women—were they the same ones in the portraits?—of cursory figures with splayed legs and the dark hairy O of their vagina and its silent roaring for discovery. Could those two genres ever be shown side-by-side or in a suspended dissolve (one of movie's innovations)? A riot was ready as peace "wrapped up" the Great War. It was there in *The Rite of Spring* (1913), in cubism (1910 onward) and the montage of Joyce's *Dubliners* (1914)—which was a modest departure next to the lovely teeming filth in his letters to Nora Barnacle. Joyce was banned for his straight prose, but if society had read those letters, it might have exploded. Orgasm can be a bomb.

Safeguards were imposed. Some historians complain about the narrow-minded restrictions of the Production Code Administration (1934). There is justice in that: many ideas and realities were pushed out of sight. But that misses the way censored restraint accentuated desire and the seductiveness of things suggested but never quite seen. As in horror movies, the action imagined is more potent than the enactment itself.

These movies seemed to be about romance and its ultimate climax, but the arousal of appearance and then a fade-out was formative. Even after censorship's collapse (in the 1960s and 1970s), we are not sure that this isn't the case. And for a Banton—and all the other artistes of appearance who were gay—that withholding was a delicious endorsement of their sardonic view: that straight sex was laborious and rather silly with its pantechnicon of love, marriage, and growing old together.

So consider *The Devil Is a Woman* (1935), the last film made by the triangle of Josef von Sternberg, Marlene Dietrich, and Travis Banton. Jonas Stern (1894–1969) had been born in Vienna. He was brought to the U.S. when he was seven. Sternberg, as he became, had little education, but he would be a supreme know-all. He edged into the picture business in New York and by the late 1920s he was directing: *The Salvation Hunters, The Docks of New York, Underworld,* and *The Last Command.*

That reputation peaked in 1929–30 when he went to Berlin to make *Der Blaue Engel—The Blue Angel*—in which an insolent cabaret singer seduces and then discards a self-important schoolteacher. The metaphor was appealing for the new culture: a lovely slut could triumph over academe and respectability—it was a suggestion that movie was more important than importance. To play that slut, Lola Lola, singing in a weary way and making a casual show of her half-clothed body,

Sternberg had discovered an actress named Marlene Dietrich. *The Blue Angel* got her a contract with Paramount. She enthralled Sternberg.

He was a fatalistic heterosexual, sardonic about the effort in winning a woman and persuading himself he might be in love with her "forever." He did win Marlene for a few moments. They were lovers, no matter that they were both married. But then Marlene, an easygoing bisexual, dumped Sternberg, and they kept working together. The American code of love was being undermined.

If cupid has wings, is that so he can fly away again? That was the epigraph to Jean Renoir's great movie of 1939, *La Règle du Jeu.* But parts of our society still insist that love is the big contract in life, the necessary thing. Dietrich's quizzical gaze saw more dangerous prospects and was not perturbed. Marlene was Sternberg's creation (she was never the same in other directorial hands), and once she had spurned him he could concentrate on the work. Truly, a director may woo an actress in casting and rehearsal, but once shooting starts the carnal needs in the woman go into hiding or concentrate on her look.

That discretion shines in the movies the couple made together, from *Morocco* (1930), where Dietrich is a cabaret singer (in male evening dress with a top hat—her own clothes, she said), all the way to *The Devil Is a Woman.* Sternberg's achievement as an artist was to signal contempt for traditional romance. As if he had learned by looking at movies, he decided that the light, the appearance, and the false texture of filmed clothes, decor, and skin were the lurking heart of the matter.

The credits say John Dos Passos did the screenplay for *The Devil Is a Woman.* Is it possible that this prolix novelist, the assembler of *U.S.A.* (1,312 pages in the Library of America edition), the conscientious social realist, wrote the whiplash taunts uttered by Concha Pérez, the "devil" in the case, like "Wait a minute and I'll kiss you" or "Kiss me and I'll break your heart"?

I can't hear Dos Passos when I see the movie. So it is reassuring, in Sternberg's memoir, *Fun in a Chinese Laundry* (1965), to learn that the writer was in bed with "undulant fever" at the time of the film's making. Perhaps it was a Spanish flu, for one effrontery of the picture says we are in Spain at fiesta time. That permits a froth of carnival streamers, flowers, birds, masks, confetti, capriccio, false noses, and the shimmer of light falling on veils, scrims, lattices, and disguises (to say nothing of the mamba gaze of Dietrich). The film is a visual pandemonium of artifice, fever, and ecstasy, as well as the luminous paint Sternberg applied everywhere. The real Spain got huffy over this portrait and threatened to ban all Paramount movies. Sternberg was giving up the ghost as he made his most personal work, in which Concha and Dietrich turn on the forlorn male with, "Are you my father? No. Are you my husband? No. Are you my lover? No. Well, I must say, you're content with very little."

Was Sternberg reading that epitaph into his actress's mouth, or was he intent on exquisite clothes and barbed lines, the metastasis of black and white, the parade of humiliated men, and Marlene Dietrich's Concha, with kiss curls painted on her brow, as artificial as Groucho's mustache? This has little of the "story" provided in *Morocco* or *Shanghai Express.* Those films have enough narrative for us to believe that Amy Jolly and Shanghai Lily have yielded to "love" for their men, Gary Cooper and Clive Brook.

It was on *The Scarlet Empress* that Sternberg had elevated his sacred monster beyond happy endings. Now, it was ecstasy or nothing. Sternberg guessed his days at Paramount were running out, and knew Dietrich was not to be owned; he replaced story with a ritual of frustrated desire. If this would be their last film, its format could have gone on forever, with Concha inspecting the manhood of Spain, pricking every hombre with a vampiric kiss before erasing him. All that required was an infantry line of toy lovers, handsome, mustached, and looking like Sternberg as much as Lionel Atwill does in *Devil,* the officer and the gentleman belittled as "my Pasqualito." Sternberg was doing the unthinkable in making a fool of the American hero and the studio system's lies about romance, marriage, and the whole routine.

At Paramount, Sternberg now found himself under the production control of Ernst Lubitsch. That seemed an amiable arrangement, but Lubitsch the Berliner disapproved of Sternberg the Viennese. Sternberg wasn't pledged to making tidy entertainments or falling for romance. The *Devil* title was actually Lubitsch's imposition. Sternberg had wanted "Capriccio Espagnole," as if offering a set of stylistic variations. Lubitsch wearied at the stress on style; he shortened the picture from ninety-three minutes to seventy-six, and cut a second song sung by Dietrich, "If It Isn't Pain, Then It Isn't Love."

There's no need for Concha to spell out the pain factor. Bringing that on is her vocation, like goosing the starched humiliation in Lionel Atwill's face. Maybe that mortification is what kept Dietrich attached to Sternberg beyond their pearled string of films and the curious cold aura of their enchantment—until Lubitsch decided that a responsible film studio had had enough.

Lubitsch and Sternberg could never stay friendly. Lubitsch was a sardonic careerist, while Sternberg was self-destructive and averse to the spurious codes of humanism assembled for Hollywood entertainment. But Concha is the epitome of desire eclipsing human hope. Not that Dietrich went along with that so easily. No matter how sophisticated she looked, she was a sentimental woman who sighed and rolled her eyes when Sternberg had her do reaction shots over and over, and then berated her in public if she wasn't quite right. Dietrich grew bored and hurt by the posing he required. She was also a practical hausfrau who brought sandwiches for their lunchtime trysts in Sternberg's office.

If Dietrich was becoming disobedient, that suited Concha's hostility to romantic contentment. Sternberg wanted a ravishing icon who treated men like flies. The result is wildly beautiful but as beyond reason as a cigarette-factory girl wearing a different Travis Banton costume in every scene, going from lavish black splendor to glowing white lace. No impoverished screen woman ever had such inexplicable luxury or wore clothes and light to glorify her cynicism. If it was gay to furnish movies with supreme clothes, then it was a gay insight that admitted how fraudulent American romance was in the depth of the Depression.

The relationship between Josef and Marlene had drained away. Her rapport with Travis Banton never wavered. Those two were bosom pals, all the more secure in that they had no thought of making a sexual move on each other. Their subjects were clothes, her look, and his genius. She loved what he could do and she understood that his dresses were more important than Sternberg's sketchy scripts. Hers was a professional delight in Banton, and the cultivation of narcissism.

All three of them understood the look on her close-up face, staring at Sternberg himself (she knew he was there in the dark beyond the lights), and intimating, Well, you can't sleep with my photo, can you? This ironic limitation extends to all of us in our dark.

What keeps *The Devil Is a Woman* alive is the realization that Concha has no pretense to being a real woman: she is an actress, a star, or what we now call a celebrity—a photographed attitude, an advertisement for depravity who has never entirely experienced that condition because she is always acting it out. She is intensely photographed but suggests no existence apart from her riveting gaze. She is ex machina.

For a movie so attentive to sex, it is oddly nonphysical. Dietrich moves very little; she seems aware that her face has consumed the rest of her. It's not that she was ever an actress who excelled in motion (like Louise Brooks, Bette Davis, or Jeanne Moreau) but in *The Blue Angel* we know her shot-putter thighs and that sensual slouch when she sits. In *Morocco* there is the hesitation and the shy dip as she kisses a girl in the cabaret audience. In *Blonde Venus,* she shrugs off the gorilla suit like someone being smothered. But in *The Devil,* she becomes nearly still to emphasize her avid eyes. Everyone knows Marlene had famous legs: she understood that Sternberg had deliberately put her in pants in the first scene of *Morocco* to create another hideaway. As a nightclub singer, she pioneered sheer gowns in which she seemed naked above the waist. She did have breasts; she was proud of them. But who ever noticed them in a Sternberg film? They threatened the smooth line of Banton's clothes.

Breasts were often ogled by masculine directors and masturbating boys, but designers preferred legs. Another gay designer, Orry-Kelly, had horrible problems at Warners with Bette Davis and her breasts. These were quite extensive but inclined to fall. Edith Head reported that Bette "refused to wear brassieres with underwires because she thought that the wire would cause breast cancer. When strapless bras became available, Kelly bought one and tried to get her to wear it, but she threw it at him!" Time and again, under gay costumiers, the lissome women resemble boys.

In the Pierre Louÿs novel that inspired *The Devil Is a Woman,* the stooge hero, Don Mateo, eventually turns on Conchita's endless flirtations with other men, thrashes her, and takes her to bed—only to discover that his femme fatale is a virgin. There is a gesture toward that in the film, but censorship got in the way. We hear the beating. There is even a glimpse of the otherwise immaculate Concha ravaged and untidy after sex (with a dull but available matador). What a film it would be—and how true to Sternberg's sadomasochism—if we had seen the beating and the bedding and then discovered that Concha was as empty as, say, Alicia Vikander's skeletal robot Ava in *Ex Machina* (2015). The seed of our modern fascination with androids or synthetic humans goes back to the 1930s. The movies were always guiding us toward virtual reality as opposed to the real thing.

The repressed comedy of *The Devil Is a Woman* and the aplomb of its imagery have nowhere to escape to. There is even a withheld tumescence that suggests imminent pornography. The fantasy is on the brink of outrage yet incapable of going there because of the Code. You wonder if murder is the only way out. "If you had loved me enough, you would have killed yourself," Concha tells Pasqual, and there is much talk of love leading to death.

Dietrich's repertoire of glances, pouts, flounces, and wide-eyed disbelief are captivating—if you're as ready to be tortured or drowned in them as Sternberg must have been. (He did photograph some of the film himself.) The caprice is heady until one feels its lack of character. This is beyond worldly, Lubitsch-like comedy; it's a measure of nihilism and of dismay at the stupid facility of photographic beauty. That's the secret to the film's duel done in pouring rain on a small set: the moment-by-moment passage of light on surfaces and the flicker of action is intoxicating, but the aftertaste brims with poison.

There we are, in 1935, with a great director and a magical face at the point of seeing that the movies may kill romance by letting us forget love and sex.

As Steven Bach suggested in his biography *Marlene Dietrich* (1992), there is something airless in the perfection of the "most unrelenting film Sternberg ever made." The enchantment perceives its own dead end. Movie beauty has seldom been as bleak. Sternberg was never the same again, just as Dietrich had lasting difficulty emerging from Concha-ism and finding the actress she may have hoped to be.

These Sternberg-Dietrich-Banton films have not dated. They are exercises in stinging beauty, comedy without laughter, and mortification. And that triangle functioned for six films—none really successful at the box office—before Paramount said enough. Sternberg drifted away into increasing obscurity. In 1935, he commissioned Richard Neutra to design his personal hideaway—10000 Tampa Avenue, in the San Fernando Valley. It was a daring modern house with many refinements: Neutra did as instructed and made the bathrooms without locks—Sternberg believed that rooms with locks were a hideaway temptation to suicide. (In *Sunset Blvd.,* the butler has removed all locks from Norma Desmond's doors.) Later on, Ayn Rand lived in the Tampa Avenue house.

Banton was dropped by Paramount (he moved on to Fox and then to designing clothes for fashion houses). He was replaced by Edith Head, good but not as reckless as Banton, and an adroit careerist. She had trained herself to mask her own sexual ambiguity. But Banton was not victimized because he was gay. His life was accepted, and his work was required. There were gays who prospered naturally for decades in Hollywood (we are coming to the most fruitful of the hideaways, the home of George Cukor). They did not think to impose their own private habits on their pictures. But, as I said, they intuited that the medium was detached or ironic about life's conventional ideals and heavenly marriages. The medium understood transience and promiscuity—the alleged liberties that straights sometimes envied in gay life.

In 1977, Luis Buñuel revisited the situation of *Devil* in *That Obscure Object of Desire* (male cinema's ultimate title?). He cast Maria Schneider as Concha, but she was "difficult," so he replaced her with two actresses—Angela Molina and Carole Bouquet—and his stupid, suave hero (the impeccable but peccable Fernando Rey) couldn't tell them apart. Casting and allegiance blew up in one sweet, comic bomb.

5

Codes and Codebreakers

Designer Travis Banton and designed Ruth Taylor, while making
Gentlemen Prefer Blondes (1928), when clothes were the stuff of dreams.
Banton designed the film and Taylor was its Lorelei Lee.
Two years later, she would be Buck Henry's mother.

THE PRODUCTION CODE for American movies was more a buffer system than a theory of moral principle. In the 1920s, there had been protestations of concern over the scandals associated with Hollywood. This humbug usually turned on young successes suddenly loaded with money and widespread adoration, acting out. These hot kids screwed around in a new way for America. They drank and took drugs. They behaved badly. There were a few premature deaths. This prompted dismay in Washington, the churches, in academe, and among parents. The taste for scandal became a media mainstay, more beguiling than most movies.

The business was unfazed by the scandals. Too many of them implicated the so-called leaders of the town. But everyone was worried lest the public took it into its head that tales of bad behavior should stop them paying to enter the dreamy dark. The worry was foolish: the more naughtiness the better if you're dreaming in a medium founded on showing forbidden things. So a former postmaster general, Will Hays, an alleged worthy who had been involved in the Teapot Dome Scandal, was appointed to lead a cleanup operation. In turn that led to the Code, in force by 1934, and surely accelerated by the ways the recent addition of sound could be extra suggestive.

But by then, the dilemma of what to do about Hollywood had been aggravated by widening rifts in economic opportunity. Why should beautiful young fools not spend their money as if it might not last? Wasn't the money as raw as the kids—and didn't America lust after new money as the old kind disappeared? In *Gold Diggers of 1933,* Joan Blondell led the singing of "Remember My Forgotten Man." The country was properly moved: it is a high point in American film and an anthem for Roosevelt's new plans. But America disdains its past and is addicted to forgetting.

The language of the Production Code was draconian but naive, for it grew out of extensive ignorance. The key guideline was that "no picture shall be produced that will lower the moral standards of those who see it." We guess that means whatever the moralists want it to mean, but it seems to say that if a picture offends a few hundred people then it should be banned for a hundred million. That threat was not friendly to the picture business, so the Code sprang up to distract or appease watchdogs.

This required large compromises with general theories of civic well-being. The Code said murder should not be glorified in any way, though it did not say it *could not* be shown, because the business had learned that scenes of killing reliably excited the public. The Code did not demand that black people be presented decently in films, though it did decree that miscegenation could not be shown. To take this argument a little further: how far does it undermine morality to suggest, over years, that beautiful people in beautiful clothes are an ideal, and deserving of happiness? Is it encouraging or immoral *not* to admit that common or unpretty people may have a tough time in a godly country?

So the Code endorsed a status quo that the picture business and all business wanted to have protected. This supported a very practical aim in the Code: that national guidelines would forestall local censorship and interference with the movie trade. Hollywood had always feared individual states like Kansas asserting their moral principles and banning such wonders as Mae West, because she was lewd, funny, and unapologetic.

When the Production Code required that "the sanctity of the institution of marriage and the home shall be upheld" it was acting on movies being a date-night event after which men and women would get hitched and have children who would themselves go to the movies one day. This scheme flourished even as the Hollywood community was breaking fresh statistics with divorce—and wondering if their failure to uphold the institution was prompting the country as a whole. People learned to smoke and kiss at the movies, and they felt easier about looser social habits because of gossip about the town (a genre ardently encouraged by the business).

Another rule said, "sex perversion or any reference to it is forbidden." Again, you can guess what they were afraid of, but the vagueness of "perversion" is problematic, especially when sexual relations between blacks and whites were considered taboo. So what came of all this?

It sounds as if gay practitioners would have had a hard time finding employment under the Code. But far from being outlawed, the creative industry of gay people in Hollywood developed very nicely.

I don't intend to compile a list of gay careers. Nor do I want to "out" people, though that word carries absurd connotations of something illicit or shameful. Rather, I want to extend the proposal that the atmosphere of all movies had a gay air—as in a mounting suspicion that America's approved romantic formulae might be demented.

In the 1930s, in black-and-white films, the Hollywood screen had a sheen and a luster that furnished what we call glamour. Photography itself had a shining quality that came from silver salts, the aura of focused lighting, the decisions over framing, and the ideology behind the close-up. That shining was technical (experts labored over it), but it was spiritual, too. It believed in the face as an open window, whereas in life we often treat it as a veiled question. Grant this process has been at work for over a century and we may wonder how far visual attraction has suppressed large areas of personality and meaning.

So, what does Isabel Archer look like in *The Portrait of a Lady* (1881)? Henry James does not dare describe her—nor does John Banville in *Mrs. Osmond,* his 2017 sequel to James. Not even the faces of Suzanne Neve and Nicole Kidman, who played Isabel in 1968 and 1996, get in reading's way. James's portrait is blind and inward; reading has its precious dark. The novel attempts to summon a young woman with the world before her. The attempt is absorbing, though it never begins to explain the folly that prompts Ms. Archer to marry the wretched Gilbert Osmond. That the novel is so good is proved by its overcoming that narrative abyss. If we wonder what Isabel looks like, James insists on her as a creature in whom appearance does not count.

By contrast, a close-up of Garbo, say, in the 1936 *Camille,* compels adoration. It is not a face subject to indecision or mistake. Camille's passionate "error" with Armand is as immaculate as a statue's gaze. Hers is a destined face we must accept. There's no point in watching the film if you don't feel that. In James's novel Isabel is full of doubts and wonderings, yet hardly *there.* She has no body, just years of mind. You never think to fall for her. With Garbo, your falling for *or into* her in fantasy is so compelling, you have less chance of thinking *about* her. Attractiveness in film has supplanted the thing James called moral being. It relies on a voyeurist impulse freed by photography and film: I may look at you—I may spy on you—without acknowledging your rights as a soul. Film assumes a slavery in which citizenship depends on being good-looking.

Camille was part of Garbo's long attempt to seem "beautiful," but it is also an aspect of cinematography that soaks up light, that believes in framing and in archetypes more than individuality. That is how most stars were the same until their age became inescapable. Garbo stopped when she questioned her own beauty (after a film called *Two-Faced Woman,* made when she was thirty-six). So her films are a bank that stocks Garbo's face and only her face, an imprint of idealized womanhood with the sadness of Garbo's wounded gaze. She usually saw love as a doomed predicament or an attempt to deny solitude; while *Camille* was shooting, her friend and advisor, Irving Thalberg, died.

Exactly the same condition affects our view of Robert Taylor's Armand, or Lionel Barrymore, Henry Daniell, and Elizabeth Allen in the same film. Hollywood did not do ordinary.

In the 1930s, cinematography was dedicated to an exquisite pinnacle of emotional radiance, and that condition is more important than George Cukor, the director of *Camille,* being gay. He admired Garbo because "she was rather cool, but seething underneath." She had realized that being adored in the detachment of cinema was more sustaining than actual contacts life might throw up. She had seen through sex or love in the rapture of being looked at. Her mantra, "I want to be alone" (whispered to herself in *Grand Hotel,* 1932), was a diagram of desire, distance, and the close-up—the triangulation that made the medium erotic.

Note that the men who photographed *Camille,* William Daniels and Karl Freund, were not gay. The surface elements the camera saw might be provided by gay talent, but the guardians of seeing were ritually heterosexual. The orientation of film's eye is still a masculine preserve. In 2014, just 3 percent of American cinematographers were female. For the Oscars of 2017 Rachel Morris was nominated for photographing *Mudbound,* the first female to be nominated in that category.

Yet in still photography the country counts Dorothea Lange, Diane Arbus, Helen Levitt, Lee Miller, and hundreds of others. The thrust of movie-looking, or spying, remains male, and I'm not sure that cinema (the engine called desire) can survive the wise reform that imbalance cries out for. The revelations of 2017, the litany of sexual harassment, never quite got to a key question: what are movies without male lust? Could the whole show lapse, like dinosaurs?

The costumes for *Camille* were done by Adrian (real name Adrian Adolph Greenburg). As a young man, he had been hired by Natacha Rambova to do costumes for Rudolph Valentino, and he would become a mainstay at MGM. Joan Crawford swore by his value as being beyond that of husbands or lovers. "He never made me feel as though I was being used as a clotheshorse," she said. But that didn't mean she wasn't often the horse. Adrian made her shoulders into a national monument or part of our genome. The head-and-shoulder shot has structured our appraisal of identity.

Dead at fifty-six, Adrian had over 250 credits as a costume designer. He was also gay, while being married to the actress Janet Gaynor, who had her own gay life; Adrian and Janet were fond companions and useful beards for each other. There were many such partnerships of convenience to forestall gossip and media criticism and to simplify crowded lives. Not all stars have the time or the energy for affairs. They need to have sex with the camera. Other strenuous sex can impair their looks and leave them fatigued. Gary Cooper's attentive mother strove to get him married just to slow the rate of his screwing around.

I am not saying that Adrian designed homosexual clothes. He did *The Wizard of Oz, Ninotchka, The Philadelphia Story,* and *Woman of the Year* as well as *Camille.* He was a conscientious professional, expert at making women look iconic on screen without arousing an audience to frenzy. He did the all-in-white Fred Astaire and Eleanor Powell against a bright black floor for "Begin the Beguine" in *Broadway Melody of 1940.* He made ladies of his female stars, obeying the factory rule "Put the light where the money is."

So the shine on the screen was as commercial as it was romantic.

It was as innocent and lucrative as sunlight in the Western. And just as Westerns promoted tourism, so movie glamour helped sell clothes. In the Depression years, many Hollywood films shrugged off tact and exulted in wealth, making its characters fashion plates, ridiculously elegant and sophisticated for audiences who could barely afford the price of admission. This veiled insolence was not a conspiracy among the studios. It arose naturally in the optimism that prevailed. But since the 1930s, this ecstatic couture has never quite returned. Costumes today are eccentric, quirky, or outrageous. They are more "real" and seldom content with expensive perfection.

There's a stirring of a gay sensibility in the scene from *Morocco* mentioned earlier. It involves Foreign Legionnaire Tom Brown and a saloon singer named Amy Jolly. The simple setup was a vehicle for Sternberg's way of looking, enough to start you thinking that if all the color systems on film are straight, or real, then black-and-white—a lovely, droll dismissal of realism—is a dream.

Tom is as beautiful as Amy. In part that is Cooper's own looks; for several years he was an Adonis of motion pictures, with a cocksman reputation to match. He was tall and lean, and known to have been raised in Montana, a land of sun and cowboys. His three years at school in Dunstable, in England, were overlooked. He had a Montana look at a time when suntan became fashionable. It looked especially good in black-and-white. Onscreen, Coop was laconic to a point of parody and an actor who seemed to do very little—as if to support the notion that acting was not manly.

He had tastes beyond the open range. During his affair with Dorothy di Frasso, a woman from upstate New York who had married an Italian aristocrat and put on airs, he fell in love with clothes. Cecil Beaton remarked on how his eyes had "black eyelashes as the lower lid and on the upper." Beaton liked to photograph Cooper, and found him "nothing like his stereotype of the slow-talking cowboy. Erudite, charming, spectacularly constructed man." He said that the gay director Edmund Goulding "worshipped" the star—"twice a day." Beaton claimed that he himself had had a brief affair with Cooper.

A hero like Coop was not unaffected by his own beauty or by the narcissism of a job where one is praised and paid for looking gorgeous. So many actors nurse the fear that acting is not virile. But in the early 1930s especially, and in *Morocco,* the process of film makes him lovely for all comers.

In *Morocco,* he wears his legion uniform like a male model in a fashion spread (or like Valentino in the *Four Horsemen* tango). He has long boots, swag white pants, a belted dress tunic (with medals!), and a tilted kepi, and he lounges in the café audience in suggestive ease—not unlike Dietrich's open-legged stance in *The Blue Angel.* He is lit with as much care as Dietrich.

Amy wears a man's black tuxedo, a top hat, and a white bow tie. This provokes indignation in the café crowd until Tom hushes them. (It prompted a similar dismay in Paramount executives who told their director that their wives always wore skirts. One of them complained that a guy can't lift pants.) Sternberg said, "I not only wished to touch lightly on a Lesbian accent . . . but also demonstrate that her sensual appeal was not entirely due to the classic formation of her legs."

Amy sings a song, "Give Me the Man," directing a lazy but inviting salute at Tom. He grins and responds. Then, as the song concludes, and in the applause that greets it, Amy notices a pretty, dark-haired woman in the crowd with a flower in her hair. She starts to back away but hesitates, and then makes a stealthy and enigmatic advance. The young woman, intimidated, begins to giggle. And Amy—but it is Marlene, too—goes up to her and takes her flower. Then she lifts the girl's dainty chin and kisses her on the lips. Is this the first subversive embrace in an American movie?

Amy acts aloof, but she will commit herself to Tom. She is independent in many ways, and daring, but she admits to loving Tom, while he takes that for granted. In time Sternberg would develop Dietrich as the authority figure in relationships, with men as her fools. This was a pattern he was himself learning with Dietrich, who praised him constantly as a great director but would not be directed by him in life. So their films involve more and more male characters, mustached lovers who endure her arbitrary authority without a tear.

At the end of *Morocco* Amy casts off her expensive shoes and trudges barefoot into the desert, mingling with Arab women as a camp follower. Sternberg was a tight-lipped poet of sexual abandon, in the position of the audience—desperate to watch but forbidden to touch. There is a feeling of infinite sexual possibility hanging over the film and an air of some languid orgy about to break like a thunderstorm. The restraints under which it was made are vital to that tension. The film is exquisite, absurd, and poetic, and that's not a comfortable mix for all viewers. Sternberg was a perverse romantic, a man who seemed to believe in images more than action.

In his mordantly funny memoir, *Fun in a Chinese Laundry,* he describes how he sometimes directed Marlene: "Turn your shoulders away from me. . . . Drop your voice an octave and don't lisp. . . . Count to six and look at that lamp as if you could no longer live without it." After they parted, Sternberg said he was told a story how on her later films Dietrich would often go through a scene and finish it by whispering through the microphone, "Where are you, Jo?" Desire and imagining, and a scene from an unmade film.

Elsewhere in the factory system, everyone who knew him liked Hermes Pan (real name Hermes Panagiotopoulos). He was from Memphis, a dancer and a choreographer who fell in with Fred Astaire in 1933 and became his career-long assistant and collaborator. He encouraged Fred in his dances, he suggested moves and entire routines, he made life easier for the perfectionist, he partnered Ginger Rogers in rehearsals, and it was a standing joke that he looked just like Fred. Pan was also discreetly gay.

He talked about a significant problem with film dance: the fact that audiences tied to realism felt uncomfortable when ordinary small talk turned into something as stylized as song and dance. This comment concerns "Isn't This a Lovely Day" from *Top Hat:*

> I would work with Astaire and we would figure out how to get into the number without it jarring, because people were beginning to be horrified by the idea of a person bursting into song or dance without a reason. So the main trick was to get into a dance before you realized they were into a dance, to get in so gradually from the spoken word to the visual.

So it was that the smoothness of those fairy-tale musicals at RKO came from the skidpan studio floors, the elasticity of Fred and Ginger, and their being handled by someone as adept as Hermes Pan so that the bumps didn't intrude. Astaire was married with children and very conservative, but he was wild about beautiful movement and thus as superior to reality as Sternberg.

The musical genre was often regarded as a gay enclave. The most accomplished musical operation in town was at MGM from the 1940s on under the leadership of Arthur Freed—that unit was known as "Freed's Fairies." The gays on staff there included choreographer Robert Alton, dance director Charles Walters (he did the dances for *Meet Me in St. Louis,* and would go on to direct for *Lili, High Society,* and *The Unsinkable Molly Brown*), and musical arranger Roger Edens, who was especially close to Judy Garland. Another MGM musical, *On the Town,* had come from music by Leonard Bernstein and dances by Jerome Robbins, both gay. On the other hand, Gene Kelly and Stanley Donen (codirectors on *On the Town,* as well as *Singin' in the Rain*) were robustly heterosexual.

With inside knowledge or the nerve to ask, you could find gay people in most of the crafts that contributed to movie. It was easier for them to gain entry than it was for blacks. Still, you might suppose that it was harder for gays to be regular actors on the screen. That would become a cruel test in the 1950s, but it's interesting to see how many supporting actors flourished in the 1930s and 1940s without being challenged. Franklin Pangborn was treasured, by audiences and studios alike, as a gay stereotype—a nervous fusspot who liked to give orders. In plenty of films that act was eagerly employed: *Flying Down to Rio, Carefree, Easy Living, Stage Door, The Bank Dick, Sullivan's Travels,* and *The Palm Beach Story.* Pangborn lived with his mother and kept a gay life on the side. We don't know whether he was happy or indignant to play the queen, but few audiences were in doubt about his personality.

Sometimes something slipped through and acquired a stealthy, snakelike menace. In 1944 Otto Preminger was set to produce Vera Caspary's novel *Laura* for Twentieth Century Fox. Rouben Mamoulian was meant to direct. Laura Hunt is a young woman in advertising who has been taken up in society by a leading newspaper columnist,

Waldo Lydecker. (What are such names meant to tell us?) He grooms her, he dresses her, he teaches her how to talk. He directs her. Then a young woman is killed—shot in the face—and everyone assumes the victim is Laura. Mark McPherson is the detective on the case and he soon realizes that Lydecker may be more than just a bystander.

In the event, Mamoulian was fired, and Preminger took over the direction (surely his plan). McPherson was Dana Andrews and Laura was Gene Tierney. But Preminger had realized that Waldo was the most intriguing part. Mamoulian had wanted Laird Cregar in the role but Preminger thought that audiences would guess too quickly that Cregar was the killer. Instead, he thought of a stage actor who was hardly known on screen, Webb Parmelee Hollenbeck, who acted as Clifton Webb. He was ostentatiously gay, along the lines of the bitter, vicious stereotype, a man who feels so wounded by his gender casting that he will take out the pain on anyone he notices. He became Waldo Lydecker, speaking some of the most scabrous and quotable lines—"I don't use a pen, I write with a goose quill dipped in venom."

Webb was a new face and voice (silky, supercilious, and like a lash) far from wartime team spirit. Waldo is such a spidery center of attention it's far-fetched to think that Vincent Price (as Shelby Carpenter) might be the murderer. It has to be Waldo—as Nabokov would say later, in *Lolita,* "You can always count on a murderer for his fancy prose style."

The film is obliged to see Waldo as the villain, and nasty, too. So the rough masculinity of Dana Andrews imposes itself on Laura in a clumsy way that leaves us wondering how short-lived their marriage will be. Beneath the surface of the plot Laura could be a boy that her lover Waldo has schooled. It's as if the ingenious Preminger has felt his way through Hollywood humbug to the lurking situation.

Waldo is entertaining, and one of the sharpest spiteful minds in American films; he dominates the picture and Webb got a supporting actor nomination for playing him (Barry Fitzgerald won as a lovable priest in *Going My Way*). Yet it says so much about the 1940s dread of homosexuality that Waldo has to express himself through a killing and hostility: "I'm not kind," he says, "I'm vicious. It's the secret of my charm." There is no male lover in sight for Lydecker; he seems a lonely person (Webb himself lived with his mother, who died at ninety-one). The film suggests that in mentoring Laura he has become so possessive that he can't endure the thought of her marrying Shelby. But that is a demeaning projection of homosexual pessimism taking revenge on a cheerful, straight society. The un-normal do not make a habit of attacking the normal. That cruel energy usually works in the opposite direction.

Otto Preminger was heterosexual. But why slip into the fallacy that only gay people are allowed to make gay films? Filmmaking does not depend on earned experience; it feeds on vicariousness. Howard Hawks had never driven a great herd of cattle hundreds of miles until *Red River*. Victor Fleming had not lived in Georgia, Kansas, or the Emerald City, yet he directed *Gone With the Wind* and *The Wizard of Oz* that enshrined those places. Movies are about imagining more than experience.

Still, several professional directors had gay lives without boasting about it or being victimized because of it. There is one example of a director in Hollywood suffering because of his sexual inclination. The German master F. W. Murnau was gay. He had made *Nosferatu* and *The Last Laugh* in Berlin and was invited to America by Fox, where he made *Sunrise* (1927), a thing of beauty and a completely heterosexual story. He did a few more films in America, and then *Tabu* in the South Seas, an ecstatic view of godlike male bodies. But in 1931 his chauffeur (a fourteen-year-old Filipino) crashed the car on the Pacific Coast Highway and Murnau was killed. Putting a kid in charge of a Rolls-Royce is always taking a chance.

In the same pragmatic way, it is more remarkable that Dorothy Arzner was a woman than that she was a lesbian. She was the only woman director in Hollywood in her time. (And still no woman in Hollywood history has directed more films.) Born in 1898, she had planned to be a doctor, but working as a medical assistant during the Great War deterred her and she opted for film directing instead. There were women screenwriters and editors then, but Arzner was smart enough to want to be in charge. She was a feminist and she usually had a woman lover—choreographer Marion Morgan for much of her career. She made more than twenty films, including *The Wild Party* (Clara Bow's first talking picture), *Christopher Strong* (with Katharine Hepburn), *Nana,* and *Dance, Girl, Dance,* where Lucille Ball and Maureen O'Hara are rivals. Arzner's private life never seems to have impeded her and it seldom shows in her movies. After retiring, she lectured on film at UCLA, where Francis Ford Coppola was one of her students.

There was Edmund Goulding, English, who made *Grand Hotel, Dark Victory,* and the truly macabre *Nightmare Alley.* Mitchell Leisen was gay. He had done costumes for Douglas Fairbanks on *Robin Hood* and *The Thief of Bagdad* and sets for Cecil B. DeMille on *Madam Satan* and *Sign of the Cross.* Then he became a director and had a long and varied career that includes *Swing High, Swing Low; Easy Living; Midnight; Remember the Night; To Each His Own*; and *No Man of Her Own.* I detect no hint of gayness in all the entertainment Leisen provided. I will add James Whale later on and, most illustrious of all, George Cukor, but Vincente Minnelli may be the most poignant case.

Minnelli was born in Chicago in 1903, and an early job was dressing windows at Marshall Field's, the department store—those windows are so very like screens or tableaux. That led him to working on costumes and sets for the stage, and then to a similar job at Radio City Music Hall. After that came movies, starting with *Cabin in the Sky* (1943), an all-black story (Minnelli was not black). His pictures are vivid with sets, clothes, color, and dream sequences. They include *Meet Me in St. Louis, The Clock, The Pirate, An American in Paris, The Bad and the Beautiful,* and *Lust for Life. Meet Me in St. Louis* may or may not be "great," but as I said earlier it is one of the films I love most, for the nostalgic décor, the songs, the house and its family, and for delicious performances from Margaret O'Brien, Mary Astor, and Judy Garland.

A case could be made that Garland was never closer to looking beautiful than in *Meet Me in St. Louis* (the fall of her lush amber wig surely helped). It is plain that she is being looked at with love; she may have felt that herself when she saw the dailies. Actresses often cultivate gay men for the comforting deal of affection and flattery without sexual intrusion. Most actors need to be admired—to fail in that aggravates the constant insecurity of being turned down for parts, trashed in reviews, and booed by audiences. Insecurity was Judy's way of being. It was her vulnerability that added to the identification with her in the gay community, along with its knowledge of Garland's own lesbian affairs. She was bisexual and very inquisitive about sex. She had affairs with Betty Asher, a publicist at MGM (and maid of honor at her marriage to Minnelli), and with Kay Thompson, singer, songwriter, and the author of the Eloise books that owed something to the neglect of Garland's daughter, Liza Minnelli, at New York's Plaza Hotel.

Minnelli had had a gay life in Chicago, but in 1945 he married Garland—his first marriage, her second. She had previously wed MGM musical arranger David Rose. Being with Vincente didn't last long, and it must have been a strain for both parties as professional attitudes struggled with instinct, but they worked together again on *The Clock* and *The Pirate*. After Garland, Minnelli would be married three more times. His gay life may have stopped or diminished in Hollywood, but his pictures are delighted by pretending and creating décor as a window that we want to buy into emotionally.

I was going to say that Minnelli never took on gay material, but then I remembered *Tea and Sympathy* (1956), one of his poorest films. It comes from a play by Robert Anderson, and it kept the lead actors from the stage production. A sensitive and artistic youth (John Kerr) is bullied in school. Nothing says he is gay except the unkindness of strangers and the slur of being "unmanly." But the wife (Deborah Kerr) of a teacher at the school becomes his friend and then, to settle his uneasy mind, she . . . donates herself to him? . . . she makes a noble sacrifice? . . . commits statutory rape? . . . has sex with him. Granted the censorship of the time the intercourse stayed off screen. Even in *From Here to Eternity* (1953) Deborah Kerr had not gone beyond being a spectacular prize on the Oahu beach in an orgasm-free picture. That was exciting just because it involved the hitherto ladylike Deborah Kerr. She and John Kerr (not related) do decent jobs in *Tea and Sympathy* and perhaps the film helped some lives. It may have meant a lot to Minnelli himself.

How much more value it could have had if the boy had realized he was gay, and the film had said that was okay, too. In 1956 that candor was still out of bounds. But the woman utters an infamous line that is an albatross in our culture. Before their lovemaking, she tells him, "Years from now, when you talk about this—and you will—be kind."

6

The Goddamn Monster

An intense close-up of Elsa Lanchester in *The Bride of Frankenstein* (1935)—
the greatest woman in horror until Mrs. Bates in *Psycho*

IT'S NOT JUST HOW WE LOVE OTHER PEOPLE, strangers still after many years. Their otherness is vital and hard to protect—it's a chance of dispute and politics, of profound association. Long before five years is up you'll realize your need for something alien or *difficult* in your other. Face it, in the nicest way, you want a hint of the unknown.

Frankenstein and his monster predate the movies, but would they have lasted without the medium's greedy aptitude for a new version of life? Monsters on screen helped us see how most movie characters were innately fabricated, more or less lifelike, but fantasy incarnate. The stitching in Boris Karloff's head as the monster prefigures the way CGI (computer generated imagery) can bring anything to life. That helped us see how the hideous could be glamorous. In Thomas Harris's books, Hannibal Lecter is loathsome, but on screen, with the dreamy, malicious Anthony Hopkins, he acquired an eerie charm (and an Oscar). He was sexy, even if driven by desires that were "unnatural." We are more inclined to go to bed with demons—just ask your lover.

This movie legacy starts with a remarkable gay director, who liked to pass as a regular fellow. James Whale was born in Dudley in the English Midlands in 1889. His father was a blast-furnace operator, the head of a family with six children living in a four-room house. In 1957, Whale would drown himself in his own swimming pool in his hideaway on Amalfi Drive in Pacific Palisades. He had dressed carefully for his big finish, and he was depressed from the several strokes he had had. He was rich, famous once, a movie director with a few classics to his name. He left a note that said, "Do not grieve for me. My nerves are all shot and for the last year I have been in agony day and night."

He got a basic education, joined the Army in 1914 and was taken prisoner by the Germans in Flanders in 1917. It was in that all-male world that he became excited by the prisoners' theatrical productions—recall the enchanting moment in Jean Renoir's *La Grande Illusion* (1937) where the French prisoners putting on an amateur show are hushed and captivated when one of them masquerades as a pretty woman.

At the end of the war, Whale plunged into London theater doing any work he could find. He was handsome, with red hair going white, and he wore clothes well. It was believed that he was gay, but in the early 1920s he had a relationship with a striking stage designer, Doris Zinkeisen, so intense that some friends—the actor John Gielgud and Elsa Lanchester included—believed the pair were engaged.

In 1928, Whale found the play that would change his life: *Journey's End,* by R. C. Sherriff, set in a trench bivouac in the Great War, and one of the most popular renderings of that war's experience. Whale directed an experimental one-night performance of the play (with Laurence Olivier in the lead role of Captain Stanhope); he then did the proper London production with Colin Clive, and the Broadway production with Colin Keith-Johnston. For all of these stagings, Whale also designed the sets—he had an instinct for places being turned into dreams. In 1930, he directed the movie in Los Angeles, with Clive restored to the role of Stanhope. At every step, *Journey's End* was a hit, and Whale was lifted higher on its success. The play has an all-male cast: it is a study of officers under the pressure of hopeless attacks, alcoholism, and imminent death. It shows these men developing affection and caring for one another in the ordeal of being afraid. What can military segregation do but uncover sexual inclinations in its crisis of fear? Medals were distributed in the Great War, but its deepest lesson was the universality of terror. Armies are gatherings against fear. So why are some military men still hostile to women in uniform? Are they afraid of the male regiment being seduced?

On arriving in Los Angeles, Whale met a young American producer, David Lewis, and they were lovers until 1952 when, on a trip to Paris, Whale fell for Pierre Foegel, a bartender who was his junior by more than thirty-five years. Lewis then quit the house and the relationship as Foegel became Whale's new companion. When Whale's health declined he began to open his house and his pool to young trade in the Los Angeles area. The director George Cukor felt that Whale had rather let the gay side down by being so unrestrained in his later life. But the union with Lewis was a marriage, before such pacts were common, and Lewis would become nearly as well known in the picture business as Whale. He worked steadily at Warner Bros. and had credits on *Each Dawn I Die, Dark Victory,* and *Kings Row.*

No one suggests that Whale and Lewis got into any "trouble" during their relationship, or that they were treated unfairly or unkindly by the business. They were regularly together. Neither man ever resorted to acquiring a female mask for public events. Whale did not go out soliciting or run the risk of public scandal. But he never behaved as if gay life required concealment.

People close to Whale believed English privacy meant more to him than owning up to a cause. Why not? We do not expect happy heterosexuals to speak proudly and lustily about the pleasures of sex with women. If they do yield to that boasting—think of it as the culture of professed pussy grabbing—we conclude that the talk is in bad taste and probably a fraud.

But the orderly Whale did have an instinct for melodrama. By 1931, he had directed some dialogue scenes for Howard Hughes's *Hell's Angels* as well as *Journey's End.* He was under contract to Universal and the studio wondered what else he could do. In February 1931, they had released *Dracula,* directed by Tod Browning, with Bela Lugosi as the vampire. It was a landmark, ushering in the era of the sound horror film. Universal was anxious to cash in on the success, and that urge was led by "Junior" Laemmle, the enthusiastic son of Carl Laemmle, who had founded the studio.

Laemmle put the idea of *Frankenstein* to James Whale. The director thought the proposal was a gag. He knew hardly anyone who had read Mary Shelley's book, written in 1818. That neglect is still current, just as many assume that Frankenstein must be the name of the monster, not the doctor. But Whale became intrigued as he explored the idea of a genius making a new human creature only for it to run amok. Here was the germ of a new being, and a metaphor for outcast members of society. Horror was always an inviting kingdom for lost souls. Scriptwriting was assigned to John Balderston, who had written the script for *Dracula* from his revision of the play text.

It had been taken for granted that Bela Lugosi would be in the new film—as the monster. But Whale thought having Lugosi in both films would be confusing. So he searched until he saw a play, *The Criminal Code,* in which a young actor did a menacing piece of physical action, stalking a man he meant to kill. Something about that killer reached out for pathos. There was pain in his eyes. You can still see it in the film Howard Hawks made of *The Criminal Code*. That actor's birth name was William Henry Pratt, and he too was English. He had changed his name to Boris Karloff, as if he had a glimmering of what was to come—it is so forbidding a name it's comic. With that name, his height (Mary Shelley's monster is eight feet tall, Karloff was six feet, but his shoes were built up and made extra heavy), his sepulchral English voice, and his sad gaze slipped into place. David Lewis looked at the script and at Karloff himself and had a crucial insight—"I was sorry for the goddamn monster!" That was the key to opening the door to a room that would one day house Norman Bates.

Karloff gave us something else. Lugosi can be honored, but he was always close to camp or madness. We seldom cared for him. But Karloff restored the undisputed human anguish of Lon Chaney (1883–1930), the original poetic bearer of disturbance in film horror. Chaney died as sound appeared, and so he is too little appreciated today.

By now, we know it's not enough for movie monsters to be scary. After all, they are safely removed from us in a cage called the screen, and no matter how alarming they seem we know we can contemplate them from our safe dark. Sympathy may bloom in that contemplation along with dread. It was all very well to take the surface view of vampirism in *Dracula* and be horrified at having one's blood sucked. But as you watched, a new depth appeared in which the fatal kiss might be as ravishing as other kisses, and the Count's obsession with female necks and breasts permitted a traditional erotic excitement. The vampiric embrace is a poisoned parody of the movie kiss. Sucking awakens such primal urges. The Dracula myth is a metaphor for young virginal women being raped and liking it. We're not supposed to think that—but that makes it irresistible.

Is there a subtext in *Frankenstein* waiting to be perceived? Suppose a black actor were to be cast as the Monster. Automatically, that would underline the opportunity in the story for a seismic reappraisal of "the other"—a human being outside the traditions that most of the species have assumed. What is a monster but some force that is simply different from us, with that difference serving as a threat? Most monsters are unaware of being monstrous, so the word "monster" reflects back critically on the wholesome society that employs it. Victor Frankenstein makes a new creature in the name of science. He also longs to escape himself. That allows a contrast between the shrill Colin Clive as the doctor (he was bisexual and alcoholic) and the grave and strangely restful Karloff. That creative disharmony carries the film beyond horror. There's an exquisite scene in *Frankenstein* where the creature sits with a little girl at a pond floating flowers on the water. Whale begs us to imagine what will become of that idyll. It's not just that we feel compassion (as well as dread) for the Monster; we are enthralled by his drugged pace and unexpected delicacy.

The narrative situation is as open as we might want: the creature could be deformed, or as beautiful as Dorian Gray. He could be an ET run amok or the demon in *Alien* ready to flirt with Sigourney Weaver's talented Ms. Ripley. The creature could be a gorilla like *King Kong* (made just two years after *Frankenstein*); it could be invisible (Whale did *The Invisible Man* in 1933). One of the lurking possibilities in science fiction and horror is the surreal juxtaposition of a norm and an abnormal. It's what made Norman Bates such a turning point in film, the kindest person in *Psycho,* yet the worst.

James Whale died three years before Alfred Hitchcock's *Psycho,* but why bar him from these possibilities? Movie is a medium where anything can be beautiful or arresting because it has been photographed and because one thing can become another on a cut in less time than it takes to close your eyes or your mind. The brink of metaphor never disappears.

Years after Whale's death, Bill Condon (another gay filmmaker) made *Gods and Monsters* (1998), in which Ian McKellen, a proudly gay actor, played Whale, and there was no doubt but that the Monster in the 1931 film was a kind of escaped prisoner, a spirit in need of rescue or understanding.

Universal and the Laemmle family pounced on horror, as any industrious studio would have done. The genre lasted for them more than twenty years as they ran permutations on Dracula, Frankenstein, and the Wolf Man. Many of those subsequent films were crude exploitation, hurried and trashy, as well as good fun. But sometimes sequels can benefit from first lessons in their own process. So, in looking for more, Universal prevailed on Whale to make another Frankenstein film in 1935. They talked about "the return" and there was a speculative script that Whale said "stinks to heaven."

Still, he entertained the idea of a sequel to help promote other projects he had in mind. But then John Balderston went away to do more work on a script, and went back to Mary Shelley and discovered that in 1818 there had been a notion that the creature deserved a mate. This was not Whale's idea, and yet the picture was made because of his enthusiasm, and it was he who determined that it ought to be called *The Bride of Frankenstein*. He guessed it was an enduring title, no matter if it involved nonsense, for the bride would be for the Monster, not for Victor.

Other writers worked on the script, and Whale oversaw the process. He supported Balderston's plan for a prologue, set in 1818, with Shelley, Byron, and Mary Shelley herself discussing the story. Whale insisted on this against studio fears that it would delay the essential horror stuff. Doctor Frankenstein appeared (it would be Colin Clive again), but much of his place in the narrative was taken by Dr. Pretorius, an older mad-scientist figure. For that role, Whale hired Ernest Thesiger, a London actor known for his flamboyant homosexuality and for being a querulous, waspish queer in life, on the stage and on the screen. Thesiger had noticed Whale in the early 1920s and become a mentor to him. They were both soldiers from the Great War and Thesiger apparently hoped to coax Whale out of his restrained life as a gay man. In 1932, Whale had cast Thesiger in a supporting part in *The Old Dark House,* which can be seen as the first camp horror film. So now Thesiger was brought over from London to play a funny but spiteful Pretorius.

It is Pretorius who helps Frankenstein assemble a mate for Karloff's Monster. In both films, the Monster was a makeup challenge, but the bride is from a new world. She qualifies as female, but she may be the first woman in American film who seems other than human. It's as if she is also made of electricity (the animating force used to bring her body parts to life). There were thoughts of casting the young Phyllis Brooks or the German actress Brigitte Helm, who had been stunning as both the good girl and the robot temptress in Fritz Lang's *Metropolis*. But Whale had another candidate from the London theater world of the 1920s.

Few performers then had been as vivid or daring, yet as hard to cast, as Elsa Lanchester. She was actress and clown, comedienne and improv artist, long before that mixture was appreciated. She was pretty in a pop-eyed way, smart and impulsive, and what was called bohemian in London in the 1920s. She had studied with Isadora Duncan (and disliked her) and made experimental films with Ivor Montagu. But her talent was odd, not glamorous or beguiling, and few knew how to place it.

She met Charles Laughton as they acted in the play *Mr. Prohack* in 1927, and they were soon living together. By 1929 they were married. They had sex, for she had to have an abortion. Then she discovered what he called "his homosexual streak" and nothing was the same again. They still acted together: she was Ariel to his Prospero and Peter Pan to his Captain Hook. But there was no more sex and not much affection. "If I had known all this before we were married," she wrote in *Elsa Lanchester, Myself,* "it might have been very different." They stayed together in mounting acrimony. Laughton's biographer Simon Callow suggests that they became worthy of Strindberg or Albee. "How they tormented each other!" said Don Bachardy, Christopher Isherwood's lover.

Laughton was increasingly promiscuous but never at peace with his homosexuality. Though refined, urbane, and very intelligent, he was a self-conscious monster compelled to draw attention to what he regarded as his ugliness. Cinema did not like to have "bad-looking" people in lead roles. Laughton often did lurid villains, but he was drawn to the pathos he felt about himself. He was a lecherous rogue winning an Oscar in *The Private Life of Henry VIII,* and then unfairly overlooked as a soulful *Rembrandt*. Quasimodo was his signature role in *The Hunchback of Notre Dame,* and he had more than his share of corpulent villains. True to his time, he never dared take a gay role. Yet he had to endure rebukes. As Laughton was directing the stage premiere of *The Caine Mutiny Court Martial* (1954), he had trouble with one of his actors, Henry Fonda. Laughton tried to give the actor notes on military detail when Fonda (Lincoln, Tom Joad, and Juror No. 8) turned on him: "What do you know about men, you fat faggot?"

Despite Laughton's lifestyle, it seems that Lanchester stayed faithful—neglected and sometimes cruel in retaliation. For Laughton that may have been balm; he had a masochistic side that led him to wallow in guilt, and which made his own ugliness a source of shame. Lanchester reported that he often said he didn't quite belong to the human race—a creature? The theatrical marriage of gay and straight may negotiate public life, but it can be agony, and marriage is a stage for revenge and even murder.

The bride is the best role Lanchester ever had. One can see this as an acting job in which she soars on the otherworldly wings of her creature. There was also the bonus that she would play Mary Shelley in the prologue, enriching the notion that the aliens in the story might be related to their creators and expressions of their forbidden desires. She is very pretty as Mary, cute even, though her hairstyle is going prematurely eccentric on one side. That is prelude to the sheer cinematic presence of the bride, luminous in anger and hostility.

Whale presided over her look, like a makeup man or a production designer (Jack Pierce was actually credited for the makeup). There were bold stitches to indicate what had been her severed head. Though oblivious to seduction or tenderness, she was perversely desirable. She was a mummy wrapped in white gauze. But above all it was her hair, which did not fall naturally but seemed to jut out from her head like the zigzag lines of lightning in a comic book. Her wig was immense and as possessed as a dark hive, with streaks of savage white that resembled musical scoring. The effect was startling and "perfect," but it had an air of damage, too, or of toxic wounds. Then there was how she sounded. The bride had nothing as ordinary as dialogue—that naturalism would have spoiled her frenzy. But she made hissing noises that Lanchester said were based on her study of swans in London parks—elemental, inhuman, warning sounds.

Where did this leave the bride? Well, not as a female partner with whom any creature could mate. Not that she wasn't riveting and alluring, even if by 1935 the Production Code would have protected us against anything overt. This bride could not approach nakedness—but what *would* she have looked like in that state? Abstract, harsh realistic, demented expressionist, or cubist? She is a gender mutant not part of any known world, and horrified because of it. Karloff's Monster likes himself, no matter his limitations, but the Bride seethes in distress—she has come into this world with hatred and misgiving like a feral child snatched from a state of antinature. She is arresting yet at war, entirely trans, with no fixed emotional abode. The making of her seems like a rape. This is one of the first films with a feeling for gender insurrection.

Frankenstein and his monster do not recede. There are so many films, ballets, and operas on the theme. By the early twenty-first century, fascination with laboratory humanoids was more current than it had been in 1818 or 1935. (We think robots may be cuddly confidants now.) Let me add the monster who comes down from the movie screen in a desolate Spanish village and enters the mind of a child in Victor Erice's *Spirit of the Beehive* (1973). In 2011 at London's National Theatre there was a play by Nick Dear in which Benedict Cumberbatch and Jonny Lee Miller alternated in the roles of Frankenstein and the Monster. Wasn't that the most acute rendering of the fine margin between the two?

Then in 2018 came the publication of Ahmed Saadawi's Arabic novel, translated into English as *Frankenstein in Baghdad*. There, in scenes of surreal mayhem, not far from the devastation left by the real war in Iraq, a peddler collects body parts from slaughter and starts stitching them together. The product of that compilation becomes a phenomenon and then a celebrity. Saadawi had an inspired grasp of how the monster could represent the everyday monstrousness that surrounded him. That's how the monster figure has the chance to stand for a new unsexed enigma in a straight but warped world. More and more movie characters are leaning toward "the other" just as gender fluidity in life makes it harder to pin down people in set schemes of romantic identity.

There has also been talk of a remake of *The Bride of Frankenstein,* to be directed by Bill Condon, the director of *Gods and Monsters.* This project was taking a long time, but there were suggestions of Javier Bardem as the Monster, with the Bride to be played by Angelina Jolie.

That's alive.

And sometimes the most "beautiful" screen creatures become like monsters.

7

Gable and Cukor

Spencer Tracy, Katharine Hepburn, and George Cukor from 1949—it must be
Adam's Rib—on their best behavior

LOOKING THROUGH HOLLYWOOD HISTORY, it is hard to find careers restricted because of gayness.

By contrast, spasms of indignation and aversion therapy once went through motion pictures at the suggestion that they might be communistic, as if the steady commercial for America in entertainment pictures was ever in question. In protecting our money, we can fall for any voodoo. So Rudolph Valentino was mocked in life and despised by some men, but his career soared. It's clear that AIDS killed Rock Hudson—but his own fears over homosexuality had undermined him long before that.

We admit how often those hostilities existed but stayed masked or hidden; prejudice has its own closet. We know about it because the fears still operate. If there was public revelation now that, say—*I'm just saying this, for the sake of argument*—Brad Pitt, Matt Damon, and George Clooney were gay, their marketable power as merry guys would be drastically reassessed, their green light would dim, no matter that all of them, and all the modern moviemaking community, would recite the solemn oath that, Well, of course, it's perfectly decent and *normal* to be homosexual. Unless you're a movie star.

So the gay director George Cukor came close to career trouble. In February 1939, as the shooting of *Gone With the Wind* at last got under way, as the film's assigned director, Cukor was fired by his old friend, the producer, David O. Selznick.

Selznick International Pictures had bought the film rights to Margaret Mitchell's novel in the summer of 1936 for $50,000. Once that ponderous book became a best-seller, the movie had to be an immense production, involving romance in the old South, the drama-queen selfishness of Scarlett O'Hara, and some skirmishes from the Civil War. The production also loomed as decisive in Selznick's passage from being a regular studio producer to having his own independent production company. The Southern romance might take all his resources—and more. That scale excited Selznick but it terrified him, too. As the film opened, in December 1939, there were still people in Hollywood who believed ruin awaited a production that had cost $4 million and was running over three hours.

In early trepidation, in 1936, as soon as he had the rights to the novel, Selznick hired the playwright Sidney Howard to do a screenplay and announced that George Cukor would direct the picture. No one was surprised at that: Cukor had worked for Selznick on *What Price Hollywood?*, *Our Betters*, *A Bill of Divorcement*, *Dinner at Eight*, and *David Copperfield* (and they had set up *Little Women* together before Selznick moved on from RKO to MGM). The two men were in sympathy. Selznick liked to feel he shared Cukor's literary taste, and he was personally drawn to stories about women such as Cukor excelled at. Selznick could be an arrogant womanizer in life, but the stories he preferred were tender to women. The pictures with Cukor had been made tidily and they had done well. When *David Copperfield* opened in 1935, it was the film of which Selznick was most proud, and it had a sweet, gentle boy as its protagonist. It was also the first of his films to be nominated for Best Picture. To make it, he, Cukor, and Selznick's wife, Irene, had traveled to England in bubbly spirits. The two men were friends—they had running jokes about how they looked alike and how their mothers hated the comparison—and that was strengthened by the fondness between George and Irene. Selznick never thought twice about engaging Cukor; he felt encouraged to have George at his side.

But friendly hiring left both men feeling they were being taken advantage of. By January 1938, Selznick was startled to find that Cukor had already earned $155,000 on the film's budget, and for what? From Cukor's stance, it was for visiting Sidney Howard and Margaret Mitchell to discuss and develop the script; for going all over the country on inane talent searches, most of which had more thought of raising public interest than finding a Scarlett O'Hara in the hills; and then in testing so many actresses, some known, some not, in that key role. In addition, George had to be available to reassure David about this scary project, and to read or endure his memos, which might run on for several thousand words without reaching useful decisions.

Cukor thought of himself as a professional director (he was never a writer), but he felt uneasy when not directing films, so he took some time off from searching for Scarlett to do *Camille*, *Holiday*, and *Zaza* elsewhere. He had seen the *Wind* script grow and bury itself in Selznick's indecision; he was doing tests of the same scenes over and over again with many actresses. The film is a classic now, of course, but those scenes were not always the greatest, not after Cukor had labored through them twenty times: they were earnest love scenes, without the edge of wit or immediacy at which Cukor excelled. They had become congealed or habitual, while Cukor valued freshness. Moreover, the tests were aimed at the central female role—Rhett seldom appeared in these tryouts, and when he did he was played by any available actor or stand-in. It's possible that Cukor was growing bored with *Gone With the Wind* and with having to appease Selznick's insecurity. Selznick could wear anyone out on a sprawling timetable that ignored other people's plans. And now we can see that *Wind* is a bore.

George Cukor was gay, had been since around the age of three, and had set out to organize his Hollywood life accordingly. He created a life of separate compartments where any insider "knew" that Cukor was homosexual and carried on regardless. This was not referred to publicly. David and Irene Selznick enjoyed his lunches and his parties, but they wouldn't have gone to his less famous and more private evenings. David would have overlooked his chum's sex life, though Irene was open to learning more. That education would lead her to a discreet lesbian existence of her own.

Cukor's best biographer, Patrick McGilligan, reported that when George was in his late teens, while directing plays in Rochester, New York, he became very close to a young dancer, Stella Bloch, and her cousin, Mortimer Offner, an actor and photographer. Cukor, a lively young man, liked to make fun of homosexuals then, and seemed to relish joking about them. Young men and women falling in love often ward off their beloveds in a bantering way. Love and commitment can be intimidating—we are raised to think of them as our big test. It was in this mood that Stella sometimes wondered if George was falling in love with Morty Offner.

Cukor was twenty in 1919. Stella said that George flirted with her and was drawn to her; he would describe her as someone he watched closely, an early intimation of his special talent as a film director. She also felt he could be "slippery" and "evasive," or not comfortable revealing himself. It was in seeing his feeling for Morty that she began to guess George's true nature, not that George talked about it with her or ever reflected on his homosexuality in the interviews he gave later as a director. George carried off his life as a polished act. There was only one area in which he seemed unsure: his weight fluctuated wildly, as if he was torn over the attempt to be good-looking.

In 1922, Stella and Morty confronted George and tried to get him to admit what they suspected. He laughed them off with what in 1922 could have been called gaiety. "You'll find out about me ten years from now," he told them. "The mystery will be solved."

It never was solved, not in any open way. We may ascribe that to the habits of the 1920s and to Cukor's insecurity over his sexual status or over having it known. That caution, and its need for secrecy, affects many people who have never dreamed of show business, and it is still active (yet furtive) nearly a hundred years later. It may be especially potent, or far-reaching, in those engaged in the intricate rites of pretending called theater, the movies, and show business, where sometimes the show can be a means of masking one's inner being.

At forty, Cukor was known as a sophisticate. He was stimulated by talking pictures and the shift from bold visual action to explorations of inner behavior. People didn't get much violence or showy action in Cukor films. He flourished with comedy and character, often while working for David Selznick, and while he was justly celebrated as a man who had helped discover and educate the unconventional personality of Katharine Hepburn, he had also delivered a number of fine performances from men: Lowell Sherman as the alcoholic movie director in *What Price Hollywood?*, John Barrymore in *A Bill of Divorcement*, and W. C. Fields as Mr. Micawber in *David Copperfield*. In *Camille*, he had directed a famous love story, not just one of Garbo's best performances but also Robert Taylor's handsome and convincing Armand.

He also did as he was told; he was by nature timid or obedient. His *Romeo and Juliet* (with Norma Shearer and Leslie Howard, deep into their thirties) turned out a bloodless version of young sexual heat, but it had ended up a prestige production. He had wanted the English designer Oliver Messel to make the Shakespeare feel Mediterranean and earthy, but the studio and its design chief, Cedric Gibbons, had insisted on a bland, indeterminate period luxury—like a kind of hotel. Cukor lost that battle.

Cukor was esteemed for good scripts and literary adaptations, with special sympathy for actors, and as a compromiser. He was an acknowledged pro, even if he might have seemed miscast as the director of *Gone With the Wind*. That project required action, adventure, and an overwhelming Rhett as well as a complicated Scarlett.

Cukor had also established himself as a Hollywood bachelor and host. He had a fine house built on Cordell Drive, a quiet lane that climbed into the hills above Sunset Boulevard. It was the epitome of a hideaway, and great work would pour from it. The six-acre plot was arranged as a citadel against the outside world, protected from spying eyes by a high brick wall. In time, it would be landscaped with terraces, gardens, and an elegant pool, as well as several cottages on the grounds kept for close friends. (Katharine Hepburn and Spencer Tracy were among those who stayed there, but not necessarily together.) The whole thing was done in a Mediterranean style. There was modern art on the walls—Matisse, Braque, Picasso, Graham Sutherland, a study of Ethel Barrymore by John Singer Sargent—as well as inscribed celebrity portraits and movie memorabilia, all part of the Hollywood wish to seem like arbiters of taste on the Western frontier. Picture people wanted to believe they had class in a culture where some decried the movies as trash. Cukor's house on Cordell Drive had an extra luster: it said that talented gay people could do very well in Hollywood and make a secure club for themselves.

Many private residences in Hollywood resembled motion picture sets. This became more pronounced as America at large suffered the Depression. When Sidney Howard visited the Cukor house in 1937 (while he and Cukor were in script consultations for *Gone With the Wind*), he told his wife, "each room is, in the most nance sense, a perfect show window rather than a room." That's discerning, but moderately disparaging. At Cukor's house there would have been many amusing put-downs for the follies and hypocrisy of straight lives. Twenty-five years later, for *Something's Got to Give,* the project canceled just before the death of Marilyn Monroe, an exact re-creation of Cukor's house and pool was constructed for the movie. Cordell Drive was a hideaway home meant to impress Hollywood.

In the 1930s, the actress Ruth Gordon, coming to town to make a film, had asked Cukor if she could stay with him. They had known each other for years, going back to Cukor's life as a stage director in Rochester. Of course, he said, but for no more than two weeks; he was urbane and amusing about how after a fortnight hospitality could turn into a prison. "The house, like its owner, is elevated and private," wrote Gavin Lambert in 1972 about the sanctum he had access to as Cukor's friend, and as a writer doing a book about the director. Lambert was starstruck enough to perceive the house as an appointed setting: as he wrote in *On Cukor,* "Inside, a private world begins immediately. It's as sudden as opening the door of a sound stage and finding yourself on a lighted set." Cukor would not have been offended by that description; he felt he was directing his life.

Hollywood could be a tough factory town, without much grace at its busy studios. So its best practitioners liked to live up in the hills with the guarantee of not being seen. "Supremely well run and staffed without making a point of it, this house is one of those rare affluent sanctuaries that exist for the personal enjoyment of its owner," said Lambert. Cukor loved his films and worked hard at them, but Cordell Drive was his cherished production, a movie for intimates. "Cukor's social life is conducted with a kind of intense discrimination," said Lambert. It was the empowering place for a man who went in some fear of being exposed. If gays walked a tightrope in Hollywood, at home they liked to strut.

He would invite big stars to the house as well as younger people who might be inspired. It was the site for Hollywood lunches and less formal male get-togethers in the evenings when Cukor was surrounded by occasional actors and decorators along with newcomers from gay trade, sometimes sailors picked up in the shore life south of Los Angeles. These were the compartments of a life in which Cukor had to separate the private from the professional. There were risks, and they required courage. Cukor had an active sex life by night, generally away from Hollywood, in Laguna Beach or Long Beach, but he went carefully for fear of being arrested for soliciting. In fact, this had happened to him a couple of times, probably in 1936, the year of *Camille,* his first great box-office success, as well as his hiring for *Gone With the Wind.* At that point, he had so much to lose.

Patrick McGilligan (a very good researcher) is certain those arrests occurred (though he has found no hard dates or police records). He also believes that executives at MGM had had the charges quashed and hushed up. Under its publicity chief, Howard Strickling, the studio had influence enough with the police and the D.A. to smother many scandals—or to threaten them for unruly contract artists. So Irving Thalberg and David Selznick would have been in no doubt about Cukor's homosexuality while being personally indifferent to it. They had bigger problems: Clark Gable had once killed a woman while driving; there were drugs and all the normal exploitations of heterosexual sex—things like rape, abortion, and brutality. By comparison, gay sex was tidier and did less damage. But there was that risk of scandal hitting the press and ruining a career.

"Moral turpitude," as we've seen, was the clause in many contracts that could let studios dump their own wayward properties. That had happened to William "Billy" Haines, a handsome and very successful actor at the end of the silent era. He had been arrested, too, at a downtown YMCA in 1933—he seems to have been a less cautious gay adventurer than Cukor. At that time, MGM had told Haines to get married (for convenience) or face disgrace. Haines had refused to compromise, so the studio claimed his voice was not good enough for talkies. Whereupon he withdrew from screen acting; he became effectively married to his longtime partner, Jimmie Shields, and the two men started an interior design business together in which they were taken up by a number of Hollywood stars who hated to see Haines ruined. Cukor had hired Haines, a good friend, to supervise the décor on the Cordell Drive house. Years later, even the disapproving Louis B. Mayer hired him for a decorating job.

The link to Haines is important in what was about to happen on *Gone With the Wind.* From the outset, the public (and Margaret Mitchell herself) had felt that Clark Gable was obvious casting for Rhett Butler. He excelled as a raffish adventurer, a man's man, adored

by women. He confirmed every stereotype about men and women, and
he did it with growling charm and a wink of his knowing eye. The
mustache had made him; he looked uneasy without it.

Selznick had resisted that casting. He had thought of Gary Cooper
and then Ronald Colman for Rhett. He even envisaged Errol Flynn as
he contemplated a production alliance with Warner Bros. that would
have supplied Bette Davis as Scarlett. Then in the growing crisis of
really doing the film, he declined the Warners offer and took a complicated package deal with MGM (and his father-in-law) that supplied
a necessary $1.25 million along with Gable as Rhett, with MGM dis-
tributing the finished product. Gable was not happy about this. As the
alleged "king" at MGM he did not like to be treated as an actor being
loaned out. He was assigned without any contract adjustment, ordered
to do a part in the face of massive public expectations. How could any
actor carry off Rhett, he complained, when the public knew the character so well?

There were the qualms over Cukor fitting the adventure elements of
Gone With the Wind. Action was not his forte. He was shy of violence.
Some feeling against him was growing at MGM, and Gable may have
added to that. The actor would have known the general estimate that
Cukor tended to give his pictures to the actresses. But there was more
than that, or there is now. A rumor has spread in film commentary that
as a young beginner in movies (in the 1920s), Gable had once slept with
Billy Haines—for money or the chance to get ahead. There is no surviving evidence of this encounter but Patrick McGilligan reports it on
the strength of "impeccable" sources—friends of Cukor's who talked
to him in confidence as he prepared his book, *George Cukor: A Double
Life,* published in 1991. McGilligan claims that in 1938 or early 1939 a
member of the Cukor entourage blurted out this Haines story and so
it spread around Hollywood as a joke at the king's expense.

This may be just one of several reasons for Cukor being dismissed.
On December 10, 1938, for the first shoot on the picture, Selznick took
on the big action spectacle of the burning of Atlanta. He set fire to
several standing sets on the lot, with long-shot substitutes serving for
Rhett and Scarlett in their escape by carriage. This was an elaborate
night shoot, involving fire brigades and every Technicolor camera that

could be found (Cukor had not worked in color before). He was there, wrapped up in a warm coat, while the designer/director William Cameron Menzies was in charge of the shooting. Even then it was felt that Cukor was not suited to the splashy spectacle. For a year, Selznick had believed Menzies was vital to the movie. He asked the designer to work out a "pre-edited" film, shot by shot, and he often spoke about Menzies running "the physical production." In that scheme, Cukor would handle the actors.

As it happened that night, Cukor picked up another task, exactly suited to him, when Vivien Leigh was brought to the set and introduced by David's brother, Myron Selznick. The English actress's face was avid in the firelight. Could she be Scarlett? Within minutes Cukor had taken Leigh to an office and was reading scenes with her—and finding that she knew them already. Leigh had seized on the book in London when it was published, and she knew some of it by heart. She believed she was born to be Scarlett. Next came the shooting of tests with Leigh, adding to the series Cukor had already done with Paulette Goddard, Jean Arthur, Joan Bennett, Frances Dee, Susan Hayward, Lana Turner, Anne Shirley, and many others.

These tests were from a script growing more muddied by Selznick's rewriting. Many movies began then (and now) without adequate preparation. That can be a handicap, but the mood of haste and improvisation can also stimulate filmmakers and aid immediacy. The prolonged rehearsal for *Gone With the Wind* had crushed some of its life. Cukor the alert observer of natural behavior felt the scenes had turned into monuments to a forgotten cause. And that's how the first scenes seemed when officially filmed. Selznick was distressed that they lacked pace and edge. The picture fell behind schedule from the start. Some said Cukor had gone slow on the material, and was favoring the women. Others felt the script confusion was betraying every attempt to be exciting.

It was in that disarray in mid-February that Cukor was fired. A halt was called after just two weeks' shooting for reappraisal. Ben Hecht was given the emergency job of repairing the script, and Victor Fleming was hired in from MGM to take over the direction. Fleming was a good director and a buddy to Gable: they had done *Red Dust*, *The*

White Sister, and *Test Pilot* together, films that had boosted Gable's reputation for wry manliness. There's no doubt that Fleming made Gable more comfortable, but he also quickened the pace of the film, aided by Hecht's rediscovery of Sidney Howard's original script with a story that worked. Vivien Leigh and Olivia de Havilland were in distress at the directorial change, and they continued to take private instruction from Cukor—in secret, at the house on Cordell Drive. They both delivered fine performances under Fleming. Leigh may have been all the better because of her anguish at losing Cukor.

Who now cares whether the young Gable ever turned a trick with Billy Haines, or whether Haines would have remembered? There were years in Gable's life when he lived on the edge of failure. In 1924, he found an acting coach seventeen years his senior, and married her. That woman, Josephine Dillon, had his teeth remade; she taught him to lower his voice; and she wanted to make him the confident, good-humored guy with a grin in his voice, the one we would fall for. Gable later on tried to forget Josephine, and there may have been other details in his life of which he felt ashamed. He was braver on screen than in life. An amiable man's guy then was not supposed to have had homosexual incidents in his past. The king could have been horrified in 1938–39 to have such gossip passed around.

There is a yearning in us for the famous having dark secrets that might destroy them. As much as we love that celebrity and polish it, we want to bring it down. And it was natural that in the despised or disdained homosexual community there might be relish over embarrassments for straight icons. That society knows all about the insecurities in sexual reputation and has always hoped for more enlightenment. There can be a mischief or malice at work, an envy and an urge to be vengeful. This is the more regrettable in that the gay community surely understands the awkwardness with which most young people make their way in the sexual world. Suppose the kid Bill Gable experimented. Wasn't that his right? Don't we allow as much to our children and ourselves?

Still, the legend of Gable and Cukor and *Gone With the Wind* is in place now, the safer for being beyond proof. Allow that something happened that might have made Gable edgy. But that's way short of an actor altering the course of so important a project, and one on which he had already been assigned, like a suit of clothes. As Cukor put it, decades later, "As stars went, he was powerful, but that was little better than impotence, in those days." It's more likely that Cukor had lost his confidence with a picture to which he was never well suited, and that both Selznick and Louis B. Mayer were in a panic over the drift on $4 million.

The situation required decisive business action, and Victor Fleming was that kind of director. Fleming himself never crowed or viewed the project too seriously. Emergency room doctors may not notice the face or the life they are saving. Fleming took the picture over and brought it home (with assistance and interference). He directed Vivien Leigh toward an Oscar for a landmark performance. He placed Gable in the story. And he never said a word against Cukor for being gay or swish or even slow. Indeed, he praised what Cukor had done with the actresses. The director's one area of being nasty was kept for Selznick, because the producer was one of the Jew boys who ran the picture business and sometimes irked professionals like Vic Fleming.

For Cukor's ambition, this was a serious setback and even a mark of ignominy, though he admitted to some people that he had let the film down. He became more controlled after *Wind:* he directed a series of dramas and comedies with style and insight. A lot of this work was at MGM, which could have been hostile to him. He won them over in a new post-Selznick compartment to his life. His pictures invariably attended to women but not at the expense of men. So he handled Ingrid Bergman and Charles Boyer with equal skill in *Gaslight* (she won an Oscar, he was nominated). He directed Cary Grant and James Stewart as well as Katharine Hepburn in the magnificent *The Philadelphia Story* (Stewart won the Oscar). He was as good with James Mason as with Judy Garland on the remake of *A Star Is Born* (they were both nominated). He guided Ronald Colman to an Oscar in *A Double Life.* He handled both Judy Holliday and Broderick Crawford in *Born Yesterday* (she won for it). He understood Aldo Ray in *The Marrying Kind* and *Pat and Mike.* More to the point, he was instrumental in defining the unique onscreen chemistry between Hepburn and Spencer Tracy in three pictures: *Keeper of the Flame* (still neglected), *Adam's Rib* (a very smart screwball feminist comedy), and *Pat and Mike.*

None of those pictures had an overtly gay sensibility, for Cukor was circumspect and eager to be a mainstream success. He had tried an experiment, in 1935, with *Sylvia Scarlett,* where Hepburn dressed and masqueraded as a boy, while Cary Grant began to find his feet in irony. That film was more daring than the 1950s could have managed. Hepburn had found the Compton MacKenzie novel and urged that they do it; there was an illusion that the film could be poised on the brink of some gender revolution (there were new ideas in movies in the mid-1930s that would pass away in the solemnity of war). Cukor never quite owned up to this rare film: "I don't remember what I thought. I'd always liked the book, and it struck me that Kate had that quality they used to call garçonne [a rebellious young woman, with lesbian suggestions], and I thought it would be a perfect part for her." Mortimer Offner had helped write that film. It proved a signal flop; it is a vivacious mess, as if no one was sure what was being attempted, let alone whether the attempt was wise. Hepburn confided in her diary, "I don't know what the hell I'm doing," but her exhilaration on screen is still plain. She would never get as close again to her lesbian inclinations or the liberated humor of role reversal.

So *Sylvia Scarlett* was courage withdrawn, and it earned some disapproval in gay circles. Parker Tyler thought it showed homosexuality being "used as a Halloween masquerade to play slyly on the subject of the homosexual as if he were not real but a sort of charade person." That's very discerning on Hollywood's protective irony, and it means all the more because of Tyler's brilliant account of what Hepburn had done in the film:

> Young, fashionably angular, always like a lanky schoolgirl in the flush of saying "I am a woman" for the first time, she fit into the role of Sylvia Scarlett as into a young man's glove, all slim questing fingers, tingling confidence, and hard knuckles. Her bosom was nowhere. But she didn't need it.

One summer's day in 1935, as *Sylvia Scarlett* was being shot on Trancas Beach in Malibu, Howard Hughes landed his Sikorsky flying boat as if to pay a call. Katharine Hepburn took it for granted that Hughes had come to see her, but her biographer William Mann thinks Hughes's real purpose was to show off for a more trusted pal, Cary Grant. It was the first meeting of Hepburn and Hughes and it didn't seem to take. But the beach landing was part of the fun of making that picture. Later, Cukor would be rebuked by the studio for having attempted the film, but at the time he felt like every day was Christmas. Was it intended as a breakthrough? The guarded Cukor said no, that wasn't what troubled people. It was simply that no one thought it funny. He always preferred the professional approach.

Still, *Sylvia Scarlett* has a flair, in keeping with Cukor's best films, that amounts to emotional sophistication. So many of his characters examine their own feelings in ways that exceed the standards of American action and adventure films. A lot of his people make fools of themselves, but they are wise enough to admit it. His best pictures have a natural air of comedy, the quality in Cukor the person that people enjoyed. He does not "reveal" himself in his work; he thought that attempt was vulgar and demeaning. "The whole auteur theory disconcerts me," he said. Years later, Hepburn would say this about George: "People were his interest. . . . He was dealing in values of love . . . and hate . . . and sex. . . . He could do that for a thousand years and would never date. . . . He's not easily shocked."

Does that tribute describe a gay sensibility? Not unless you feel inclined to call Astaire, Charlie Parker, or Matisse gay, though such labeling does not transfer smoothly to non-narrative arts. There was no way, between 1930 and 1960, that any audience would have come out of a Cukor picture sure that a homosexual had made it. But in the Hollywood climate of manly films, directors alert to gay feelings made some of our most gentle, generous pictures and some with uncommon sympathy for women. Cukor made top-rate entertainments for literate audiences, while conducting a private gay life with some intensity (he admitted that he needed sex as much as movies) but without putting it on display. He exemplified the attitude that a man could be a first-class moviemaker in Hollywood without taking ads in *Variety* to declare that he was gay, alcoholic, a Christian Scientist, left-handed, or insane. He was doing a job, not making art, and he understood how at nearly every level there were homosexuals in Hollywood who were thriving. He was better than *Gone With the Wind*.

George Cukor was an establishment figure by the end of the 1960s. In 1965, on his fifth nomination, he won the Best Director Oscar for *My Fair Lady* (far from his best work), which also won Best Picture. It was the sixth of his films to be nominated for Best Picture. He was a very social figure in Hollywood who took pride in his army of friends and his standing as a host. "Everyone" of stature in the town knew he was gay and no one thought to use that as a lever against him, or even as a vehicle for tasteless jokes. There was a more urbane understanding of what a "woman's director" might be, which had to do with a more grown-up sexual sensibility creeping slowly across the screen—and the world.

The whole concept of "women's films" was condescending and damaging. As if commercial branding could really compartmentalize the audience and dictate its concerns. The scheme of women's pictures was based on a belief that the male audience is primary, no matter that more women went to see films than men. But pushed to one side, the women's picture became as open to adventure as the B movie. So under that demeaning label, we get the social criticism of Douglas Sirk movies in the 1950s. And that is only a first step toward the riotous inner meanings in television soap operas, the genre that best predicts the social-sexual disintegration of America. To take that in properly you might have to surrender your life to soaps, but in the 1950s we were watching the television screen more and more already.

George did not make a picture with overtly gay characters until *Rich and Famous* (1981), his last film, about a long friendship between two women (played by Candice Bergen and Jacqueline Bisset) in which Bisset is a sexual adventurer (like a man?) and there are gay characters as well as a new level of sexual action. Cukor did not seem at ease with that (there's a scene in an airplane lavatory, a fucking scene—you have to call it that) which many found nervous and awkward, anathema to Cukor. In the end it was not very sexy. He was out of step with an age that no longer had enough faith in talking well.

Still, Cukor the public figure died discreet. He had a fear of being rebuked by Hollywood conservatism; he had his own respect for the innate reticence of good movies. (He is a good example of a director who had flourished in the alleged wasteland of the Production Code; there were others: Howard Hawks, John Ford, Preston Sturges, Billy Wilder, and Alfred Hitchcock among them.) So it was plain that in the book *On Cukor* (1972) he was going to stay tight-lipped about personal matters. That book was important because the English critic Gavin Lambert had chosen to do a book-length conversation on a director's career. Lambert was openly gay, and he had been a friend of Cukor's since coming to Los Angeles in the 1950s. It is not that the book attempts to open up Cukor's secret life; protective ground rules had been agreed in advance. Yet surely Lambert—a very good writer and observer of films—was sometimes frustrated by Cukor's tact. So many gender orthodoxies were bending by 1972—and so much more needed to be discussed. The book could have been more valuable if Cukor had been prepared to talk about his gay life and how that had influenced his movies and made his life problematic. But he was locked in the composure of seeming unruffled.

Let us be clear about something. By 1977 (when he died), it was clear to Hollywood, as it was to those who loved his movies, that Howard Hawks was a habitual womanizer who discovered young actresses for pictures (it's a roll of honor) and then had affairs with some of them, for a while. His wives knew him as a faithless searcher, a liar, and a fantasist. A similar life story could have been pinned on many other Hollywood directors.

In 1982, another good critic, Joseph McBride, published *Hawks on Hawks,* as entertaining an interview book as *On Cukor* had been. He never came close to asking Hawks with whom he had had sex . . . or what it had been like. Nobody wondered why not. A great deal of heterosexual sex (yours, perhaps) has always preferred to be more confidential than the flirt, the glances, the skin, and the kisses that are such a rapture in the light of the screen, when it's Bogart and Bacall in their *Big Sleep* and our sweet dream.

.   .   .

George Cukor lived and died as the master of 9166 Cordell Drive. The compartmentalization had worked. There might have been narrow escapes—*Sylvia Scarlett, Gone With the Wind*—and there were mishaps along the way, like *Two-Faced Woman* (Garbo's last film), *A Star Is Born* (a spoiled version of what it might have been), *Bhowani Junction* (a great subject that falls short—Cukor had been in love with India as well as with his promiscuous heroine, but the studio muffled both feelings). On the other hand, Cukor's reputation depends on *David Copperfield, Holiday, The Philadelphia Story, Gaslight, Adam's Rib, Born Yesterday, Pat and Mike,* and a few others. So many of those pictures deal with versions of marriage, in which fond people try to stay together—or think of murder. Cukor had never been married or had long-term companions until George Towers from about 1960 onward. I doubt he had ever had sex with a woman or wanted to. It is also possible that Howard Hawks never took Lauren Bacall to bed—he seems to have been forestalled in that by her meeting Humphrey Bogart on *To Have and Have Not.* But maybe that thwarting only intensified the giddy yet cool fantasy Hawks put on screen in that dream and *The Big Sleep.* (And it's arguable that Bacall was never again as desirable in movie light.)

Cukor made grown-up married pictures, as if in a spirit of wistfulness or envy. There's an air of regret in Cukor's closing years and even a feeling that compartments can become cells or prison structures. Only a couple of years before his death, Cukor consented to an interview with Boze Hadleigh, a young man without Gavin Lambert's credentials. These interviews were published in 1986, in *Conversations with My Elders,* a book that sought to open up the lives of several movie people who had been gay—Cukor, Rock Hudson, Cecil Beaton, Sal Mineo, Luchino Visconti, and Rainer Werner Fassbinder. The opening up is often tentative or coy, and the book was not published until all its subjects were dead.

So it's an uneasy book, with Cukor less intelligent or relaxed than he had been with Lambert. Hadleigh was not as adept an interviewer. But perhaps his naiveté and awkwardness, as well as his own unconcealed gayness, charmed Cukor occasionally. Knowing what Hadleigh is after, he teases his young questioner. He becomes like the great host he was at home—witty, bright, and not unkind as he ignores or dismisses crude questions:

QUESTION: Were there one or two great romances or relationships in your life?
CUKOR: I don't know. It would be embarrassing to reach so far back.
QUESTION: Do gentlemen never tell?
CUKOR: *Gentlemen* don't. Besides, who would care? I'm an old man now.

Hadleigh asked whether he would ever direct "a gay-themed motion picture," and Cukor hedged, as if he still felt an answer might be incriminating. That was thirty years ago, an interval in which so many positive or enlightening changes seem to have occurred. Still, I don't think Hollywood, in the sense of the American mainstream, is much closer to a "gay-themed motion picture," just as actors with homosexual lives are usually not eager to have that plain truth—that normality—revealed. There are independent movies, like *Brokeback Mountain*. But the mainstream—the big pictures, the ones that gross nine figures—have been regressing toward a preoccupation with macho fantasy and the erotics of technology.

That leads to a paradox. There have been institutional and commercial impediments to the movies going gay. For decades, the picture business dreamed it was a heterosexual task force in a nation founded on male confidence. Yet the practice of making movies is so well supplied with gay people; it was once a sanctuary for them and is now a large club where homosexuals are employed beyond their numerical standing in society, and which has no need of sanctuary. It is normal. That alone would make it remarkable that so little gay experience or action finds a direct way into mainstream films. What is more strange and revealing is that the medium and the technology of movies may be the single strongest instrument in the enlightenment that has opened up a society of vaunted *real men* to the possibility of being gay—of falling for men as much as women—while still being American.

An example may help explain that. Earlier in this chapter, *for the sake of argument,* I offered the hypothetical possibility that Brad Pitt, Matt Damon, and George Clooney might be gay (and what that would do to their status if revealed). I chose them because they are the stalwart guys in the *Ocean's* films. They are Danny, Rusty, and Linus (it hardly matters which is which), leaders of the brotherhood out to pull capers on casinos. They are good-looking, hip (Linus can be a dork), witty, assured, infinitely clever and brave, and captivated by their group huddle. There are women in some of the films: Julia Roberts is a valiant love interest and Catherine Zeta-Jones does some flirting. But women don't penetrate the gang or its complacent thinking. (Not until *Ocean's 8* in 2018.)

Those three films were enormous successes, and now they look like a last gasp of the mainstream movie in which elegant, gentlemanly crime is a source of smart entertainment. I enjoy the films at their streamlined, moneyed level—I can even believe that George Cukor could have handled one of them, for they are nearly as old-fashioned and nonviolent as, say, Ernst Lubitsch's *Trouble in Paradise* (1932). I doubt that the director, Steven Soderbergh, or the guys regarded the movies as gay parables. But look again, and treasure the knowing esteem they have, the adoration, nearly, for male companionship and beauty. There they are, sailing along, mainstream pictures that are inherently gay.

It's another kind of compartmentalization. And a hint that compartmentalization is not always enough. Yes, it served George Cukor and his long, illustrious career. But it served the Hollywood system in more far-reaching ways, for it whispered to a Cukor that everything would be okay if he made discreet, urbane comedies of manners along with movies that searched into male and female natures seldom seen in such staples as the Western, the crime film, the war story, or even the famous woman's picture. I think Cukor was naturally polite and fond of elegance, and not a director to match the passion or the outrage in directors like Jean Vigo, Luis Buñuel, Robert Bresson, Ingmar Bergman, Rainer Werner Fassbinder, or Jane Campion. He abided by the American system's feeling that movies should be polite, calming, and reassuring. It was not their duty to admit that life might be out of control, for disruption could spoil business.

Well, that business looks bereft now, and loss of control in the world keeps mounting. There comes a moment when art should not tolerate compartments. We have to face the entirety of our existence. This is like admitting that the attractive living rooms where the party is held adjoin a kitchen where animals have been slaughtered, a bathroom where a cook has OD'd, and a bedroom with blood and semen on the unmade sheets. A house is all of those rooms, so it is a white lie that we can enjoy the party and ignore the chaos that surrounds it. George Cukor did not get to the chaos: he never made a film about a young Gable who might have had to turn a trick to survive. Perhaps American cinema still goes in terror of that turmoil.

So *real men* still have an iron grip—nothing else protects them from their fear and the plain dread that an actual America need not be the advertised greatest place. Do we really have to be brave to live here?

Can't we admit how much American experience has been rooted in fear?

8

Tracy and Hepburn

A still from the making of *Sylvia Scarlett* (1935). Is it the sexiest picture of
Hepburn you ever saw? It's over eighty years old now, but if it was
from a film that opened yesterday—*Personal Shopper,* say—you wouldn't
be surprised about being surprised.

SPENCER TRACY AND KATHARINE HEPBURN—we run the names together now, as if history or some alchemy had ordained it that way. They have become a given, and so they were in their own time, whether they intended it or not. There was a way in which they presented themselves as unusually straightforward actors—as distinct from the drama queens, the neurotics, and the unrestrained egotists of the film world. Say your lines and don't bump into the furniture, Tracy advised, while Hepburn declared she was against fuss and unhealthy introspection. She liked to say that Spence was a meat-and-potatoes actor. But it was not as simple as that. There are few stable actors with respect for the furniture. And it's hard to claim that Tracy and Hepburn still look the cozy way they did in the 1940s and the 1950s. Healthy Kate could be crackers.

It's important to admit that, when they met, in 1942, they were in grave need of each other. Their careers were on the edge, like their ages.

Hepburn was thirty-five, born in Hartford, Connecticut, the daughter of a urologist and a feminist campaigner. Her family was devoted to physical and mental health, sports, and outdoor activities. She grew up a tomboy who cut her hair short and excelled at tennis, swimming, and athletics. She was smart; she had graduated from Bryn Mawr, though she pursued acting and golf there as much as her academic studies. She was irked at having to be considered in the company of other young women. She took it for granted that she stood out.

She never lost her faith in intelligent problem-solving, a clear mind, and positive thinking. But she was set back by the early suicide of her brother Tom in 1921 and the failure of her marriage, in 1928, to Ludlow Ogden Smith. Perhaps it was more than that; perhaps educated problem-solving let her down—it disappoints so many of us.

Tom Hepburn was fifteen in 1921, and Kate was nearly fourteen. They were very close. He was known as an anxious boy, afraid of not pleasing his father. The two of them were in Greenwich Village on a holiday vacation. One morning, Katharine went to wake her brother in the attic room at their aunt's house. The door was locked. Knocking brought no answer. She broke into the room and found Tom strangled in a way that indicated he had done it himself. She adored her older brother, but she had long felt the need to care for him because of his insecurities. Why the suicide? Some said a girl had jilted Tom. Katharine once said it might have been a boy. No one ever knew, or gave, an adequate answer. Katharine said she took his lost soul and the wounded boy on herself.

Ludlow Ogden Smith, or "Luddy," was an old friend. But no one who knew them believed their bond was stronger than that. Many felt the marriage came out of absurd hurry. Indeed, she had been more interested in another man, who was married. She was a young actress understudying the lead in *Holiday* on stage when she apparently walked away from the theater in dislike or dismay (or because she wasn't playing the lead?) and seized upon Luddy for marriage (December 12, 1928). She said they had gone to bed together, once at least, and the wedding was arranged quickly, or impulsively. But in just a few months she quit the marriage and went back to acting. It was as if she had tested real life and had given up on it.

She and Luddy divorced after a few years and stayed friends, but Hepburn had closed the book on a good, practical marriage to the kind of Connecticut man her parents might have approved. Instead, the woman who was often noisy about being open, decent, and honest (and she could excel in all three) decided to go in for pretending and acting. To the end, she had the manner and attitudes of a teacher or a political figure, but she also nursed an urge to be cherished by strangers, which is never simply rational.

Spencer Tracy did not seem like her kind of man. Born in Milwaukee in 1900, the son of a man in the construction trade, he had grown up Catholic and troubled. He did poorly in school. He was known as a difficult boy who brooded over difficulties (a tendency Hepburn disdained). But at Ripon College and then at the American Academy of Dramatic Arts he showed talent as an actor. He was not handsome, and he never quite looked "young." In 1923, he married an actress, Louise Treadwell, and their son, John, was born in 1924. The boy was born deaf. Tracy fell into despair over this and entertained irrational ideas that the deafness might be linked to a venereal disease he had contracted. (Hepburn's father had written learned papers on such diseases and done research on treating them.) Tracy began to withdraw from his marriage and to live apart, though he would go home on weekends.

Tracy and Hepburn were both elevated by talking pictures. Neither of them had the vivid immediacy—call it attractiveness—that silent pictures required. He was solid and persistent, as if glamour alarmed him. She experimented with her look: she could be austere, a tomboy, or even a sexy kitten. Nothing convinced her. But they had distinctive voices, full of character, and a faith in speaking candidly without becoming humorless. As time would show, their voices went well together, just as they seemed to be two idiosyncratic nonmovielike personalities who clicked—in movies. They were famous already in the 1930s. Hepburn had won an Oscar playing a headstrong young actress in *Morning Glory,* and she had been nominated for *Alice Adams.* Tracy had won two Oscars—for *Captains Courageous* and *Boys Town,* and been nominated for *San Francisco.* He played priests in the latter two, and in the first he's a Portuguese fisherman who mentors a rich kid played by Freddie Bartholomew.

These parts were loners, and the public felt Tracy's incompleteness. In an age of heady romantic fusion on the movie screen, he had got his Oscars playing men without women, unaware of romantic rapture. In his strongest film of that era, Fritz Lang's *Fury,* he starts out with Sylvia Sidney as a girlfriend but soon becomes a man apart, consumed by anger and a need for revenge. He would be an adventurer in remote places in *Stanley and Livingstone* and *Northwest Passage.* Separated from his wife by the mid-1930s, Tracy had had an affair with Loretta Young and shown romantic rapport with her in *Man's Castle* (1933). But he was rarely in love on screen, much less carried away with it. He was not anyone audiences were encouraged to fantasize over. That may be what makes Tracy seem uncommonly grown up and impressive now, but it was a casting problem by the early 1940s.

Hepburn had been following a similar course. In *Morning Glory* and *Alice Adams* she had played arrogant egotists oblivious to what others thought of her. She had been driven by passion as Mary, Queen of Scots, but off in her own royal world. In several films she had been a lone pursuer of career or fulfillment—the aristocratic and suicidal aviatrix in *Christopher Strong,* a hillbilly faith healer mired in rural accent in *Spitfire*, a composer in *Break of Hearts*, a defiant feminist in *A Woman Rebels*. But none of those films had gained a large audience.

She had done great work—with Cary Grant in *Bringing Up Baby*. In that masterpiece they were years ahead of their time, playing mad children lost in the midnight woods of Connecticut instead of figures we could imagine going to bed together (or with us). That screwball comedy had done poorly at the box office. Hepburn could seem eccentric, opinionated, superior, chilly, and nearly harsh sometimes. By the late 1930s *Variety* had called her "box-office poison." At that moment, she had campaigned to get the part of Scarlett O'Hara (aided by her admirer Howard Hughes). George Cukor must have been party to those discussions, yet he never talked about them, and Selznick had turned her down because he felt she could not deliver sex appeal on screen. If Cukor had claimed she *could* do sex, that might have been another reason for Selznick to doubt his suitability on the picture.

How was Kate in life? This is a tricky issue, if only because Hepburn became in her last few decades such a talisman for enlightened social politics, longevity, good work, and sheer lack of nonsense. One reason people liked her was because they felt she had cared for Spencer Tracy and looked after him in his unhappy times. Any trace of poison had turned into a nourishing drink, not sweet, but tart and wholesome.

I can attest to some of this. One day in November 1990, Hepburn took me from her house in Manhattan to New Jersey to introduce me to Laura Harding. I sought this meeting because Harding had had a romance with David Selznick in the 1930s and I was writing Selznick's biography. Hepburn and Harding (an heiress) had been close friends since the early 1930s. When Hepburn first arrived in Hollywood, Harding was her companion. They won extra attention because they both wore stylish pants and seemed unimpressed with men or Hollywood. Indeed, Kate and Laura had been closer than ever David and Laura managed.

Hepburn could not have been more decisive or helpful on our day together. We got in her chauffeur-driven car with tubs of borscht that Hepburn had made for the ailing Harding. As we drove, talking all the time, the car blew a tire on that network of ramps and flyovers on the Jersey shore. Hepburn suggested we get out of the car while the chauffeur, Jimmy, changed the tire—all done very professionally. So she and I sat on the curb, talking about Cary Grant and *Bringing Up Baby,* while semis thundered past. They started to honk their horns. She waved to the drivers. "They know it's *me,*" she said, merrily, "and they love me." She was right on both accounts, and she was a heady companion that day—yet cold and regal and ecstatic as truckers saluted her.

When she published her own book—it was called *Me,* just to make things clear—Hepburn was candid about her zeal at self-promotion and her delight in being Katharine Hepburn. This was a palpable side of her, and it has struck some of her biographers, notably William Mann, author of *Kate: The Woman Who Was Hepburn,* an exemplary book in its understanding of how a movie star could work at her image and reputation as if creating a great role—the one she deserved.

Hepburn had had that marriage to Luddy and a divorce. She was later linked in the press to Leland Hayward (her agent, and talent doesn't often have sex with their agents; emotional percentages are delicate matters), to John Ford (who had directed her in *Mary of Scotland*) and Howard Hughes, who plainly thought the world of her and her thrill at flying. Once, with Hughes as her copilot, Kate had flown a plane beneath the Fifty-Ninth Street Bridge in New York.

Mann is not convinced she went to bed as a habit with any of the men she knew. No one is ever going to know the answer, and it doesn't matter too much. If I had to bet, I'd suspect that Hughes got closest to her physically, and there was talk for a while that they were going to be married. But in *Me,* talking of Hughes, Hepburn sounded like the woman I met: "He was sort of the top of the available men—and I of the women. It seemed logical for us to be together. . . . We each had a wild desire to be famous." Wild and logical in the same breath gives a hint of how tricky Katharine Hepburn could be.

Desire can take many forms, and in the movie business some people simply desire to be desirable, while enthralled by the isolated rapture of being on a screen or in a hideaway where no one can ever touch you. Hepburn favored strong, successful, *male* men—she even flirted with her boss at MGM, Louis B. Mayer (and seduced his daughter, Irene). This is not outing anyone; it is just an attempt to describe desire and sexuality in the movies and their world. Movie stars need to be loved by strangers, and sometimes that makes it hard to fix on real people, especially if they are in the business and full of their own ego. Everyone is a "me" in show business; it's a survival drill. Hepburn had had some sex with men, but I share Mann's view that she was not stirred by the concept of intercourse. Indeed, I don't think she often took the women whose company she cherished to bed. She loved herself in a shining, unequivocal way that acting can take for granted. It must have amazed Tracy, who was so gloomy about himself and his guilt. But of all the men after Tom, Tracy was the one who most needed looking after.

Tracy and Hepburn met at MGM, in preparations for the film *Woman of the Year*. Hepburn was more in charge of this project than Tracy. She had previously brought *The Philadelphia Story* to MGM; it had been a play by Philip Barry that she had sponsored and done on stage first, in 1939, with the quiet financial support of Howard Hughes. It was a good play, and part of Hepburn's campaign to make herself more sexually appealing, to escape that "poison" tag. Then *The Philadelphia Story* became a hit movie in 1941. She had thought first of Tracy for the James Stewart role, but he had been unavailable. *Woman of the Year* was an idea of Garson Kanin's, written by Ring Lardner Jr. and Michael Kanin (Garson's brother) when Garson joined the military. Hepburn promoted the project at the studio, through the producer Joseph L. Mankiewicz, and she proposed Tracy for the male lead. She had seen him on stage and liked his films, but they had not met.

Woman of the Year is about two newspaper writers, a high-flying woman columnist and a male sportswriter, apparently ill-suited to each other, yet tailor made for a movie marriage. George Stevens would direct (he had worked with Hepburn before, on *Alice Adams* and *Quality Street*). When the two actors met for the first time Kate was wearing high heels and she observed that she might be a little tall for Tracy. That's the story. But he reassured her: he would cut her down to size, he said. That's folklore now, so it's worth adding that Tracy was two inches taller than Hepburn.

As the picture was first set up, the woman character, Tess, went some way to educating the man, Sam. The couple have married, but their union is in jeopardy because the man is uneasy with so smart a woman (and that was a wariness that studio movies fostered in the audience). The film was shot and cut, but when it previewed the public flinched at the ending's endorsement of the woman's superiority. In 1942, at war, guys needed to feel in charge. Then something happened that cuts against the grain of Katharine Hepburn's legend. A new ending was ordered in which the wife would be disciplined and reduced. Another writer was brought in, and, as Lardner recalled in *Backstory 3,* "They [the studio] felt that the woman character having been so strong throughout, should be somehow subjugated and tamed. . . . The whole theory behind it seemed to be that there had to be some comeuppance for the female character." Tess was now supposed to cook breakfast for Sam, but she didn't know how to do it. So that task made a fool of her. How could a woman of the year not manage bacon and eggs? Louis B. Mayer had insisted on putting this scene in the picture, and he liked his own traditional breakfast every day.

Hepburn shot those humiliating scenes: she appreciated Tracy by then, and although she was an avowed feminist she was obedient to Mayer's wishes and the studio's commercial formula. She had gone wild once, on *Sylvia Scarlett,* but then learned to behave herself. The result is still there on the screen, betraying creative intent and social reform. But the picture was a hit, the screenplay won an Oscar, and the studio was eager to do more Tracy-Hepburn pictures. Tracy had a woman at last on screen, and Hepburn no longer seemed so arrogant because he had given her a warning look that said, Watch out, sister. Whatever the understanding the two actors had between them in life, they could not deny the new commercial opportunity. They made eight more movies together, six of them at MGM. Hepburn began to become beloved, while Tracy had a mate for whom he didn't have to give up his dignity or his depression. She would look at him with adoration, an attitude she had seldom tried before on screen.

The working bond between Tracy and Hepburn became the basis for a very effective club. This was rather organized by George Cukor, who had established some rights on Hepburn's offscreen persona in five films by 1940 (*A Bill of Divorcement, Little Women, Sylvia Scarlett, Holiday,* and *The Philadelphia Story*). But two other people were essential to the gang. Garson Kanin was a writer-director married to his writing partner, the actress Ruth Gordon. He was a skilled director who had only once come close to a hit (with *My Favorite Wife*). But Kanin was a heartfelt careerist who discovered himself as a writer and vital to the Cukor who was never able to initiate scripts but who presided over the work of others.

They had fun, too. On *Pat and Mike,* Cukor said, "I remember the readings we had here, in this room [on Cordell Drive], for this picture. Spence sat in the corner, his glasses on, and read absolutely brilliantly. Kate read her part, and Ruth and Garson and I took the others. It was a most happy period for everybody." Hepburn had the same warm memories, though she recalled Tracy sitting in his corner, away from the group, listening attentively but not contributing. In turn, Cukor rarely gave Tracy notes, yet somehow the actor came up with everything the director wanted.

The motif of their films was the argument between men and women who were fond and loyal but too understanding to be swept off their own feet by love or sex. Kanin's play *Born Yesterday* opened on Broadway in 1946 and played over 1,600 performances with Paul Douglas as the crude gangster, and a newcomer, Judy Holliday, as Billie Dawn, the shrewd "dumb" blonde who gets an education and outwits her gangster. It was a funny play, a model of conventional liberalism, and it depended on Holliday's unique personality (one that makes Marilyn Monroe look foolish or unfocused now). The movie version came along in 1950, with Cukor as its director. Kanin and Gordon also wrote *A Double Life* for Cukor, in which Ronald Colman plays an unhinged actor. It was then that the team assembled for what may be their best film.

Adam's Rib has Tracy and Hepburn playing lawyers, married for some years, fond of each other but also accustomed to each other's follies. This is the first work in which the team have no burden of romantic love or sexual glamour. They are nearly middle-aged, childless, and happily set in their ways—until they find themselves on opposite sides in a case of marital abuse: Judy Holliday has attacked her husband, Tom Ewell, because he's a cad and a snake who deserves no less. *Adam's Rib* is the kind of adult comedy Cukor handled very well, including a long scene that shows off Holliday in which Hepburn serves as her obliging and largely passive backup. The team were doing what they could to urge Holliday upon Harry Cohn, the boss at Columbia who had bought the rights to *Born Yesterday*. Cukor wanted to direct the Kanin script, and they all believed that Judy should repeat her stage success (though Cohn was blunt about her being too heavy—Tracy was plump, too, but that went unmentioned).

Judy Holliday was seldom at ease or convinced by her own stardom, but for a few years, on stage and screen, she was a personality audiences rejoiced in. She was unusually smart (in terms of IQ) but then quickly typed in dumb roles—most notably Billie Dawn. Judy was pretty, and in moments she could be beautiful. But she had regular problems with her weight and she seemed to think glamour was stupid or demeaning. She was apparently wild about men, often unsuitable or impatient men—Nicholas Ray, for one, then Sidney Chaplin, Peter Lawford, and the jazz musician Gerry Mulligan. There was a failed marriage and a child from it. And she died tragically early, at forty-three.

She had had a lesbian relationship as a young woman. Holliday stayed friends with the woman and regarded the bond as a learning experience. This was a mark of the way her creative circle saw nothing surprising in a life that swung both ways (assuming there were only two ways). As Joan Schenkar researched her book about the novelist Patricia Highsmith, *The Talented Miss Highsmith* (2009), she found in her files a photograph of Holliday in that moment from *Adam's Rib* where her character is suddenly seen as a man—in a suit and tie, with hair done in a manly way, and Judy's eyes gazing out from what is either a prison or a threatened haven. Schenkar believes that Highsmith and Holliday had been lovers.

The Cukor-Kanin-Gordon club made Judy Holliday—she is one of its jewels. I doubt she could have managed the trick on her own. Even then, she was too defiantly a complicated person instead of a vehicle for our fantasies. The comparison with Monroe is fascinating. Holliday was as professional as Marilyn was hit-and-miss, increasingly disruptive of factory filmmaking yet ready to be the very sex goddess on screen that offended her in life.

It was not easy getting Judy Holliday for *Adam's Rib*. Kanin and Cukor thought the part was made for her: a blowsy, uneducated, untidy, overweight wife being two-timed. But Holliday declined the offer. So

Hepburn went to her and urged good sense. What she discovered was that the "overweight" tag upset Holliday just because that issue dogged her in life. Hepburn reported this news and Kanin rewrote the part leaner and more attractive.

When the production of *Adam's Rib* came to the big interview scene between lawyer and client, Cukor shot it on Holliday in an unbroken long take, seeing just Hepburn's back. The scene went perfectly—it is a great sustained moment—but Cukor the pro thought he should do a covering shot on Hepburn's reactions. Kate wouldn't have it. "Forget it, George," she said. "The scene is fine and it should belong to Judy, anyway." That's the take-charge woman at her best, but some felt Hepburn was getting very fond of Holliday.

Many of these plans were hatched at the Cordell Drive house, not just a showcase for Cukor's domestic style but also a cockpit of smart comic invention. For a few years, this select club dominated literate humor. Cukor called it his *entente cordiale*. But if he presided over it, Kanin was often the creative initiator or the plot man. He had married Ruth Gordon in 1942, though she was his senior by sixteen years. There are marriages like that in life, of course, but they are more common in show business because they can be covers. William Mann and others reckon Kanin had a gay life, too, and Mann quotes a rather bitchy Gavin Lambert on it: "He'd show up in his velvet suits with his little old lady wife and was really convinced he'd fooled people." So at least three members of the entente had gay experience. I think Gordon made it four sometimes. Tracy was not there as often as the others, and seemingly bonded with Kate. The years from *Keeper of the Flame* to *Adam's Rib* were the most intense in their relationship.

Adam's Rib is in the pantheon of American marital comedies, thriving on the bickering interplay of Hepburn and Tracy, but not a movie romance. Whatever those two felt for each other in real life, on screen they needed to be at cross-purposes. His character, a cool reporter, came to admire hers in *Keeper of the Flame,* and she was never more beautiful than in that film, or so sexy, with her hair long enough to fall onto her shoulders. If there was passion between them, I suspect it was then. She has glamour in that film, as if she felt she was being dreamed over, and he succumbs to her in a way never repeated. But neither Kate nor Tracy did love with ease. They were in their element as difficult individuals who happened to be together and argued a good deal. They were so blessed by this that a mature public fell in love with them (they were never fodder for kids), and in 1949 when the film was made they were both in their forties—Tracy was nearly fifty. Their appeal had a lot to do with their ennobling of a middle-aged couple who had decided to be together—so long as they had something as good as the court case in *Adam's Rib* over which they could disagree.

This is a special situation from life that Hollywood did not often pursue: a marriage in which the partners are past first romance and swooning lovemaking, and have settled into a companionship built on argument, passing hurts, and the realization that perfect mates can become quite different or opposed. They have no children, and in Hollywood pictures kids were a nearly automatic lock in marriage. So many movies ended on clinging embraces between two lovely people that left the public to discover that marriage could turn out a tougher proposition. So it's worth stressing that this innovation emerged from a group of gay people for whom heterosexual raptures could be regarded from a detached distance or with a pinch of salt. Some gay people have special humorous fondness or tolerance for conventional romance, sex, and conjugal love. It reaches from Oscar Wilde and Marcel Proust to Stephen Sondheim and David Bowie.

The vexed partnership in *Adam's Rib* had a real-life model in the marriage of Kanin and Ruth Gordon. She had been married before and she had had a child by the director Jed Harris, who had produced her in *Serena Blandish*. In her book, *My Side*, dry, cryptic, and allusive, Gordon mentions meeting Kanin without a flicker of feeling or losing control in the manner recommended in so many movies. I'm sure that's an underplaying wit that actually signals affection. If theirs was a marriage of convenience, let us hail convenience in such partnerships. It can be more comfortable than inconvenience, neglect, or betrayal. Why should the possibility of two people talking together (and arguing) for years and decades not stand comparison with gratification of the bed?

Gordon was at least as funny as Kanin, and he always trusted her actor's sense of how a line played. They had more in common: they were both susceptible to gay experience and endlessly curious about the sexual variations that could be observed in show business. They were also on a meal ticket. Gordon was not easily cast in big roles—until she became the rogue old lady in *Harold and Maude* and *Rosemary's Baby*. Kanin was eager to stay on top as a writer, and money-minded. So Cukor was a vehicle for them along with the Tracy-Hepburn arrangement. Gordon and Kanin wrote for Cukor without a studio contract, confident that their work would not be interfered with. It was an enchanted relationship. Gordon adapted her own play, *Years Ago,* so that Cukor could make *The Actress* (where Tracy played Jean Simmons's gruff but loving father). Kanin and Gordon together wrote two more films for Cukor—*Pat and Mike* (for Hepburn and Tracy) and *The Marrying Kind*—while Kanin wrote *It Should Happen to You.* Everyone in the team was doing very nicely, and this was in a movie age when new kids were the rage: Elizabeth Taylor, Marlon Brando, James Dean, Elvis Presley, not forgetting that other kid on the block, television. So if people nearing middle age could get away with it, good for them.

Along that way, Tracy and Hepburn had become unique middle-aged stars. Hepburn had seldom been seductive on screen or unduly romantic, but her pairing with Tracy had made her seem spunky, smart, talkative, and interesting. She had found balance and a character. Apart from the films they made together, this persona was assisted by *The African Queen* (where she was teamed sexlessly with Bogart), *Summertime* (about a lovelorn spinster on vacation in Venice), and then by her performance as the drug-addict mother in *Long Day's Journey into Night,* opposite Ralph Richardson. It's an intriguing question as to whether Tracy could have let himself be emotionally naked enough to play that O'Neill material with her.

Cukor said there might have been one more reunion of the charmed club. It was *Cat and Mouse,* a Kanin script with Tracy as the leader of a currency racket (in drag in some scenes) and Hepburn as a Treasury Department agent tracking him down. (Does it sound like *The Thomas Crown Affair?*) This seemed promising, but Tracy said they were too old for it. Perhaps Hepburn was thinking he had been too old for Gene Tierney (his most recent romance as they made the inane *Plymouth Adventure* together).

Tracy still managed to represent tough-minded, virtuous, white-haired guys who knew their own mind and who spoke in the actor's measured but slightly threatening way. That's the Tracy in *Bad Day at Black Rock,* a supposedly rugged desert film still hailed for realism despite being a serene fantasy made for armchair guys (and again Tracy is not bothered with a love interest—honor is his bride). That veneer of veteran fortitude evaporated when Tracy tried to play the fisherman in *The Old Man and the Sea,* Hemingway's most stilted and sentimental book, with the overweight actor sweating in front of ocean projections while marlins frolic in the distance. The steady Tracy returned, opposite Fredric March, in *Inherit the Wind,* playing the skeptical Clarence Darrow–like lawyer, and so much happier with cross talk instead of Hemingway's intoned prose.

In fact, Hepburn and Tracy worked sparingly at the end of the 1950s and into the 1960s, and the legend was gently cultivated that she was looking after him because . . . well, there were a lot of reasons to choose from. He was unhappily married, with that deaf son and the consequent torments. He was lonely, despite torrid affairs with at least Ingrid Bergman and Tierney. Tracy took women to bed, sober or not. He was a bad drunk, often disabled and seriously ill because of it. Why did he drink? Was it because of Catholic guilt, an insoluble Irishness in his soul? Because he was an actor and an addictive personality? Or was it also because from time to time he slept with men?

Don't overlook "because he was an actor" in that list of reasons. The public regards movie actors as beautiful or assured as simply themselves—Tracy, John Wayne, and Fred Astaire, say, were not beautiful in the way of Gregory Peck, Tyrone Power, or the young Marlon Brando. But they were so confident in their looks, or so we thought, hardly noticing how far casting, writing, the camera, the lighting, and the situations of their films accounted for that glory, to say nothing of the publicity that went with the films. Many actors have been humbled by the processes of auditioning and refusal and by not always being liked. They nurse a growing certainty that they may be short on self, which helps them to go long on pretending, booze, and behaving badly. And they have come to see themselves as commercial properties that have to be nursed and catered to, as opposed to artists who come to every fresh role in the spirit of creative endeavor and adventure. Do not minimize the way Tracy and Hepburn recognized each other as a supportive and profitable crutch, and do not forget the helplessness and humiliation that can go with that. An actor like Spencer Tracy seemingly embodied a trusty reliability and midwestern integrity—it equipped him as the judge in *Judgment at Nuremberg*—but don't rule out the possibility that drunk, in and out of affairs, torn over his sexuality, the man was a wreck desperate to seem seaworthy and secure, and someone who found the best opportunity for that acting in movies. He was only sixty-seven when he died. The strain can be enormous. Surely something in Tracy needed comfort or peace.

Around the time he was making *Pat and Mike,* Tracy apparently telephoned Scotty Bowers, who did some work as a handyman. Tracy had met Bowers as a barman at one of George Cukor's parties. Bowers was good-looking, glib, and friendly—he seemed to know a lot of people. So he went over to Tracy's house and worked on the actor's hot-water tank. They started talking, and *Pat and Mike* and working with Hepburn came up:

> Something deep inside him was unleashed. He launched into a tirade about her. This was not the cool, calm, collected Spencer Tracy we were all familiar with through the characters he played on screen. This was an angry, bitter, bruised man. He had been hurt by her. Slurring and stumbling over his words he told me she was always rude to him, that she treated him like dirt, that she was contemptuous of him. Nothing about their great tabloid romance matched up with what Spence was telling me that evening as night fell.

Bowers was about to leave but Tracy begged him to stay and Scotty took pity on the actor's "desperate need." They got into bed together. Scotty hugged Spence and told him to sleep. "Instead, he lay his head down at my groin, took hold of my penis and began nibbling on my foreskin. This was the last guy on earth that I expected an overture like that from, but I was more than happy to oblige him and despite his inebriated state we had an hour or so of pretty good sex."

A lot of people make love when drunk, and the sex can be good enough. Much happy lovemaking is forgotten, and maybe even more is enshrined or armored as memory—even if it is only what one of the parties would recall.

The account I've quoted is from a book called *Full Service,* written by Bowers with Lionel Friedberg, and published by Grove Press in 2012. The jacket of the book carried this assurance, from Gore Vidal, "Scotty doesn't lie—the stars sometimes do—and he knows everybody." But I've known Vidal to get things wrong, and no other person has ever given such direct testimony about Tracy as Bowers. So, coming from a confessed hustler, *Full Service* is suspect. A year earlier, James Curtis, a distinguished writer of good biographies on movie people (W. C. Fields, Preston Sturges, and James Whale), published *Spencer Tracy,* which went over a thousand pages and was the fruit of six years' research and writing. Curtis dismissed Bowers (as quoted in William Mann's book about Hepburn) as an opportunist and a fabricator (and a man who had waited until his subjects were dead before publishing a book subtitled *My Adventures in Hollywood and the Secret Sex Lives of the Stars*). It's not hard to present Bowers as one of those authors who, long after the events described and without valid source notes, or anyone accountable, chooses to allege that nearly everyone in pictures was gay and/or sex mad. Curtis concluded, "There is no hint of homosexual activity in the Tracy papers nor in anything I have seen or learned elsewhere during the course of researching this book."

I don't trust Scotty Bowers, but I can't forget him. While I sympathize with a dedicated biographer who has spent six years on a subject without finding a trace of this or that in the surviving paperwork, I don't necessarily rely on that blankness. I worked six years on the David Selznick biography I mentioned earlier and spent a great deal of time with Irene Selznick, his first wife. I knew her and loved her, even if she was one of the fiercest people I have ever met. But you don't learn everything, especially with people who have had a training in pretending. I always guessed she was keeping a lot to herself; it was a way the old woman had of making sure I kept calling on her at the Pierre Hotel. After Irene was dead, when the book was published, I was in Toronto for a reading. When it was over, a smart, well-spoken woman came up to talk to me. She told me that her mother had had a lengthy affair with Irene. Then she hurried away. Perhaps she was pretending.

The things in the Bowers story that stay with me are Tracy's abject state, for I think he could go very low on self-esteem, and the way he might feel angry at Kate because of her condescending, hectoring ways. She was a bossy person, if one who liked to turn demure with powerful men. Apparently she was half-soft on the monstrous Louis B. Mayer because of the power he held at MGM. When Tracy had his very physical affair with Gene Tierney (just after *Pat and Mike*) it's possible that Kate made some cruel fun of his infatuation. (He had offered to marry Tierney.)

Tracy was often morose, despairing, drunk, and helpless—I don't think he always knew what he was doing. So I don't rule out the chance that sometimes he went to bed with men in an attempt to find some comfort. For sure, he knew Hepburn well enough to understand that she was capable of being bisexual. That antiromantic view of themselves may have been what held them together, just as it helps explain the uncommonly shrewd if unsentimental view of love that gay people might have in that time and place.

As Tracy's health declined, he and Hepburn worked less. She was looking after him, and they sometimes lived in separate cottages on George Cukor's estate. He had a place with an entrance on St. Ives; hers was off Cordell itself. She lived with her companion, Phyllis Wilbourn, an English woman who, from about 1957 onward, alleviated Kate's horror of being alone. Tracy was not just alone—he was a natural solitary. In this time they were often together but they slept in their own cottages. Tracy was only in his sixties, but he had increased trouble breathing.

There was one last film, *Guess Who's Coming to Dinner*, directed by Stanley Kramer, in which they costarred with Sidney Poitier and Hepburn's niece Katherine Houghton. It is an interracial love story, if that's what you want to call it and if you can overlook the radiant social-spiritual whiteness of Sidney Poitier. Tracy's work pattern was erratic, and Hepburn was watching over him all the time. When the filming was complete they lived in the cottages on Cukor's estate. Tracy had given up smoking under orders, and when he couldn't sleep he watched old movies on television, even his own, and Kate and Phyllis sometimes joined him to criticize the pictures.

A couple of weeks after he finished *Guess Who's Coming to Dinner,* on June 12, 1967, in the middle of the night, Tracy dropped dead at a table drinking tea. He had had a heart attack. Hepburn called Louise Tracy with the news, and when Louise arrived, she looked at Hepburn and said, "I thought you were a rumor." We have that just from Hepburn's memoir *Me,* where she reported the remark in anger, for it seems like a line calculated to hurt and disparage. Others believe Louise knew all along.

Guess Who's Coming to Dinner was an enormous hit, not just for the novelty of its interracial romance but because it was the finale for Tracy and Hepburn. They were both nominated for Oscars, and she won, in a triumph of sentiment over reason. Her teary performance beat out Anne Bancroft in *The Graduate,* Faye Dunaway in *Bonnie and Clyde,* Edith Evans in *The Whisperers,* and Audrey Hepburn in *Wait Until Dark.* It was a travesty. But there could not have been a screen event more certain of completing the legend of the two of them.

Only a few years after Tracy died, in 1971, the legend was delivered as perfectly as any have ever been managed when Garson Kanin published a book called *Tracy and Hepburn,* subtitled *An Intimate Memoir.* The entente cordiale had broken down by the late 1960s; it's not clear why. Cukor worked less past sixty and he mixed the grand production of *My Fair Lady* with offbeat failures like *The Chapman Report* (an awkward attempt to film a Kinsey-like survey of sexual behavior) and *Justine,* a disastrous version of the Lawrence Durrell novels. The place of adult comic romances was far more uncertain by then.

For reasons never made clear, Kanin and Gordon stopped writing as a team in the mid-1950s, without separating. They never divorced, and Kanin spoke warmly about their relationship: "We civilize each other, don't we? That's why good relationships and good influences are so important." That may be a profound insight on the example homosexual ties can set for people of all genders. Straight people often mock and envy gays for their promiscuity—but gay people can experience a lasting attachment that is for its own sake and not contingent on children or contracts. Adam and Amanda in *Adam's Rib* fight a lot—maybe as much as Tracy and Hepburn did in life—but they have decided not to part, if only because you cannot really leave another person after a deep relationship.

Kanin went back to directing and wrote more plays (he said he preferred the unfettered authorship on stage), which flopped. Thus, after Tracy's death, he needed money and saw the opportunity for a book about the apparent late-life romance of two quirky actors. He did not tell Hepburn what he was doing, as if foreseeing her wrath (and her urge to interfere). She was duly horrified when the book appeared, though in time she had to realize not just that it was a big best-seller but that it converted her from being a celebrated movie actress to a national treasure and an icon of how to behave. The book portrayed Tracy and Hepburn as lovers held together in caring, though Kanin sometimes admitted that he never claimed they actually made love.

Kanin had known his two subjects for a specific time in their lives, and he saw less of them after about 1955. His book delivered chunks of living dialogue that could hardly have been remembered. Kanin might have argued that he helped write some of the best dialogue Tracy and Hepburn ever had on screen, so why stop, just because they were out of earshot? His book cannot be relied on, but it guided a way the public—moviegoers and truckers alike—wanted to think warmly of the couple. So they became for us crusty, cranky lovers (an admirable version of your parents), just like Pat and Mike or Adam and Amanda, and in that process the curious and unresolved relationship of two people in romantic and gender confusion was lost. The real muddle, like that between your own parents, was erased, and that may be an easier way of getting through life than searching for the truth and insisting on doing your own long day's journey into night. *Tracy and Hepburn* worked wonders with obstinate and unresolved fact, and the book made a lot of money. Garson Kanin and the others in the Cordell Drive club had always reckoned that's what you had to do, that's what kept you going.

As for Hepburn, she told one journalist how she and Tracy had "had a secret understanding, a total understanding." Humans always hope for such precious empathy—sometimes we vest it in animals (who ask fewer question than we do). Years later, when she wrote *Me,* Hepburn conceded that the affection and the ties rested on uncertainty and knowing that she had never got to the bottom of what troubled Spencer Tracy so much. "What was it, Spence?" she called out, like an actress playing herself.

9

Buddies and Cowboys

Millard Mitchell and James Stewart in *Winchester 73* (1950).
The longer you look, the more it seems that dressing grown men in
cowboy gear was pretty silly—unless you really needed the game.

SOMETIMES IN OLD WAR FILMS and Westerns there's a male togetherness that believes it's natural and normal. But the longer you look at it, the more worrying this heroic pose becomes. Are these men made to be pals, or do they fear and dislike women? By 1960, fissures were appearing in macho confidence, as they were in the entire film business.

Hollywood was cracking, and national politics were being led by TV toward celebrity and being good on the box. Big male stars were aging. Male supremacy had excelled in the Second World War and just after, but wars in Korea and Vietnam without victory took their toll. Large showcases for triumphant males—like John Wayne's *The Alamo*—felt stranded. From 1957 to 1961, Humphrey Bogart, Tyrone Power, Ronald Colman, Errol Flynn, Clark Gable, and Gary Cooper died. *Some Like It Hot* and *Psycho* flourished. Hemingway killed himself.

Could the classic American man still handle the world? In *Bad Day at Black Rock* (1955), Black Rock is a barely inhabited town built for the movie outside Lone Pine on US Route 395 in eastern California near the Nevada border. Lone Pine was a pleasant resort town (population around 2,000) able to support a film crew on location for Metro-Goldwyn-Mayer. Black Rock is meant to be a hellish furnace at the back of beyond, a ghost town where the ghosts don't know they have been abandoned. Few trains stop there, until one blazing day a steel leviathan halts and a one-armed Spencer Tracy gets off. He is as much a man alone as Gary Cooper in *High Noon*.

But this man, Macreedy, is not a lawman. His character has a self-appointed task, to find Komoko, a Japanese who once lived outside Black Rock at Adobe Flats. Those flats are empty now save for a burned-out house. The visitor wants to know what happened to Komoko, and he has no one to ask but a group of exceptional supporting actors who seem to have retired to the desert for the dry air. There's Robert Ryan, Dean Jagger, Walter Brennan, John Ericson, Ernest Borgnine, and Lee Marvin, and they don't know nothing at all.

They don't even know why they're there in Black Rock. Ericson runs a hotel, a place without apparent function, except to tell Tracy it has no rooms available. There's no money or business in the burnt hills. There's no theater or ballet, no restaurants or shopping malls. There's no "civilization," as in a place where Ernest Borgnine or Lee Marvin could have a good time (is ballroom dancing their passion?). Las Vegas is 230 miles away; Reno, 260; and San Francisco, 352. There is one female in Black Rock, the pretty Anne Francis, who is Ericson's sister and apparently Ryan's lover (though that was seldom a comfortable assignment in the movies). Is she being imprisoned? Her womanliness is ignored—that was often the dead end for actresses in adventure films. Brennan and Jagger are "mature" in years and seemingly melancholy, though Marvin and Borgnine look like men who might think of sexual company sometimes on a Saturday night. If they can recall which day is Saturday. Who have they got apart from each other? I'm not making any suggestions about Lee and Ernie, tough men, we all know. But, honestly, what do they do?

This practicality can seem facetious, but it's a way of drawing attention to the implications of male groupings in a lot of American action films—and *Bad Day at Black Rock* is still regarded as a classic, even if it gets thin after a first viewing. We're meant to think of Marvin and Borgnine as nasty hoodlums—we're also supposed to accept that a one-armed Tracy disposes of both of them, which tells you about the fantasy in this gritty film.

What could these bad or lonely fellows do in Black Rock? If you're Marvin, imagine talking to Borgnine all day, every day. Well, you say, you never bothered to think about that, and does it really matter? Not in most ways, and not if you're content with the modest excitement of this John Sturges film (done five years before *The Magnificent Seven;* and don't ask about *them*). But imagine hundreds of American movies in which the empire of the guys is self-sufficient, iconic, and just a little constipated. What would you think if Tracy reached Black Rock and found a town inhabited by six supporting actresses—Beulah Bondi, Agnes Moorehead, Eve Arden, Spring Byington, Margaret Wycherly, and even Natalie Wood? (You can make substitutions if you're inclined.) Is that more startling than what we have? Or just more fun?

Or to phrase it a littler more pointedly: If there were some homosexual comings and goings in Black Rock, would that seem natural or unnatural? If you would have been nervous to put that question to Lee Marvin, then you know what "unnatural" used to mean.

There was an age when American adventure films were taken with unblinking respect—to have them teased or dismantled would have seemed un-American. Ordeal by adventure was the test that awaited happy endings. Black Rock in 1955 was an appropriate cockpit for American movie courage. In the age when "un-American" meant so much, in the late 1940s and early 1950s, I was a kid who watched Westerns and epics of adventure (one way or another horses were involved). I recall squirming at those embarrassing moments when the cowboy had to kiss the girl—kids wiped away the impact of those kisses with an indignant forearm. I longed for my boy to get back together with the other boys. If he happened to be alone, then he could talk to the horse.

There is a poignant moment in the film *Winchester 73* (1950). Its hero is Lin McAdam (James Stewart), who seems to be a wandering cowboy and a reminder of the romantic myth that such fellows did roam the prairie in 1876, with a saddle and a gun, good teeth, and horse insurance. But Lin is not alone: he has a companion, a sidekick. People do have friends, especially in stories where they need to talk and tell us how they are feeling. "Sidekick" has a Western flavor as a person who helps and spends a lot of time with someone who is usually more important or powerful. You could argue that a lot of wives in films of that era were sidekicks, along with yes-men, entourage men, assistant cops, and that fellow you'd been riding the range with for years until it became second nature.

Lin's sidekick is "High-Spade" Frankie Wilson (Millard Mitchell). High-Spade suggests a gambling career, but Frankie has none of those unreliable airs. He is tall, lean, losing his hair, and has a gruff voice. Lin can count on High-Spade. They arrive in Dodge City just as Wyatt Earp himself is about to conduct a marksmanship contest in which a Winchester 73 is the prize—one of the best rifles the Winchester company ever made, one in a thousand. Lin wins the contest, but he is cheated by "Dutch" Henry Brown (Stephen McNally), someone he has always known and hated. Why? Because Dutch Henry happens to be his brother—a dark other. Dutch Henry goes off with the sacred rifle and so begins the pursuit, or the ronde, that makes *Winchester 73*.

Broken fraternity means a lot in these parables. Brothers can be eternal kin: think of the Earps and the James brothers. They can also be your worst betrayers: think of Cal and Aaron Trask in *East of Eden*—or remember the unceasing unalikeness of the Marx Brothers. It's when your brother has let you down that you need a pal and a comfort. In so many movies that bond is glossed over. It's just there. But in *Winchester 73*, Lin and High-Spade do have a scene.

It is night on the prairie, at a camp in the moonlight, and it seems romantic in black-and-white, photographed by William H. Daniels, who had shot Garbo in *Camille* and Margaret Sullavan in *The Shop Around the Corner*. This camp is a hallowed and pretty sight, a place we want to be. Even if it's the panhandle in summer, you long for the warmth; somehow or other a dinner is going to be conjured up out of the few things a wandering cowboy has (where do they shop?); and without company, or a book to read, a cowpoke might have panic attacks.

HIGH-SPADE: How do you figure to hit Tascosa?
LIN (cleaning his gun): Around two or three tomorrow.
HIGH-SPADE (looking at Lin's deftness with the gun): I remember when you were taught that trick. Long time ago.
LIN: Yeah. Long time.
HIGH-SPADE: You ever think what he'd think about you? Hunting down Dutch Henry?
LIN: He'd understand. He taught me to hunt.
HIGH-SPADE: Not men. Hunting for food, that's all right. Hunting a man to kill him? You're beginning to like it.
LIN: That's where you're wrong. I don't like it. Some things a man has to do, so he does it.
HIGH-SPADE: What happens when the hunt is over? Then what?
LIN: Hadn't given it much thought.
HIGH-SPADE: Now might be a good time.
LIN: Maybe you're right. You've been real fine people, High-Spade, riding along with me.

HIGH-SPADE: That's what friends are for, isn't it? Leastways that's the way your dad said it.
LIN: Yeah, he did, didn't he? Said if a man had one friend he was rich. I'm rich.

Neither the writer of the scene, Borden Chase, nor the director of *Winchester 73,* Anthony Mann, had any record as a homosexual. Millard Mitchell was no more gay than James Stewart. The scene is not strictly necessary: you could omit it and the film would run along smoothly. Yet there it is, poised and soulful in the moonlight, as two men near the end of an adventure—and High-Spade knows Lin has recently seen a woman he likes. (The first? Lin is forty-two—is he a virgin?) The talk is taciturn, and some of it is cliché from sixty-nine years ago, but the adventure slows for a moment, and High-Spade's look is level but hesitant. A friend watched the film with me in the early 1960s and asked if the scene had a gay tone. I thought this estimate was correct, but I only realize now that "Lin" sounds like a girl's name.

Some moviemakers were becoming more alert to what might be hidden texts in their work. The same Borden Chase wrote *Red River* for Howard Hawks just a couple of years before *Winchester 73.* That film involves a scene of sly innuendo between Montgomery Clift and John Ireland. Clift was playing Matthew Garth, the adopted son, who will lead the great cattle drive in the film. Ireland plays Cherry Valance, a gunslinger hired by a nearby ranch who then decides to throw in his hand with Garth and the father-figure, Tom Dunson (played by John Wayne).

It was known on the production that Montgomery Clift was at least bisexual and probably gay, and doing his best as an actor to look like a young man of the West, learning to ride horses, use six-guns, and chew grass. From the moment Cherry appears in the form of Ireland a showdown is promised or a show-of-arms. So there's a scene in which the two cowboys show each other their six-guns and engage in a shooting contest. They are a match, but Cherry boasts to Matthew that his gun is bigger—a Hawks biographer, Todd McCarthy, says this was a reference to the rumored size of Ireland's member.

It's a scene played with humor. Seen today, it's hard to conclude that anyone involved didn't get the point. Hawks was not gay, but he had a shrewd intelligence about men in action, and his films have subtle asides on sexuality, courage, and manly style. Hawks knew innuendo before anything else, and I'm sure he understood the wordplay and may have enjoyed the joke on Clift. But I don't think audiences got that point in 1948, when the film opened.

When did the Western break down as a fixed fable about American manhood and honor? In some ways it never has. We had two gay cowboys in *Brokeback Mountain,* a decent, touching film, but if you're inclined to value that as a "breakthrough," just go look at Andy Warhol's *Lonesome Cowboys* (1968), which is a very funny demolition of Western buddy-ism.

Western righteousness has not suffered much. In the living theater of the nation, the cowboy is less present but still revered. Ronald Reagan appropriated the West as his atmosphere. Clint Eastwood took his *Unforgiven* as seriously as John Ford and John Wayne ever took *The Searchers.* Politicians still put on Stetsons to establish their good intentions. For them, William Munny and Ethan Edwards were credible men of the West facing immense challenges with rocklike perseverance. They are also heroes who seem to have undertaken silent vows of chastity or forbearance. On the other hand, the gang in Sam Peckinpah's *The Wild Bunch* (William Holden, Ernest Borgnine, Ben Johnson, and Warren Oates) are rough, rowdy fellows, without fuss or illusion: they are set on getting money, being free, and bathing with a gang of Mexican whores when the opportunity arises. One accepts Peckinpah's suggestion: this is how men lived in that time and place, and our America now might as well face up to it.

In the same year as *The Wild Bunch,* 1969, there was a hugely successful film that could not be approached as anything but a "camp" Western in which the hallowed realism of the camp firelight had given way to the knowing prettiness of modern actors having fun teasing the Western genre. When I say that sensibility was camp, we are on the way to recognizing that certain Western icons had become coy gods of irony. The men in *Butch Cassidy and the Sundance Kid* were adorable, *and they knew it.* They were sexy for women, but they were sexy for guys, too. The ambiguity shone out of their very names.

No, we're not outing Paul Newman or Robert Redford, though by 1969 both actors would have agreed that there was nothing wrong in being gay. That was just one of the several civil rights that were being collected in the new age. That does not mean they would have dared play a gay character. It doesn't suggest that Redford would do so even now. (Though he did it once in *Inside Daisy Clover.*) The one current movie star who is gay, and who has owned up to it, is Kevin Spacey, not just out now, but erased.

Still, Butch and Sundance are resplendent versions of Lin and High-Spade. It's not that they've come out but that they're turned inside out; they have converted the uncertainties of life on the run to looking like lovable models from a Sundance gift catalogue. They are costumed (by Edith Head, no less). Pursued across the badlands of Wyoming and then exposed to the privations of Bolivia, the boys have apparent access to dermatology and a barber shop—Sundance manages to keep his mustache trimmed without ever stooping to that dandyish refinement himself on screen. Above and beyond those cosmetic assets, they have something more blessed—an ability to crack wise with poker-faced repartee. They had a writer (as well as a barber), and his name was William Goldman.

No one complained (*Butch Cassidy* is a very easygoing movie—"I think it's really a nice picture," said Goldman), but a part of the enjoyment is saying goodbye to standard Westerns and relaxing with a pair of cool and rather swish dudes. No, they don't screw on screen or get close to what Jake Gyllenhaal and Heath Ledger managed in *Brokeback Mountain,* but they had an edge on those later "pioneers" in that they were having such fun. Annie Proulx's Wyoming shepherds, Ennis and Jack, are tragic and uneducated figures, but Butch and Sundance are swingers. Even their demise is enshrined in a frozen frame.

One of the sure marks of their privilege was their curious handling of women. Sundance has his girl, Etta Place (Katharine Ross), said to be a schoolteacher. She is introduced in a special way. As she comes back to her dark house at night Sundance is there, like a waiting rapist.

He orders her to take off her clothes (certified period underwear from Ms. Head), and she seems stricken until we realize that this rape routine is just their sex game. Pretending is their thing, and their charade is being in the West. Etta is Sundance's girl, but she makes it plain in an ordinary way that she loves Butch, too. Though Butch has to make do without female companionship, he has the comfort of that dopey showstopper song, "Raindrops Keep Falling on My Head," as he cycles around the postcoital slumbering of Etta and Sundance.

It would have been a bolder film, and funnier, if Etta had screwed both men—which may have been truer to the period. Etta is not just a teacher but nearly maternal. She knows the boys' escapism needs a precious or spoiled level of existence, but she warns them that when their danger becomes too great she will quit. She doesn't intend to see them perish. The idea that the boys are happier together fits the tongue-in-cheek daydream. That freeze-frame means we don't have to see them slaughtered, either.

Butch Cassidy and the Sundance Kid was a modish update on the buddy film, a genre that was deep-seated while the movies kept pace with a succession of American military conflicts, and the way gangs of young people still went to the movies together. That male companionship was rowdy and blithe at the same time, swapping jokes and taunts, performing for the silent girl outliers who waited for their kiss goodnight. Teenage gangs still function in similar ways, if less often at movie theaters. They also bear out a young male fear of testing female company: are the girls going to want to talk about *stuff*—like life, ideas, future, furniture, families, and Emily Dickinson—or can they be kept in their place as knockout trophies who will provide carnal satisfaction and children (thus the future) as and when the time arises? Boys just wanna have fun and store away the treasure trove of buddy memories to sustain them past twenty-three or twenty-four.

The movies catered to those urges with unquestioning obedience. Gangs became the working system of many movies, with the star as the gangleader: that is the nutshell that explains the dynamism of James Cagney, even if he had a passion for action, movement, and surprise that were all his own. Those gangs had girls or dolls, who tended to be sweethearts or sluts, and even killers had to be able to distinguish one from the other. The gang roared into life with sound, its wisecracks, its machine-gun fire, and the smack of punches. A Cagney would be lost without his Warners sidekicks, Pat O'Brien, Frank McHugh, and Alan Hale, and his sweethearts, like Joan Blondell, Ann Dvorak, and Mae Clarke. The sexual-familial setup was locked in, and it carried over into war films where soldiers bursting with comradely vitality (what else hides fear?) were rivals for pretty women who seldom questioned the male code. That is what fed us at the movies—gender stereotypes that took for granted a fixed society and a surging economy.

What Price Glory? is a keystone in this tradition. It was a hit on Broadway in 1924–25, a play by Maxwell Anderson and Laurence Stallings in which Captain Flagg and Sergeant Quirt are a credit to the Army for their courage in combat, their rivalrous pursuit of the same dames, and their constant teasing of each other. There was a girl in contest, Charmaine, a French villager, but she was a prize and an element of fun, rather than a real character. Two years later the story was filmed, directed by Raoul Walsh, with Victor McLaglen and Edmund Lowe as Flagg and Quirt and Dolores del Rio as Charmaine—the French girl turned Spanish, but who cared? In a silent picture, she wasn't talking.

In the 1920s *What Price Glory?* was hailed for its realism with war, men, and their language, but that only shows how robust our innocence can be. It was filmed again in 1952 (by John Ford) with Cagney and Dan Dailey in the lead roles. By then it was just another war-buddy film amid the glut of others and the increasingly desperate hope that if war had done nothing else it had provided friendships. Yet there were some pioneering war pictures that said service and combat might be isolating experiences to the point of breakdown—*Twelve O'Clock High*, *Act of Violence* (rueful with postwar reappraisal), and even *From Here to Eternity,* which involves two loner soldiers.

Lin and High-Spade are in that buddy tradition, and it is akin to the bonding that still dominates cop shows—that cops go in pairs because it's dangerous out there. So sometimes these cops are in their car talking quietly and bitterly about having no home life, like Gene Hackman and Roy Scheider in *The French Connection.* But the movies always had mixed feelings about home life—going out to the show meant getting out of the house and escaping from its tedium or its impossible fights. In all its virtues and fantasies, *Red River* is about a band of guys who go off on a camping trip together, with cows as company. Just before they reach the railhead, they discover a maidenhead in the form of Joanne Dru, and rapidly Matthew Garth defeats Cherry Valance in the contest for her (though in life it was that sly John Ireland who ended up marrying Dru).

In the Howard Hawks film, the cowpokes eat their beans and handle a stampede, they run riffs on false teeth and how the boss Mr. Dunson is getting tougher by the day. They do not walk off into the brush to masturbate; no one asks Cherry how he got that name; they do not go to the chuck wagon where Dunson might have a couple of hookers alive and ready. They do not rape Indian women discovered on the trail—and that happened in the West. They do not read poetry or whittle away at wooden sculptures. And in the middle of the nineteenth century they could not look at Laurel and Hardy movies, to see the dumb softies that buddies might be.

Stan and Ollie were not just two guys pushed into keeping company. They had little other existence beyond being one half of the whole. They were very different: Oliver Hardy was from Georgia in the American South; Stan was from Ulverston in Lancashire. The one weighed about twice what the other did. Ollie was officious, bossy, a know-it-all; Stan was demure, foolish, and innocent. They both wore silly derby hats, ill-fitting suits with frock coats, and gestures toward smart ties. They noticed ladies; they were polite to them, they tipped their hats and became sheepish with them. But they had no thought of what to do with girls. Their life was a series of calamities sent by fate and their own daft natures. It was one fine mess after another, as Ollie never stopped reminding Stan. For them to have anything like a business—delivering pianos?—was to explore the details of disaster. They had no money or family and little in the way of a home. But they had each other. Indeed, they could not escape being together. They were a couple doomed by marriage, but sustained by it.

The veteran watcher of their films waits for the obvious mishaps and the chance of surreal escape. In *Way Out West* (1937), Stan allows Ollie to fall through the roof of a hut; amid the wreckage, he seeks a ladder to help rescue his fat friend; while he is doing that, turned away, Ollie extricates himself. When Stan notices this, he still says, "I've got a ladder to help him get out." It's a simple, sweet joke; at such moments, vaudeville routines can slip into *Waiting for Godot*, another stalemate of two men by a tree on the road (going nowhere).

Here comes another moment when, hearing the twang and sway of cowboys singing, in a lovely withdrawn full shot, the accident-prone boys feel their limbs tugged at by dance. In a moment they're in a side-shuffling pas de deux, enough to show us that Oliver Hardy was a very dainty mover. *Way Out West* is credited as "a Stan Laurel Production" and I daresay he shaped the routines, but the more you look at the boys the clearer it is that Ollie was the most graceful fat man on the American screen. He's like a Margaret Dumont who hears rhythm—does that leave Stan as his husband?

No, these boys do not have sex—like so many settled married couples. They did not know how to and if anyone had told them they would have got it wrong. They did not seem subject to aging, let alone hormones. They were often aimed at childish audiences; they could be the last two people left on Earth, or was it the first two? They acted on the principle that as soon as two people come together an engine of disorder exists. On the second day, God said, let there be misunderstanding—now we're cooking. And it's clear from this reading of history that Mrs. God had left the big guy long ago, in despair. So God made Laurel and Hardy as a tribute to what little he recalled of the comedy of marriage. There are famous screen marriages in the age of Laurel and Hardy: Nick and Nora Charles, the family tree of Andy Hardy, Ma and Pa Kettle, and we can even include Lucy and Desi, who started just a few years after the boys stopped (1945). So many films were blundering their way toward happy endings that closed on an embrace in which some Robin Hood and Maid Marian would furnish a Levittown with society, good values, and bridge.

The great body of happy-ending cinema did not spend too much time on that subsequent bliss. It was terrified of what came next. That was what followed the advertisement, and it might be divorce, disobedient kids, or buyer's remorse. But Laurel and Hardy could never divorce. Just as they had made no decision to be together, so they lacked the option or the willpower to part. If you were schematically minded you might say Stan was the female and Ollie the alpha. But those schemes dissolved because there was no more lasting guilt or memory than there was between Tom and Jerry—another great movie marriage, where cartoon antagonism is too fierce to admit tenderness. Laurel and Hardy and Tom and Jerry were forever re-enacting a theme that the critic Stanley Cavell has identified as being at the peak of American screen humor—the comedy of remarriage. So the mouse destroys the cat, and the cat is reformed so he can be destroyed again.

In fact, Mr. Laurel and Mr. Hardy had irregular personal lives. Stan was married five times and had two children; Ollie had three wives. Neither one of them was what we would call gay—look at their forlorn faces and that quaint word turns to dust. But they are typical of a movie tradition, of pals not just content with being together but unaware of other options. They are guys but nearly sexless, and so in time their bond takes on metaphorical hues.

They had many writers and directors, yet no one apart from their boss, Hal Roach, stands out from that crowd. They made their own films, and Stan was more the comedy writer than Ollie. In this discussion I don't think vision or authorship matter. They were lonely, indignant atoms in a molecule of eternal imbalance but as life-enhancing as water. Never mind their chromosomes, their nationality, their weight, or their intent, they were an odd couple that movies had to have. They are the purest version of a genre that runs to the Marx Brothers, Abbott and Costello, Dean Martin and Jerry Lewis (the marriage as torture), and De Niro and Joe Pesci in several Scorsese pictures. We treasure these odd couples.

When that title appeared—*The Odd Couple*—it was as if darkness had been blown away, revealing a model form. Neil Simon's 1965 play was never a candid, itching metaphor about being gay—I don't think Simon got that point himself—but it was a moment at which the molecular structure of Laurel and Hardy (and others) began to be transparent.

Neil Simon had a brother, Danny, who split with his wife in the early 1960s. He moved in with a friend and soon people noticed that this impromptu couple were behaving oddly, like a married couple in ordinary, everyday things, like cooking and housework and nagging. Neil Simon thought there was a play in the situation. Danny tried to write it himself but got no further than fifteen pages. So he turned it over to Neil. They had a financial arrangement out of which *The Odd Couple* opened on Broadway. Felix Ungar had been thrown out by his wife and taken up residence with his pal, Oscar Madison. Mike Nichols directed the hit show, Art Carney played the neurotically neat Felix and Walter Matthau was the ultra untidy Oscar. (Note: in preproduction, Matthau had begged to play Felix.) The show ran 964 performances. It was a transforming event and the audience thought it was all about real life and the comedy in breaking up.

Neither the text nor the production suggested that Felix or Oscar were homosexual. In fact, there were two Pigeon sisters upstairs in Oscar's building who attracted the guys. Simon named them Gwendolyn and Cecily, and when Nichols remarked on the allusion to *The Importance of Being Earnest,* Simon didn't know what he was talking about. Instructive coincidences can happen: it was in 1969 that the Stonewall riots occurred in New York City, a landmark in the need to recognize gay rights. As late as the 1960s, homosexual behavior was illegal in public, and gay bars or clubs were at risk of being shut down.

There were other iterations of *The Odd Couple:* a movie, in 1968, directed by Gene Saks, with Matthau and Jack Lemmon, and then the TV series (1970–75), with Tony Randall and Jack Klugman. By then, Simon had very little involvement in the show. It was a training ground for other writers and directors and its setup had a lasting effect on television situation comedies in which fixed gender became the sport of role-playing. One cannot grasp the widening and often confusing interpretations of marriage in America without recognizing the influence of *The Odd Couple* and the way that phrase has become so instructive in the study of innovatory relationships.

It may seem improper to wonder about the subtexts in movie buddies. To raise such questions is like undermining sacred bonds: the code of the boys' prep school, cops on duty, the military, those clubs that prefer to bar women. Augusta National Golf Club (home of the Masters) only allowed female membership in 2009 (it had been founded in 1933, like the Production Code). The issue of women in the military, in combat or in command, is still nearly as vexed as the possibility of women exercising executive rights in the film industry.

So the questions are worth raising. Earlier, I proposed the desert town of Black Rock being peopled with supporting actresses. I hope that seemed amusing—at first. The fact remains that the persistence of male buddies in film fiction has not been much extended to women. There are a few worthy examples, like *Thelma and Louise* (who feel obliged to kill themselves as payback for their brief and hopeless liberty). But where are the female couples as long-lasting as Laurel and Hardy? Is it that women are less friendly? Or do men require a secret agenda as a touchstone of superiority that lasted a hundred years and could still triumph?

10

"The Cat's in the Bag, the Bag's in the River"

Elizabeth Taylor and Montgomery Clift during *A Place in the Sun* (1951). This
shot does not appear in the film, but somehow it's like a caption or a poster for it,
and for the thwarted romance of this dreamy couple. I used to think that movie
illustrations had to be from the movie—but so many stills feel dead because
they've stopped moving. True stills—a photographer's art—can get at the inner
meaning. It's like the *Bonnie and Clyde* picture on page 3.

WHAT WERE WE MEANT to be feeling at the movies in the 1950s on hearing a line like this? What do we feel now? What is this insinuating rumor about the cat, the bag, and the river getting at? How did movies make such magic out of masked meanings?

We looked at the screen, and things there seemed so real or emphatic—the men, the women, the sky, the night, and New York. In *Sweet Smell of Success* (1957) you believed you could sniff the black-and-white stink of the city. Wasn't that in the contract as light ate into film's silver salts? But the things depicted were also elements in a dream—nothing else looks like black-and-white. And because we believe dreams have inner meanings, not meant to be understood so much as lived with, we guessed there might be a secret within the facts. Was it just a gorgeous, repellent mood in *Sweet Smell,* or was a larger odor hanging over the film?

"The cat's in the bag, the bag's in the river," Sidney Falco says to J. J. Hunsecker as information or promise, even as endearment. Those two rats play a game together called bad mouth. In 1957 in *Sweet Smell* the line had the click of hard-boiled poetry or of a gun being cocked. It said that some secret business was in hand, cool, calm, and collected but also dirty and shaming until you dressed it up in swagger. We were sinking into rotten poetry. I felt for that cat, and wondered if its death was being signaled; but I guessed the scrag of wet fur was alive still—it was a secret and secrets don't die, they only wait. The very line said, What do you think I mean? And that's what the best movies are always asking. Sometimes you revisit those 1950s movies and feel the cat's accusing eyes staring at you through the bag and the rising river.

Some people treasure *Sweet Smell of Success* because it's so unsentimental, so *gritty*. I don't buy that. Long before its close the story becomes tedious and woefully moralistic. It shuts itself down, and then the wisecrack lines are stale garnish on day-old prawn cocktail. Admit it: after sixty years, a lot of "great" films can seem better suited to museums than packed places where people want to be surprised for the first time, *now*. In museums, as on DVDs, the films can seem very fine, yet not much happens while you're watching except the working of your self-conscious respect. But power in a movie should be instant and irrational; it grabs at dread and desire and often involves more danger than contemplation.

Sweet Smell is that good or grabby for at least half an hour—and in 1957 that came close enough to horror or fascination to alarm audiences. Perhaps that's why the scabrous movie had to ease back, turn routine, go dull, whatever you want to say. Would it have been too disturbing for the movie business—which includes us, the audience—if *Sweet Smell of Success* had gone all the way and let its cat out of the bag?

As written first by Ernest Lehmann, then rewritten by Clifford Odets, and directed by Alexander Mackendrick, *Sweet Smell* is set in the old newspaper world of New York City. J. J. Hunsecker is an indecently potent gossip columnist on the *New York Globe*. The hoardings in the city call him the Eyes of Broadway, with the image of his cold stare and armored spectacles. At the time, there was talk that Hunsecker was based on a real columnist, Walter Winchell. That's not incorrect. But how many now know who Winchell was then? Whereas a lot of us still respond to the smothered hostility in Burt Lancaster and react to the gloating tension he has in the film with Tony Curtis.

Lancaster played Hunsecker; his own company (Hecht-Hill-Lancaster) produced the movie. So Burt was in charge, and he is filmed throughout the story as a monarch who sits still and orders the execution of others with the flicker of an eye or a hushed word. That verdict will be passed finally on Sidney Falco (Tony Curtis), a scuttling press agent who survives by getting items into Hunsecker's column and so can be engaged to do whatever ugly deeds J.J. requires. A refined, codependent slavery exists between them: J.J. smiles and Sidney smiles, but not at the same time. It is the toxic pact between these two that makes the film disturbing for at least thirty minutes—but it might have been a greater film still if it could have seen or admitted that their mutual loathing is the only thing that keeps them from being lovers.

This was not admitted in 1957, and no one can blame a commercial movie of that era for lacking the courage or even the self-awareness that would have been so direct about a destructive homosexual relationship. If Burt had felt that subtext, his company would never have made the picture. But Burt the man and the actor cannot resist the allure of the secret. He looks at Sidney and at his own position like a charmer looking at a snake and seeing danger. Yet *Sweet Smell* plays out finally as one more melodrama of good people and bad people—the way Hollywood liked to tell us the world worked. The radical situation of the film is that Sidney fears and needs J.J. while the columnist despises but needs Sidney. There's no room for conventional affection, let alone love, but dependency is like cigarette smoke at the nightclubs where the two rats live. And it reaches poetry in the vicious zigzag talk that joins these men at the hip.

The talk seems lifelike—you can believe you are hearing two cynical professionals whose venom is ink; the insults feel printed. But it's hard for movies to stop at that. In the conspiracy of close-ups and crosscutting, and in the pressure to hold audience attention, the talk becomes musical, rhythmic, a self-sufficient rapture, and even the subject of a film.

Sidney goes to the 21 Club, sure that J.J. will be there, in his element. They know each other like a married couple. J.J. is at his table, holding court—he is a little like Vito Corleone at the start of *The Godfather,* but not as warm or amiable. Hunsecker is receiving a U.S. senator— a weak officeholder he has known for years—a groveling talent agent, and a blonde woman the agent is touting (and providing for the senator's pleasure). The blonde is named Linda James. She maintains she is a singer. She is played by an actress named Autumn Russell who had a dozen movie credits before fading away; she is good here as a woman past youthful freshness, attractive yet desperately preserved, painfully available, and about to be humiliated.

Sidney sits down at the table, beside but a little behind Hunsecker. J.J. begins to order him away, but Sidney has a password, a way into J.J.'s need—he has something to tell him about Hunsecker's sister. So the powerful man relents and Sidney stays. Then Miss James, trying to be pleasant, wonders out loud if Sidney is an actor.

"How did you guess it, Miss James?" asks Hunsecker, scenting revenge.

"He's so pretty, that's how," she responds. And let it be said, Tony Curtis in 1957 was "pretty," or a knockout, or gorgeous . . . The list of such words is not that long, and it's nearly as problematic now as calling a woman "beautiful." Let's just say "pretty" fits, even if Sidney is torn between pleasure and resentment at hearing the word.

Then Hunsecker speaks—and in a few words we know it is one of the killer speeches of 1957.

> Mr. Falco, let it be said, is a man of forty faces, not one, none too pretty and all deceptive. See that grin? That's the charming street urchin's face. It's part of his "helpless" act—he throws himself on your mercy. He's got a half a dozen faces for the ladies, but the real cute one to me is the quick, dependable chap—nothing he won't do for you in a pinch, so he says! Mr. Falco, whom I did not invite to sit at this table, tonight, is a hungry press agent and fully up on all the tricks of his very slimy trade!

That speech is as cruel as it is literary. It helps us recognize how uncasual or nonrealistic movie talk can be. Of course Hunsecker is a writer, though it's easier to believe he dictates his column instead of putting pen to paper. But the speech relishes words and their momentum. In life, it was one of the speeches that Clifford Odets hammered out on his typewriter in a trailer parked on a Manhattan street hours ahead of the shooting. Odets had been a revered playwright in the 1930s, the husband or lover to famous actresses, and here he was, at fifty, a Hollywood writer and rewriter for hire, doctoring a screenplay for immediate performance. He knew self-loathing from the inside; observers said he was "crazed" by the shift in going from being the next Eugene O'Neill to just another script doctor. Yet Odets was good enough to build to this moment: as he concludes his assassination, Hunsecker picks up a cigarette, and says, quietly, "Match me, Sidney."

This is an ultimate humiliation; it is the blade slipping between the bull's shoulder blades; but it is a proposal, too, or an admission that a terrible wounding marriage exists between the two men, one that cannot be owned up to or escaped. The line is poison for Sidney to taste, and Tony Curtis has played the scene, in close-up, like a man with a sweet tooth for poison, on the edge of nausea. (Later on in the film, Hunsecker tells Sidney he's "a cookie filled with arsenic.")

But even a destroyed wife can sometimes get a line back. "Not just this minute, J.J.," Falco answers, and now we know there is a level between them, beneath professional cruelty and self-abasement. It is a horrible kind of love. Hunsecker smiles at the refusal, as if to admit that the wretched Falco can stick around.

There is more talk like this, and in 1957 it was courageous or even reckless: the film was never a popular success—it had rentals a million dollars less than its costs, so Burt the businessman suffered, which meant others would feel the pain. One obvious risk in the film was giving offense to real Hunsecker-like figures and undermining the integrity of what was still called "the press." But there's a deeper implication in the scene and the talk: these two men need each other; they might exchange insult and subjugation forever. Indeed, as an audience we don't want them to stop talking.

Alas, *Sweet Smell* cannot act on that realization. A complicated plot intervenes. J.J. is obsessed with his sister, Susan. This is asserted, but never explored: does he simply need to control her, or does he have a physical desire for her that he cannot express or admit? It should be added that there is no other woman in Hunsecker's life. He is disturbed that Susie seems to be in love with a young jazz musician, Steve—maybe the cleanest, whitest, dullest jazzman in all of cinema. These two characters, played by Susan Harrison and Martin Milner, are embarrassments who drag the film down. This is not an attack on the actors but despair over the concept that lets the film dwell on them. Why is J.J. obsessed? We never discover an answer. I don't necessarily want to see his incestuous yearnings; I accept his need for power and fear in others. But I want chemistry between J.J. and Susan if the threat of losing her is to be dramatic.

As it is, *Sweet Smell* degenerates into a tortured intrigue in which Sidney contrives to frame Steve on drug charges, just to make Susan turn against her guy. This leads to an ending in which two bad men get their just deserts. But that is banal and lacks feeling for "the young lovers," who trudge off together into a new day. We do learn more about Sidney's conniving nature, and the film becomes a showcase for Curtis. (That he was not nominated for his work speaks to how far Sidney unsettled Hollywood.) But we do not get enough of the two caged men clawing at each other with spiteful words. I don't think anyone could contemplate a remake of the film today without seeing that there has to be a gay relationship between columnist and press agent, a reliance that excludes the rest of life.

As the film ends, Susie has found the strength to leave her brother. "I'd rather be dead than living with you," she says. The odious cop, Kello, has beaten up Sidney on the street and carried his limp body away. Is he dead? Or would it be possible for J.J. to come down to the street to reclaim the broken body, carry it upstairs, and put it in the room left free by Susie's departure? That is not an enviable future for a very odd couple. Maybe Sidney lives in a wheelchair, crippled and needing to be looked after. Just so long as he can exchange barbed lines with J.J.

This is less film criticism—as in a review of a new film—than a reflection on the history of the medium and the way a dream evolves if it is potent enough. I can find no evidence that anyone on the picture intended the undertone I am describing, or was aware of it. I am confident that director Mackendrick and writer Odets were not homosexual, though I'm less sure that they didn't understand the possibility of that relationship and see an underground life in the casting. Tony Curtis (born Bernard Schwartz in 1925) really was a very good-looking kid, though as a Bronx boy and then a young man in the Pacific war (in submarines), he was only ordinarily good-looking. It was in the late 1940s, as he thought of a show business career, that he started working hard on his looks and his body, and when he felt people in the neighborhood were thinking he might be gay.

In those late 1940s—and still today—there is a widespread feeling that a lot of people in show business are gay. That notion exists above and beyond the fact that there are more homosexuals in show business than in most other professions. Curtis was a fascinating case, with a well-earned reputation as a ladies' man, with six marriages and six children.

Curtis was also funny, candid, and quite bold. He could sit there on screen as Sidney while other characters considered how "pretty" he was. Many lead actors of that era would not have stood for that—I'm sure Lancaster would not have sat there, absorbing it (which doesn't mean he was deaf to the undertones as he administered the lashing). Curtis grew up in the movie business with a corps of very good-looking guys, many of whom were clients of the agent Henry Willson, who cultivated gay actors who did not come out of the closet on screen—one of them was Rock Hudson, a contemporary of Curtis's at Universal. Maybe most important of all, Curtis had the courage to play Josephine in Billy Wilder's radical film, *Some Like It Hot.* How much courage? Well, it's fair to say that Jack Lemmon played Daphne in the spirit of farce and slapstick. It's not likely, watching *Some Like It Hot,* in 1959 or now, to believe that Daphne is a girl. But Curtis went for it. Josephine *is* an attractive woman. Curtis is candid in his book, *American Prince,* about the shyness he felt in wearing female clothes and then being on show in front of the crew. "After all these years of putting up with guys coming on to me and hearing rumors about my own sexuality, dressing like a woman felt like a real challenge to my manhood." So he told Wilder that Josephine needed better clothes.

Not that it matters now, but I don't believe Tony Curtis was gay, ever. Of course, that would have nothing to do with his ability as an actor to imagine or pretend to gay experience. And if Curtis was that good then he was admitting millions of people in his audience into the same experiment. One principle in this book—and it has been of enormous influence in our lives as a whole—is that in watching pretense we acquire a deeper sense of our reality but a growing uncertainty over our psychic integrity. What else are movies for? We thought we were identifying with characters for fun, but perhaps we were picking up the shiftiness of acting—for life.

The case of Burt Lancaster is more complex. He was married three times, and he had five children. But we are past believing that such credentials settle all interests. The best biography on Lancaster, deeply researched and written with care and respect by Kate Buford, does not believe he had an active gay life. That book was published in 2000. On the way to a celebration of its publication at Lincoln Center, I had dinner with an old friend, George Trescher, a man who did nothing to conceal his own homosexuality, and he assured me that in fact Lancaster had led a gay life. Later still, some documents were released from the F.B.I. and the Lancaster family that did not name names but that revealed that Lancaster had often been "depressed," that he was bisexual, and that he had had several gay relationships, though never on more than a short-term basis.

With that in mind, you might look at Lancaster's strangest film, *The Swimmer* (1968), directed by Frank Perry and taken from a John Cheever story. It's a fable about an apparent Connecticut success, Ned Merrill, who takes it into his head to swim home one summer Sunday by way of all the pools owned by his acquaintances. Cheever, who had a tormented gay life, watched the filming with awe and amusement, as Burt, at fifty-five, in simple trunks, made Ned's way from sunlight to dusk and dismay. Why did they make that movie? you'll wonder. Because Burt wanted to do it.

For much of his career, Lancaster was called a he-man or a hunk. Trained in the circus and proficient as an acrobat, he loved athletic and adventurous roles in movies for which he frequently did his own stunts. As a boy, I thrilled to him as Dardo in *The Flame and the Arrow* (1950), about a twelfth-century Robin Hood figure from Lombardy. His sidekick in that picture was played by Nick Cravat, a circus partner who kept company with Burt for decades. They made nine films together, including *The Crimson Pirate* (1952), with Burt as an archetypal grinning rogue, beautiful and physically commanding, in what went from being a straight pirate adventure to a camp romp in which Lancaster is blond, bright, and comically cheerful—in other words, the hero is a parody of himself.

There was another Lancaster, darker and more forbidding: you can see that actor in *The Killers, Brute Force,* and *Criss Cross,* and he emerged fully as Sergeant Warden in *From Here to Eternity.* That Lancaster became a good actor, but for decades he was determined to stay athletic and heroic: as late as *The Train* (1964), when he was fifty, he was doing his own stunts. But his work in *Sweet Smell* is the more interesting for being so repressed. Was he at ease like that? Orson Welles had been the original casting as J.J., but Welles was in a run of flops so Lancaster the producer elected to play the monster himself. He made the role in a way that would have been beyond Welles. It's in Hunsecker's stealth and stillness that we feel his evil—or call it a darker inner life than Burt was accustomed to showing. Only a couple of years before

Sweet Smell, he had played with Curtis in *Trapeze,* a conventional circus film that took advantage of his own physical skills.

Tony Curtis reported in his book that Lancaster was often very tense during the filming: he was at odds with Mackendrick, so that they sometimes came close to physical conflict. In one scene, Mackendrick wanted Burt to shift over on a bench seat to let Curtis sit at the table. Burt insisted that Hunsecker would not have moved for anyone—it was a good insight—and he nearly fought the director. Mackendrick was taking too long; the picture's costs were mounting. But the physical actor in Lancaster was both determined on and pressured by the role's tensions.

The film's composer, Elmer Bernstein, said, "Burt was really scary. He was a dangerous guy. He had a short fuse. He was very physical. You thought you might get punched out." Yet Lancaster was supposedly in charge, as both character and producer. Was he afraid of his own film commercially? Did he bridle at his required stillness? Was he in control of Hunsecker's blank rage? Did he guess that Tony Curtis had the more vivid role? Or was he oppressed by the implications of the film's central relationship? Did he feel the movie was a plot against him? These questions are not just gossip; they enrich one's experience of J.J.'s paranoia. Lancaster's authority and Hunsecker's power are twinned and destructive.

If we see a gay subtext in *Sweet Smell,* then the hobbled nature of its women characters becomes clearer. It is not just that pliant singer on a senator's arm. Susan is an emotional wreck, attractive in outline but drained of romantic confidence or stability. At one point Sidney tells her to start thinking with her head not her hips. Hunsecker has a secretary who has no illusions about him. Sidney has a girl who is his humbled slave. There is a well-drawn betrayed wife (nicely played by an uncredited Lurene Tuttle). And then there is the Barbara Nichols character, Rita, an illusionless hooker so degraded she will do whatever Sidney requires of her. There isn't a woman in the film with appeal or self-respect. This bleak elimination of heterosexual potential is part of the dankness in *Sweet Smell* and one more contrast with the exhilarated sparring between the male leads. Hatred or antagonism is their idiom, and we can't stop hanging on the tortured double act.

.   .   .

The 1950s was the crucial era of change in that the shifts were barely noticed yet. Blind urges were pushing to escape genre rules. In 1953, at Universal, Douglas Sirk made *Taza, Son of Cochise*, with Rock Hudson playing the Apache chief. Born and trained as a stage director, Sirk was an unusually educated or well-read director for Hollywood pictures, yet he had an instinct for popular entertainment. In what was his first (and last) Western, he also had a heightened feeling for the ambiguity of his lead character, a sensitive savage. In *Sirk on Sirk*, he says "He is my most symbolic in-between man. He is an Indian, but there has seeped into the character this element of civilization. . . ." Keep on seeping, America.

That trailing away is from an interview book (1971) with Sirk. He and Rock Hudson were a creative partnership on eight films in the 1950s, a group that includes some of Hudson's best work as well as the preparation for his stardom. *Taza* was their second film together, and the in-betweenness of Taza has something to do with this Apache being six foot five, utterly Caucasian in his features, truly beautiful, and with a bared, hairless chest that spoke of the gym and Universal's wish to put beefcake on the screen when that commodity was reckoned as honest and sustaining as real beef for dinner.

Hudson disliked the memory of *Taza*, and he could be eloquent about the travesty he felt he had made of himself as an actor: "If you scratched and scratched beneath the surface of most of the roles I played, you wouldn't find any kind of human being there. I'm not like anyone I've ever played. Roy Fitzgerald [Hudson's real name] is a different person from Rock Hudson, whom I sometimes think of as a stranger."

Hudson is obvious material in this book, not just for the tragedy of his life and the impact he had as a lesson or influence but because for so long the public chose to see what it wanted to see in him and nothing of the real in-betweenness. In his heyday, the public never noticed the cavities in "Rock."

Roy Harold Scherer had been born in Winnetka, Illinois, in 1925. His father abandoned the family when Roy was young; his mother remarried and the boy took the name of her second husband, "Fitzgerald." He was not a great student; he was an aircraft mechanic who actually sailed to the Pacific but never saw combat; on his return, he thought of trying acting. He was a guarded youth, interested in creative things but silent about them in case he was seen as a "sissy"—that barbed word was his choice, and so common in schoolyard taunts. Roy failed in drama courses at the University of Southern California, and he worked for a while as a truckdriver. He was tall and handsome, or what is still called "good looking." He came on as frank and friendly; he had an air of reliability and strength. In 1947, he sent a photograph of himself to the talent agent Henry Willson and he was taken on.

Willson was thirty-six in 1947. He had been a child in a show business family, acquainted with many stars, and homosexual despite efforts by his father to direct him toward "manly" activities. I am using the language here that was customary at the time, to characterize a life in which Henry's sexual tastes had to be hidden. But he had flourished in the business as an agent, and in 1943 he was hired to recruit talent for David O. Selznick, especially in the making of *Since You Went Away,* a story about women left at home during war, that includes a number of young servicemen. One of those was played by a Willson discovery, Guy Madison (real name, Robert Moseley).

Many Hollywood stars, a good number of them fervently heterosexual, had changed their names or had them changed for them: the star of *Since You Went Away,* Jennifer Jones, had once been Phylis Lee Isley; Robert Taylor had been born Spangler Brough; John Wayne was Marion Morrison until 1930. Aspirants to the screen often had to sacrifice their original selves.

Henry Willson's specialty, what carried him from Selznick to forming his own agency, was in devising new names and flimsy panache for handsome young men trying to get into pictures. I must stress that not all of them were gay—because it was still regarded as a debility to be gay in that business—but his roster included Guy Madison, Tab Hunter (Arthur Kelm), John Derek (Derek Harris, and then "Dare Harris" in Willson's first shot at glory), Robert Wagner, Rory Calhoun (Francis McCown), Chad Everett, Troy Donahue (Merle Johnson) . . . and Rock Hudson, the name he conjured up for Roy Fitzgerald. (Later on,

Roy cursed himself for accepting it. Can you be "Rock" at seventy-five without incurring derision?)

Fitzgerald was far and away the most successful of this group, and his career sustained the Willson agency. He had a lot to learn as an actor, but he applied himself at the Universal training school. He had a strong, deep voice; he was attentive with actresses; and he seemed to embody an ideal of physical courage that was still treated without irony or reservation in the 1950s. For Douglas Sirk he did two uplifting romances with Jane Wyman, *Magnificent Obsession* and *All That Heaven Allows*, that together grossed about $13 million.

Wyman was eight years older than Hudson; she had an established career in which she had been married to Ronald Reagan (they divorced in 1949), and had won an Oscar in *Johnny Belinda* (1948). Those two films with Rock amounted to new life for her; both Universal and audiences appreciated that the tender, romantic side to Hudson had helped her to it, without ever rivaling the chemistry that existed at that time between, say, Lancaster and Deborah Kerr or Montgomery Clift and Donna Reed in *From Here to Eternity*.

Hudson was in the ascendant, but when he was cast as the Texas rancher Bick Benedict in *Giant* (1956), he seemed bland and boyish, free from Texas dust, and not quite a compelling husband for Elizabeth Taylor's character. Hudson had become a competent star—he is better by far as the romantic journalist in *The Tarnished Angels* (a Sirk adaptation of William Faulkner's novel *Pylon*) and genuinely desperate in *Seconds* (1966).

A lot of movie fans haven't heard of *Seconds*. Rock Hudson was no great admirer of his own career, but he named *Seconds* as one underrated performance he was proud of. "No one's seen it," he said. "John Frankenheimer directed. Drama. Now it's kind of a cult film—that no one's seen."

As written by Lewis John Carlino, the film transgresses many Hollywood ideals. It involves a middle-aged, disillusioned man (played by John Randolph) who is tired of life. But then he hears of an expensive surgery, organized by "the Company," that can bring him back as a "second," restored to youth and hope. He can be his own other. He makes that deal, and comes back as a radiant playboy artist, looking like Rock Hudson. One can see why Hudson appreciated this daring, for the film is a parable about the warring brotherhood in an American man between straight and liberal sensibilities (with little faith in either!). In an age of dire remakes, one longs to see talented people take another shot at *Seconds*. And still one wonders why so few see the original, the most suggestive film Hudson ever made.

He would also develop a comic instinct for a series of coy romances with Doris Day that were big commercial hits (*Pillow Talk, Send Me No Flowers, Lover Come Back*). From 1956 for about seven years, he was not just popular but one of the top-three box-office attractions in America. That means that in the age of John F. Kennedy, Mickey Mantle, and Norman Mailer, he was accepted as an ideal male hero. Sure, the name "Rock" was smiled at, but we were less ironic then and so much less discerning.

What did people think of Rock Hudson in those years, and how did they know what to think? I was fifteen when I saw *Giant,* and I was more interested in James Dean than in Rock Hudson, because Dean felt closer to my moods or experience—call it yearning; you could be fifteen then and have had very little experience. Moreover, I went to the movies for experience, without realizing what a perilously vicarious game that might be. I had only a vague idea of what it might be to be homosexual. But homosexual behavior was against the law then in Britain, and I don't think I knew anyone who was gay or willing to have that state recognized. So Hudson appeared acceptable or credible as a male lover in both *Giant* and *A Farewell to Arms,* even if he felt less masculine than, say, William Holden, Gary Cooper, or Humphrey Bogart, or less urbane than Cary Grant or James Mason. Rock came off a little boyish—that's the word I would have used—and unusually tender or sensitive for a man of his physique. But the pictures he made with Doris Day were as popular as those with Jane Wyman, and Rock was satisfying many people as a sophisticated, if rather choosy, object of romantic interest.

Those pictures were actually famous for their suggestiveness, as the bulwarks of censorship grew less secure. *Pillow Talk* grossed $7 million, and *Lover Come Back* took $8.5 million. They made Rock rich and erased any interest he might have had in playing someone closer to himself. In the 1970s, he was asked what would happen if a gay actor came out or played a nonstereotypical gay role. He shrugged: "He could make a living on the lecture circuit—all kinds of nut do that. But I wouldn't see him getting hired to do a miniseries."

The career risk was drastic, and it was only settled when Hudson could no longer deny his AIDS. But I don't believe many in the audience of his biggest years had any suspicion that Hudson was gay. (At much the same time, my mother—an emotional intelligence I trusted—had no thought that Noël Coward might be gay. She thought he was classy.) If a few did guess about Rock, they never spoke out, because that knowledge then would have been too disruptive, and damaging to the speaker. Any convincing revelation of his own sexual status would have been as crushing to his career as evidence that he was a conscientious Communist; this was still an age in which star actors could be wiped away by rumor.

That's why Henry Willson was so anxious to protect Hudson. In the mid-1950s, the Hollywood magazine *Confidential* had heard that Hudson was homosexual. I don't think that took strenuous hearing. Hollywood then was still a closed community, alive with its own gossip and sheltered by studio publicity departments that worked to divert unwelcome attention. Tony Curtis said in his book that he and many others were well aware that Hudson was gay. There were said to be gay parties (and it would emerge decades later that Burt Lancaster had been present at some of them).

Confidential magazine had a circulation of five million in the 1950s. When it threatened to expose Hudson, Willson negotiated a compromise: if the magazine hushed up the Hudson story, he would give them information that Rory Calhoun had been in reform school and Tab Hunter had been arrested for disorderly conduct. None of this makes Henry Willson endearing, yet he would have reckoned he was doing the sensible Hollywood thing. Rock Hudson was a major property. To secure his star, Willson then made a deal with his own secretary, Phyllis Gates, so that she would marry Rock and give him cover in the media.

Gates lived with Rock for a few months. They were married in 1955, separated by 1957 and divorced a year later. Gates was awarded alimony of $250 a week for ten years. It's clear now that Gates, a lesbian, understood the deception and entered into a business relationship. This can seem disconcerting, but take note of other marriages of convenience in Hollywood—and in life at large. For centuries, many of our marriages were deals, sometimes sight unseen. It is only the age of movie romance that has trained us in the notion that marriages might be matters of true love reliant on meeting, attraction, and appearance or in line with the pursuit-of-happiness game we are meant to be playing.

That is actually far more than a game (as in a diversion). It helps to understand Hollywood's pragmatic scheme of marriage. Tony Curtis and Rock Hudson were the same age, but Tony was a little ahead—he was flashier, prettier, funnier, and more able to drive a crowd of teenage girls wild. By 1951, Universal was taking Tony very seriously as they put him in a picture called *The Prince Who Was a Thief.* His costar in that film was Piper Laurie, still only eighteen but a promising studio project who was dating Robert Goldstein, the head of talent at Universal.

Bob's brother, Leonard, was producing *The Prince Who Was a Thief,* and he dropped the idea in Tony's head that it would be smart for Tony and Piper to become "a couple," if only for fan magazine coverage. There were some obstacles to this tidy arrangement. Tony was by then attracted to another young actress, Janet Leigh. Though two years his junior, Janet had been married and divorced twice already (as a teenager), and there were stories current that she was seeing Howard Hughes (producer of the bizarre *Jet Pilot* in which she was starring with John Wayne). So Tony wanted to keep hold of her; in time he and Leigh would become a major married item of the 1950s. It was also the case that, as for Laurie, Tony "didn't find her attractive at all. . . . She was an unpleasant person, very suspicious of everybody."

Well, you can't have everything. When Universal told Tony there was a $30,000 bonus waiting if he married Piper Laurie, he *was* tempted. "Truth be told," he would admit later, "if someone had actually riffled the money right under my nose I might have taken it." (That's Falco talking.) Casting in Hollywood can be a game of chance: later on, Tony longed to be with Audrey Hepburn in the film *Two for the Road* (the part went to Albert Finney), and sometimes marriages are cast and recast, too. Janet and Tony were married for eleven years. They would do five films together and have two children as well as a load of favorable publicity and adoring two-shots in magazines. But Tony was always broad-minded enough to notice other women.

There was so much we wanted from the movies and so much we didn't know. I spoke earlier about watching James Dean as a teenager. This was a strong attraction, one of the two most powerful that I felt for movie men. On seeing *Rebel Without a Cause* I fantasized about the lives that might be lived by the Dean and Natalie Wood characters after the close of the film, and that lapped over into daydreams in which her Judy was my girlfriend. Dean might be inarticulate on screen, troubled, moody, and awkward, but he had a dark grace that left no doubt about why girls wanted him. And in the mid-1950s, in circles I knew, girls were sleepwalkers for Dean or a Deaner type just as boys bought red windbreakers to be like Jim in *Rebel* and combed their hair in a Dean-ish way. (A wayward high school kid, still he has a fantastic, groomed haircut—but he has a sedan to get to school in, too!) Few fans guessed or wanted to hear that Dean had a bisexual life—until he was dead, and then the legend of his gayness bloomed along with the male reservation that he had just been kidding.

Insiders knew much more. In searching for an actor to play the lead in *East of Eden,* director Elia Kazan went to New York to see Dean on stage: he was playing a homosexual Arab servant in a play taken from André Gide's novel *The Immoralist.* It was agreed that Dean was exceptional in the role (he won prizes for it, even if he was fired from the show for rudeness to costar Louis Jourdan; the other star, Geraldine Page, tried to defend him), but he seemed torn by the experience. Was he nervous about playing the gay role? Was he drawn to it? Or was he simply acting out the part of a difficult or impossible actor? He won *East of Eden* as a result, and the problems never stopped. Dean was apparently engaged to the Italian actress Pier Angeli, a model of romantic sweetness. Kazan heard their lovemaking and their terrible fights in a dressing room next to his office. (That great eavesdropper wanted to be close.) No one could read Dean: Was he a young mess, like the parts he was asked to play? Was he struggling with a bisexual identity? Or was he trying to imitate the turmoil he believed was expected in a Brandoesque actor? He did not live to provide answers.

It is apparent now that Dean, dead in 1955, aged twenty-four, had "experimented" with homosexual relationships. That is still the word used about him, though no one would think to say that he was "experimenting" with driving a Porsche Spyder at high speeds on the highway at Cholame, California. We are all experimenting a lot of the time: men and women happily married for thirty and forty years may still be looking to see what tomorrow brings. In other words, James Dean might have become an extraordinary and iconic gay hero in America in the late 1950s and 1960s. That surprise could have been so intense that he might have been assassinated by someone who had grown up in adoration of his old screen persona. Or Dean could have become an early victim of AIDS, in company with the Rock Hudson who is his rival for power in Texas in *Giant*.

Or Dean might have become a great and troubled movie star, a womanizer married four or five times, fitful in his politics, shallow but fierce. And a bit of a bore. That boring aspect may be the most shocking possibility. The hardest thing to imagine for Dean is a bland existence.

Such speculations have nothing but the films to feed on, and they are torn between his hope and his darkness. In *Rebel Without a Cause,* in what seems like a real Los Angeles, we find three troubled kids in high school. Natalie Wood and Sal Mineo deserved to be there: they were verifiable teenagers. Wood plays Judy, a girl who is misunderstood and shunned by a stern father modeled in concrete. Mineo is Plato, a boy who has been deserted by his parents and left in the care of a maid. In time, both are drawn to Dean's Jim Stark. Dean was in his early twenties, which gave him an air of weary fatalism in the triangle. Plato (his real name is John) has a crush on Jim, in part because he needs a hero, protection, and any kind of love. Jim senses this, and you can watch the film in a way that feels Jim's appreciation of Plato's loneliness.

As for Judy, she sees in Jim the same kind of emotional respect, all the stronger in that her previous boyfriend was a cheerful lout who kept her as a trophy. For all three characters, their coming together is a first discovery that there can be a valuable life of the emotions. It is a process of self-education when they have their night in the empty mansion, like children making a new world. Jim and Judy kiss, and it is a tender scene—I went to sleep on it for years. But they do not screw, which is what two hormonally alert kids in Los Angeles in 1955 might have attempted. It's not that the film's director, Nicholas Ray, was unaware of that urge. At the same time, he was involved with Natalie Wood while carrying on a bisexual life. Gore Vidal met Ray in those days at the Chateau Marmont and thought he was "rather openly having an affair with the adolescent Sal Mineo." If you ever loved Dean in *Rebel,* you have to allow the way Ray loved Dean, too—and looked at him with smothered adoration (always the most potent kind). Which is not to say that he and Dean were actual lovers.

Dean was a great focus of romance on screen. His quality was always that of an outsider figure, a youth available for the dreams of guys in the audience who felt themselves misunderstood or frustrated in life. In *East of Eden,* his Cal develops a love for Abra (Julie Harris) that is actually more moving than Jim's feeling for Judy—in large part because Harris was so mature and generous an actress. (Kazan said it was her sympathy that made the shoot possible for Dean. In addition, she was thirty.) Cal takes Abra from his upstanding brother, Aaron, a handsome, shallow young man who does nothing worse than be in Cal's way and own their father's favor.

The brooding but sensitive Cal ousts the conventional brother in much the way Jim Stark picks Judy out of the fraternity of high school kids. The desire felt by Dean's characters drives the films. Even in *Giant,* Dean's character, Jett, is excluded from regular romance. He is a loner who has a spot of land on Bick's enormous spread—but his wretched ground has a secret: oil, Jett's orgasm, as witness the exultant scene where he showers in his black ejaculate.

One afternoon, he entertains Bick's new wife, Leslie, for tea in his shack. Leslie is the lady of the estate, socially superior, but Dean and Elizabeth Taylor were nearly the same age; he was actually a year older. Leslie sees the Mexican woman Jett keeps around but knows that she is only a gesture or hormonal release. There is a sympathy between Leslie and Jett, though nothing can happen because he has no money or social standing. Later on, Jett and Bick fall into enmity; there is a moment when the sneaky Jett punches noble Bick in the stomach as he is restrained by others. Later still, as everyone grows older, the aged, dissolute but oil-rich Jett tries to romance Bick's daughter (played by Carroll Baker, who was only a year younger than Dean).

There are so many undertones with Dean. In *Rebel,* there is a way in which Jim "kills" Plato: he extracts the bullets from Plato's gun (such actions are surface motions resting on strata of inner meaning), but then Plato is gunned down by the police surrounding the Planetarium. It's clear that Jim feels guilt and grief for this—but he or the film has removed what could have been a compromising character. Dean was the cat in the bag of his pictures.

A commercial movie wanted to cater to every possible fantasy, whether or not it understood the balance of those desires. The several dysfunctional parental lives in *Rebel* are redeemed by the notion that Jim and Judy will remake a decent world. Aged fifteen, I aspired to the fantasy future in which those two would marry and have children of their own in an "all-right" world. But did that rosy future glow require the removal of Plato (in case his need for Jim might eclipse Judy's)?

Years after Dean's death (and not long before he was murdered in 1976), Sal Mineo talked about that aspect of the film: "[Plato] was, in a way, the first gay teenager in films. You watch it now, you *know* he had the hots for James Dean. You watch it now, and everyone knows about Jimmy, so it's like *he* had the hots for Natalie [Wood] and me. Ergo, I had to be bumped off, out of the way."

In the studio script notes for *Rebel* (apparently those of executive Steve Trilling) there is the query "Jim kisses Plato?," as if someone had suggested that onscreen possibility. There is even a book that quotes Nicholas Ray's memories of rehearsal:

I heard [Dean] explaining things to Sal. "You know how I am with Nat [Wood]. Well, why don't you pretend I'm her and you're me. . . . Pretend you want to touch my hair, but you're shy." Then Jimmy says, "I'm not shy like you. I love you. I'll touch your hair." I took one look at the kid's face . . . he was transcendent, the feeling coming out of him.

That's not in the finished film, but what is so touching about the story is how close it comes to the way kids in the audience (would-be actors, longing for a part in life) conjure with the situations being imagined.

Sal Mineo was a troubled man and a fine actor—he is good in *Rebel*, but much more in *Exodus*. He had a heterosexual relationship with Jill Haworth, his costar in that film, and they came close to being married. Apparently she opted out of the marriage when she learned that Sal was having an intense gay affair. He acknowledged being bisexual, and he was always an actor striving to be a star. But he was both vague and revealing when asked whether or not he had had an affair with Dean himself:

> He was a shitheel, sometimes. He liked being that way. But everybody had moments when they loved him—one way or another. I did, too. Did we have an affair, do you mean? . . . I might tell you some people I had affairs with—maybe. But Jimmy was special, so I don't want to say.

That's a moment in which the exaltation of stardom merges with the notoriety of a gay existence. It's revealing that Mineo feels the magic so intensely he won't confirm or deny it. Twenty years after Dean's death he seemed to have been living on the possibility. Wanting to be a star then, I think, was a resolve to be unlike others. And whereas previous guys tracking stardom had been robust, straightforward, and reliable—even Elvis was like that—there were others (Clift, Brando, Dean, Mineo) who insisted on a sensitivity that was nearly un-American and that often alarmed parents and the set traditions of acting.

Mineo was not the only person on *Rebel* with that feeling: Dennis Hopper and Nick Adams had felt it; the composer, Leonard Rosenman (he did *East of Eden*, too), was a roommate and mentor to Dean; the screenwriter on *Rebel*, Stewart Stern, was marked for life; and Ray himself never got over the loss of Dean. The actor might have lifted Ray to career perfection and a dream of personal happiness. (As if Nick Ray could ever have been happy.)

In *Giant*, Jett surpasses Bick's wealth and may think of defiling his daughter. In *East of Eden,* the film acts on Cal's longings by sending Aaron away to the war in Europe, so that Cal can curl up in another idyllic family situation with the devoted Abra and a father crippled by stroke.

I am not alone in having lived with these films for over fifty years. That is a tribute to the filmmaking, for sure, but it is also a measure of an age when films had buried secrets. So I should add a note on the best scenes James Dean ever had in *Eden* with an actress—I mean his meetings with the mother who abandoned the family years before and who nearly killed her husband, Adam, the boys' father. This mother runs a whorehouse in rowdy Monterey; the Trask farm is in the nearby and lovely Salinas. Jim discovers his mother and goes to meet her. The mother, Kate, is played by Jo Van Fleet, and it is plain that both characters understand their hopeless affinity—that of dark, needy souls, with ugly instincts, who are committed to the life of an outsider.

"Rebel Without a Cause," people say when Dean is mentioned. That was not even his best film, I think. But the title is a polite nonsense or wishful marketing. Jim may be rebellious, but he has a cause: he knows and feels more than any other character in *Rebel* or in the Los Angeles he inhabits. As for Dean, he had a cause, too, even if he and his adherents could not articulate it at the time. It was not gayness but something more profound—it was a life of true feeling in which male and female might be married not just in the household or in a marital bed but also in the rapt, contentious turmoil of consciousness.

I said there was one other male actor who stirred me as much as Dean, and you may guess that it was Montgomery Clift. More than ten years older than Dean, Clift had been born in Omaha in 1920. By 1940, he was evidently one of the most beautiful of young men as well as one of the most promising of American actors. He was also very confused. At about that time he developed an intense friendship with the actress Phyllis Thaxter. For a time, she lived with Clift and his parents, and sometimes in the mornings he would come into her bedroom, snuggle up beside her, and be served breakfast in bed with her by his mother.

You may read that with raised eyebrows or a knowing smile, but it's important to appreciate the innocence or ignorance that Monty and Phyllis might have felt at that time. Some onlookers believed the fond couple were bound to get married—being so bound was a nearly gravitational force then, not sufficiently questioned. But isn't that still true?

They never had sex, yet they were inclined to believe they should get married. Then one day Monty told Phyllis, "I've been thinking about it, darling, and I can't get married. It just wouldn't be right." Thaxter felt, "He seemed so serious and a little sad, as if he knew something I didn't. I didn't ask questions; I just said all right and we never mentioned marriage after that."

In the early 1940s, Clift began to discover himself in active affairs with men. He also emerged as an actor, on stage in *The Skin of Our Teeth, Our Town,* and *Foxhole in the Parlor.* In that play, in 1945, he was paired with the actress Ann Lincoln. It was said they were in love. Friends believed they were on the point of eloping to Mexico. But when they came back from that trip there was a gulf between them, because Monty had decided he couldn't marry her, either. He was distraught and in tears; she was angry—so much so that she went off and had a brief affair with another little-known actor in New York named Marlon Brando.

By then Clift's looks had matured, which is to say that his youthful radiance had an edge of sadness or dismay. He was made for the movies, and he was cast as the young hero, Matthew Garth, in Howard Hawks's *Red River.* This was the saga of a rancher, Tom Dunson, who adopts a lost boy and lives to see that son take over his great cattle herd on a pioneering drive from Texas to Abilene after Dunson has turned into a brute and a tyrant.

John Wayne was set to be Dunson, and it is one of his great performances and the first clear sign that he was more than a stock Western icon. Wayne was uneasy when he heard that Clift might be cast. He must have heard about Clift's reputation; he could not ignore that Clift was a lean stripling, hardly credible standing his ground in the required fistfight with Wayne. Clift was himself unsure about the project. He didn't ride; he didn't have the hips to support holstered six-guns; he felt silly in a cowboy hat. But Hawks's wife, Slim, reassured the actor that Hawks could finesse these things and that Monty would be taught what he needed to know. In fact, that education was accomplished in production by a young wrangler and stunt rider named Richard Farnsworth, who would become a valuable actor by the time he was sixty.

Red River was a triumphant fantasy for which Monty was paid $60,000. Even wearing fringed buckskins and giving away six inches, Clift was a match for Wayne as a screen presence. He was handsome, smart, brave, and emotionally tender, and he did seem to ride a horse—such things have always been handled on screen. (In one scene, it's plain now that Clift is on a rocking horse in front of a back projection—but I never noticed that at eight.) He was a youth ready to challenge a forbidding man; in hindsight, he was also sensitivity rebuking macho certainty. In *Red River,* on screen and on the set, there was a fear that Clift was not man enough to be a cowboy. In several films he would be beaten up and abused.

Matthew Garth was not quite adult compared with Dunson, and not the same hardened man of the West. But he was made for prowess, success at driving a herd all that way, the achievement of subduing his threatening father—I had such a Dad—and the ease with which he found Tess Millay (Joanne Dru) as a mate. It wasn't just natural to identify with him; it felt inevitable, a diagram of identification. My first son was called Mathew—a gesture he wisely ignores.

Just about everyone was persuaded by *Red River* except Clift. He disliked the film and thought that Hawks's ending, where Joanne Dru tells Wayne and Clift to grow up and stop fighting, was a farce. He had an instinct the film would change his life, but he insisted he was mediocre or fake in it. He was outspoken and self-critical, a victim of his own intense sincerity. About that time, he and Christopher Isherwood were attracted to each other in Santa Monica, but "Christopher found Clift touching but ugly-minded and cold" (as he wrote in his memoir *Lost Years, 1945–1951*). The actor would never overcome his unease. The director Edward Dmytryk recalled hearing Clift at a party say "Look at that disgusting fag," and then in an hour he was having sex with the guy he had been deriding.

He was a new ideal on screen, beyond his own grasp, strong but soft, pristine yet manly. That could have remained intact as a dream, especially if Clift himself had died in the mid-1950s. Instead, he took on a series of films that made him untouchable. In *A Place in the Sun,* he seemed magically cast as the poor kid who would find love and money (and his sunlight) in the society girl embodied by the eighteen-year-old Elizabeth Taylor. Those two actors were quickly drawn to each other on screen and off. They were equally ravishing; it was the most physical infatuation Clift would ever have, and it meant a great deal to the young Taylor. I'm confident that they became lovers—as an experiment or out of a deep faith in passion and casting. They were both romantic children, addicted to falling in love.

The story of the film, derived from Theodore Dreiser's *An American Tragedy,* has Clift's character (George Eastman) hopelessly compromised in romance, drawn into thoughts of murdering a pregnant girlfriend (Shelley Winters) and then executed because of her "accidental" death. *A Place in the Sun* ends in telephoto close-ups of Clift and Taylor with prison bars between them. It is one of the screen's most impassioned love raptures founded on thwarted desire. The actor was established as a tragic figure, and any dismay or confusion in his real life flooded into the role. (Their not having sex is the cat in the bag.)

Clift's was the acting career of the early 1950s, for he was soon cast to play Prewett, the rebellious soldier, in the film of James Jones's *From Here to Eternity.* In the novel, Prew is a rough Kentucky boy bruised by life; in the film, Clift makes a soldier-saint of him. (The studio had first thought of Aldo Ray in the part, a tougher, less sensitive actor.) James Jones himself, who treasured and promoted his own forceful male persona, became friendly with Clift. During the filming, Jones, Clift, and Frank Sinatra would hang out and get drunk together. Some observers asked Jones if he was gay: he did have a taste for Indian jewelry and tight jeans. In a kidding way, Jones told one friend, "I would have had an affair with him [Clift], but he never asked me." (There had been gay scenes in Jones's original text, but the publisher made him cut them.)

The metaphors in the film are extraordinary and as innocent as Burt Lancaster and Deborah Kerr rolling in the surf: so bold once, so naive now. Prewett comes to a regiment proud of its boxing team. Prew had been a good boxer until an opponent in the ring was blinded, so Prewett abandoned fighting. But now the team starts to give him the treatment to get him to join them. He is an afflicted, bullied loner, a pure figure among a gang of coarse men. His only comforts are the friendship of Maggio (Sinatra), his bugle-playing, and the love of Lorene, the genteel whore in a Honolulu cathouse.

Prew is brave (he kills the stockade sergeant, the intimidating Ernest Borgnine, who had destroyed Maggio). He is steadfast—he wants to stay in the army that has abused him. And he must be a perfect lover—you feel that in the fond eyes of Donna Reed's Lorene. But those two never do it, not even on a fade-out. They retain a ghostly virginal status, as if Lorene can remain as bourgeois as she longs to be, and Prew as immaculate as a twelve-year-old kid might aspire to. There had been far more sex in the book, but Daniel Taradash had delivered a script that tactfully overlooked it. Still, Columbia Pictures were in awe of their product—"The boldest book of our time . . . honestly, fearlessly on the screen!"

That uneasy push worked. *From Here to Eternity* was another big hit for which Clift was nominated as Best Actor (he and Lancaster lost to William Holden in *Stalag 17*). And if James Jones had been wooed into believing in Monty as tragic hero, then so would the world. At which point we should remind ourselves that the great adult movie of that moment, from a novel so famously "sexual" that Hollywood had reckoned it could never be made, relied on two actors, Clift and Lancaster, who had more complicated romantic lives than the public detected from the dark.

Monty's car crash was mistimed and cruel. On May 12, 1956, he was at a dinner party at Elizabeth Taylor's home in the hills off Coldwater Canyon. The two of them were making an overblown Southern romance called *Raintree County*. The guests at the party included Rock Hudson and Phyllis Gates (this was in the brief window of their marriage). Monty had been drinking too much, so when he left he was trying to follow his friend Kevin McCarthy in a car ahead. But descending on the twisting road from hideaway to main drag, he crashed his car violently against a telephone pole and was badly hurt. His nose and jaw were broken; his sinus cavity was damaged; several teeth were out and his lip was torn. McCarthy drove back to tell Taylor and she and some others hurried to the crash site.

This is a seminal moment of Hollywood history, with lovely soulmates in agonies of distress. The crash had collapsed the front of the car. Monty was huddled beneath the dash. Liz could only crawl in through the back door, but she managed it and then she cradled his head—there was blood all over her dress afterward—and pulled broken teeth from his throat. An ambulance arrived; and then a doctor, with the gentle strength and assistance of Rock Hudson, managed to extract Clift from the wreckage.

Monty was repaired physically, through conventional and then plastic surgery, but his face was never as clear again, and his confidence was gone. "He had been so beautiful," said Jack Clareman, his lawyer. "People used to gasp when they saw him. Now they gasped for different reasons." Clift had most of the mirrors in his home removed. He drank steadily (while talking of playing Hamlet); he had many affairs and some lasting lovers; he slept with men but cherished women; he grew older and earned less money; and he was in torment over the struggle between being a dream figure and a real homosexual. He could never reveal himself or escape being the wreck of Montgomery Clift. He kept going for a few years: in the war film *The Young Lions* (1958) he played a sensitive Jew mercilessly taunted and beaten by the other guys in his Army unit. In *Lonelyhearts* (1958), from the Nathanael West novella, he was the newspaper columnist tormented by the grief of readers and his inability to help them. He was beaten up by bullies in Kazan's *Wild River* (1960), though that proved his last great performance—it contains an unexpectedly tender love story with a woman played by Lee Remick. In *Judgment at Nuremb*erg (1961) he had been castrated by the Nazis. As *Freud* he was persecuted by his own director, John Huston, who was irritated by Clift's insecurities. No other male star had been so loyal to the role of victim—or was it martyr? Something in the actor felt he had betrayed an old Hollywood code. As Deborah Kerr said from knowing Monty, "He wanted to love women but he was attracted to men, and he crucified himself for it."

Montgomery Clift died in 1966, aged forty-five. The immediate cause was a heart attack, but drug and booze had weakened him. Rock Hudson felt the loss was greater than that of Dean. After the car crash, he said, Clift had lived "a long drawn-out hell-on-earth"—though it was not as long as the one Rock faced.

So if I look back at the movie actors I most admired or wanted to be in my formative years of the 1950s, then the list includes Clift, Dean, Lancaster, and Hudson. Is there anyone else I've not mentioned so far?

Dead Attractive: Cary Grant

So what is Cary Grant thinking, wondering, or remembering?
If you're not quite sure, you are on the threshold to his work and his life—yet
still in the dark, which is where he wanted us. Apart from anything else,
this portrait (from the mid-1940s) is proof that sincerity was finished.
Photograph an intelligent person long enough and uncertainty takes over.

IN 2011, Jennifer Grant published a book, *Good Stuff: A Reminiscence of My Father, Cary Grant*. Jennifer was his only child, born in 1966, during his marriage to Dyan Cannon. Her book is not searching about Grant the actor; he had retired from making films before Jennifer was born. He was sixty-two already at that happy event. On the other hand, *Good Stuff* is a touching account of the bond between a little girl and an elderly father. Grant died in 1986, when Jennifer was only twenty. We are in no doubt about their closeness or the emotional merriment they shared. They spent time together, and some of it was the best kind, silly time, as enjoyed by affluent people. Often in the book, Jennifer says that her father told her everything. But Archie Leach—Grant's debut role in life—had been such a victim of lies as to put a severe test on family honesty. Lying can take over lives, no matter how much we disapprove of it.

If you are reading this book to settle whether or not Cary Grant was gay, I have to warn you—hold on to some doubts. Isn't that the response Grant urges on us in his best films? The persistent thing about him is his ambivalent look. It's a gaze that few male actors in Hollywood have understood or attempted. As the author and critic Molly Haskell said to me, he's such a rare mixture of leading man and goofball. Perhaps he never made up his mind which he was.

There is a steady but vague assumption now, thirty years after his death, that Grant had a gay life. None other than Scotty Bowers has told us with some glee that he frequently tricked Grant and his pal Randolph Scott as they lived together in the late 1930s and early 1940s. Scott was between marriages: in 1936 he had married the heiress Marion duPont; they were divorced in 1939; in 1944 he married Patricia Stillman, who acted in a few films. At that same time, Grant was single, too, pending his 1942 marriage to Barbara Hutton. (These actors did appreciate rich women.)

There are exuberant photographs of Scott and Grant together that have the shallow panache of publicity pictures—as if the two men are shouting out, "Hey! Look at us!" They are happy photographs, playing with their dog, at their pool, working out. There's not a shred of privacy or professional discretion in these views of Cary and Randy. They are glossies that seem to have been taken by Paramount, to which the stars have given themselves freely and enthusiastically, as if they felt no need to be guarded about their friendship. Indeed, the pictures are not so different from those of heterosexual movie marriages when we happen to know the individual partners were less than loyal or rapturous but were putting on big smiles for public relations and their next opening.

The fan magazines that ran the pictures of Randy and Cary did not add that the two men got into what Scotty Bowers would call "A lot of sexual mischief together. Aside from the usual sucking—neither of them were into fucking, at least not fucking guys, or at least not me—what I remember most about that first encounter was that Scott really liked to cuddle, and talk, and was very gentle. Grant was nice as well, though Scott was even more of a gentleman."

Apart from that, Bowers includes a still of Grant (from a movie) with the caption "Cary Grant. Need I say more?" Well, yes, I think Bowers often needs to say more—or less. Just in 2016, in Jean Stein's *West of Eden* (an intriguing account of Hollywood lives), Jackie Park, sometime mistress of Jack Warner, was quoted as saying, "And I went out with Cary Grant for a while. The first time I ever had a date with him, he was dressed up like a woman. He had on a silk blouse, velvet pants, and gold lamé shoes. You had relationships, you know."

If we don't quite know, we can't help imagining what the lonely people in Hollywood did. I am not discounting Park's memory, though I will add that moment in *Bringing Up Baby* where Grant's character, David Huxley, is wearing an elaborate white, marabou-trimmed negligee (for good if insane movie reasons), only to be asked sternly by Susan's aunt (who may be ready to donate money to his museum) "But why are you wearing *these* clothes?" to which his frantic character replies, "Because I just went gay all of a sudden!"

I can't judge how many viewers in 1938 understood what "gay" might mean there, and I can believe it is a joke from director Howard Hawks, though there is a case for believing Grant himself ad-libbed the line. A Hawks-Grant picture was in its nature an opportunity for improv and improvement. We should also note that a star like Grant could have declined the line, so he likely said it because he thought it was funny and in keeping with the screwball comedy of *Bringing Up Baby* and because he had the instinct to tease us. Even so, gold lamé shoes feel like a stretch.

That negligee is stock in trade now in the assertion that Cary Grant was gay, though people making the case seldom explore the levels of the scene. Far fewer realize that there was another Grant-Hawks film in which the same joke is more sustained. In *I Was a Male War Bride* (1949), Grant plays a French army officer, Henri Rochard, just after the end of the war. He acquires an American lieutenant, Catherine Gates (played by Ann Sheridan), as an assistant. They start out at cross purposes, like the best Hawksian couples, but then fall in love and marry, whereupon Catherine is ordered back to the States, and the only way Henri can accompany her is as a "war bride." So Henri/Grant dresses as an army nurse on the ship going back to America. For a large part of the film, Grant is in a skirt, with comic consequences that made the film a hit (which was more than *Baby* managed).

I daresay some gossips on hearing of this film would leap at the further "proof" of Grant's secret nature. But if they saw *I Was a Male War Bride* they would discover a movie about a heterosexual romance (done with warmth and affection) in which Grant brilliantly conveys the mixed but embarrassed feelings of Henri dressing as a woman while longing for his wife. You could surmise that the situation reveals Grant's mixed feelings about gender, but then you'd have to reconcile yourself with the confidence he needed to take on the project in the first place as well as the wit and precision required to play it. Yes, the actor and the man may be alert to sexual ambiguity, but he is unintimidated by the risk of drag and the possibility of gossip being inflamed by it. It's hard to think that Burt Lancaster would have accepted the part, out of fear it would expose him. That Grant understood Henri's screwball situation and played it with relish vindicates the actor's personal security and intelligence. You have to see the film to have a chance of understanding Grant's nature. Even then, you are looking at an actor or at a personality hired to pretend, to dress up, and to entertain. Grant is a delight in the film as a man on an uneasy brink. You are left to draw your own conclusions, but note in passing that he makes not the least effort to do Henri as a Frenchman.

Wasn't he sophisticated enough already? Wouldn't it have been foolish for him to talk like "zis" and "zat"? Not that Grant didn't enjoy clowning around for daughter Jennifer and the several celebrities who might be in his house in that mood where famous people often cling together to avoid uneasiness. She leaves no doubt about the fun Grant could be. Having stopped making films, he was ready for the big role of "Dad." In Jennifer's breezy text and the family snapshots, it's easy to see Grant being loving, kind, thoughtful, and a steady source of "good stuff." Parenting had not worked well in his own life, so he would be full of hope for it in hers.

Jennifer Grant had heard rumors. "It's awkward living with public misconceptions about my father. What does one say when asked if one's famously charming, debonair, five-times-married, crooned-over father is gay? Hmmm . . . a grin escapes me. Can't blame men for wanting him, and wouldn't be surprised if Dad even mildly flirted back. If so, it manifested as witty repartee as opposed to a pat on the ass. . . . Being gay is neither here nor there, but hiding oneself from family and friends . . . not so good." But hiding can take a person over until it feels natural and your own thing.

Elsewhere in her book, Jennifer admits, "Dad's previous marriages went undiscussed as well. Nothing taboo: I simply never asked. He was married five times. I knew the names of his first three wives and vaguely knew their faces. That was all fine, and beyond that, it was history." The children of later marriages may prefer to think the world began with them.

We have to wonder what Grant intended. That's in keeping with that half-smiling, half-intimidating glance he kept for so many matters, which asked, Well, what do you think? And maybe asking that of others spared him from having to answer himself.

Jennifer Grant's *Good Stuff* may be the most thorough dismissal of gay rumors in the books about Cary Grant, but it is in step with the others. In 2016, I contributed to a documentary film about Grant by Mark Kidel (who was based in Bristol, England, Grant's original home), *Becoming Cary Grant* (2017). Kidel showed me a rough cut of his film and asked for comments. I was impressed, but I noted that he had not addressed the question of a gay personality and I wondered if that would prompt criticism in the modern climate. Kidel replied that one of his chief consultants, Mark Glancy (the latest Grant biographer), was at pains to say he had found no reliable evidence to support those theories.

In that respect Glancy was in line with several previous books on Grant, some of which had raised the possibilities and reported the rumors but had been unable to reach a firm conclusion. When Grant was in New York in the late 1920s, he roomed with Orry George Kelly, an Australian who became an outstanding production designer for movies: Kelly won three Oscars, including one for *Some Like It Hot.* His professional name was Orry-Kelly (he is the costumier who had trouble containing Bette Davis's breasts). Much later, he wrote a memoir, *Women I've Undressed,* in which he claims a youthful affair with Cary Grant. In San Francisco, in 2017, Dr. Jay Nadel (aged eighty-eight) told me that Grant had propositioned him in the early 1960s. There were male dancers in the city who said similar things.

On the other hand, as Jennifer knew, Grant had been married five times. His first wife—for six months—was the actress Virginia Cherrill (she plays the blind woman in Chaplin's *City Lights*); the second was the Woolworth heiress, Barbara Hutton; the third was another actress, Betsy Drake; the fourth was the actress Dyan Cannon; and the last (in 1981) was Barbara Harris, who had been working at a London hotel in public relations when they met.

But marriages, and children, need not exclude anyone from some gay experience or secret lives along the way. It is evident that people of both sexes in show business have entered into long-term partnerships that diverted gossip or put off legal intrusion, and that were often accompanied by some pleasure and affection without becoming steady, physical marriages (granted that we are agreed over what those are).

Still, Cary Grant looked at women with interest and had several affairs. One of the coups in Mark Kidel's film was the discovery of home movie shot by Grant himself. I have seen only the selections chosen by Kidel, but the footage is notable for the admiring or engaged way in which he films young women. Many of them are unidentified and may be forever unknown, but Phyllis Brooks is one of them and she was someone Grant came close to marrying in the late 1930s. She seems to enjoy being filmed as much as he likes training a camera on her. His way of looking at these women is sexually curious—it is sexy. And that look is natural, hard to hide, harder still to imitate. To deny that feeling or to miss it is a disqualification for anyone who prides himself in "reading" movies and the way they are shot. Cary Grant saw heterosexual possibility, which is not to say he was lewd or aggressive. But, once more, the gaze is close to that balance of interest and doubt with which the actor Cary Grant looks at the world and the stories in which he finds himself.

For much of his life, Cary Grant was under siege: he was forever imprisoned by the façade of "being Cary Grant." How hard it would be to put himself on true trial with other, new people. He could not really find *new* people or anyone for whom he was new. They felt they knew him already. So he was barred from the secrecy or privacy so many of us treasure in sexual encounters. We long to believe in the special recess where sexual curiosity may find us. It's one reason why sexual encounters are so often accompanied by immense, passionate talk between the selves unlocked. We are like Clyde Barrow: we want to hear our story told. That can make a precious feeling of something inviolably intimate being shared as it has never been before.

That may prove wishful thinking or a delusion later. But for people always on show, for show people, it can be a dream that is never satisfied. How could Cary Grant feel discovered, as opposed to being compared with "Cary Grant"? How could he or anyone else feel that some precious being had been arrived at? Isn't there the creeping air of being a fake and a failure, as brilliant and bereft an entertainer as a whore playing yourself?

So movie people may give up the ghost on their secret identity as romantic beings. That is not so far from the self-loathing that some heroic actors feel when they are esteemed for rites of courage and physical prowess they cannot claim as their own. A kind of contempt can develop—that or an exaggerated and even cruel insistence on their own virtuous violence. Sex and bravery can be filled with paranoia—and in turn that leads some of our great romantic icons to feel a desperate unease with themselves. Cary Grant could never be satisfied with anyone's belief in him. So a kind of mockery emerges: it could seem witty and sophisticated, but it might feel gay, too.

We're only talking about Grant because that look of his is so particular and so enigmatic. We are watching the difficulty of deciding about him, and surely he knows this. Grant is not lazy or casual; the closer you look, the more there is to see.

If you want one example of that, go to Alfred Hitchcock's *Notorious* (1946), which involves a tortured love affair between Grant (as Devlin, a government agent) and Ingrid Bergman (as Alicia Huberman, whose family history places her on the edge of Nazi circles). The film is famous for a prolonged kissing scene between the stars as stealthy as it is erotic. That Grant had no difficulty playing straight. The actresses he worked with never seemed impeded or dismayed. But the narrative situation keeps Devlin suspicious of Alicia, and even cold toward her, as he sets her up for a perilous investigation of a Nazi conspiracy. Jealousy has seldom been done better. Thus Devlin gets her to marry a chief suspect, Alex Sebastian (very well played by Claude Rains). That jeopardizes their love and even threatens her life.

In the end, Devlin rescues Alicia, carrying her out of a house of evil and poison. Their love comes through, but uncertainty and a kind of cruelty linger in *Notorious*. These lovers may never forget the sense of falling in love and then of just falling. In a film about trust and vulnerability, *Notorious* depends on the anguished desire in its central faces. Once you've registered that, the unease does not easily leave you. The happy ending the film provides is for suckers.

This is acting; it is professional. In the riddle of performance, Devlin's face has to be Grant's. I cannot link *Notorious* to proven details of Grant's private life, but another reference is available, and it is more cogent. Archie Leach the child lived with his mum and dad in an ordinary house in Bristol. There had been an older brother who died at the age of one. Then one day, when he was nine, the boy came home from school and his mum was not there with his tea. Archie waited. Dad came home and said the situation was a puzzler. The boy's mother, Elsie

Leach, did not come home. Archie was told she had gone away—and deserted them. She never went back to that home again.

Archie grew up. In time, his dad found another woman. The kid joined the music hall; he went to America; he became Cary Grant; he got into movies. It was a tough training, much of it in knockabout physical comedy—he was raised a goofball. But the lowly Bristol boy became an epitome of grace and charm for the wide world. One day in 1935 in Beverly Hills he got a letter from a solicitor in Bristol regretting to tell him his father had died. According to the solicitor, there were a few formalities to be tidied up. But one question was out of the ordinary or presented uncertainty: what was to be done with Elsie? Long ago she had been lodged in an asylum in Bristol, the Glenside Hospital, a place that Archie would have seen often without ever thinking about it.

Grant went back to Bristol as soon as he could. With surprising ease he was able to get his mother out of the asylum; it was plain that his father had placed her there, with some connivance from doctors, to suit his own situation. Elsie never returned to the asylum. She and the long-lost Archie did their best to repair their relationship. It would never be strong or relaxed. Elsie may not have been disabled, but that does not mean she was other than disturbed after nearly two decades being confined. She felt betrayed. Grant was horrified at what had happened, and he would admit later in life that he seldom found emotional comfort with his mother (she died in 1973, aged ninety-four). Had he let her down? Had he been deserted or deceived? Let's just say that Grant's trust and security were in ruins, and that can be a vital impulse for acting.

This is not a plea for sympathy—there's no need to plead with these extraordinary circumstances—or a hope of explaining Cary Grant in any thorough or clinical way. I remain uncertain as to whether he was homosexual for a time in his life. And there is no reason to look down on that possibility or to argue that it might have been forgivable under his circumstances. Gayness does not need forgiveness—or explanation. There is ample reason to believe Grant was upset, disturbed, or damaged—whatever word you want to use—and thus all the more driven to seem smooth, urbane, and in control. Often enough in life, he would say, "I wish I could be Cary Grant." That line got a laugh, especially in the *Evening with Cary Grant* stage shows he did in his last years and which were never filmed. But the wistfulness speaks to the way actors can feel overwhelmed by the popular image of themselves built up in a successful career. Isn't that how Roy Fitzgerald felt dismayed or displaced by the looming figure of "Rock Hudson"?

My history of watching Grant suggests that every possible meaning (and then others not thought of) should be recognized in his smile and his bleaker stare. He is not simply heterosexual in the breathless *His Girl Friday,* where he treats his ex-wife and his wife-to-be (both of them Rosalind Russell) with a furious, competitive cunning that manages to be beguiling and alarming as well as comic. He only once came close to playing a gay character, but that Cole Porter was not allowed to be his homosexual self in the foolish and sanitized *Night and Day.* With magnificent aplomb he let a blue-chiffon Grace Kelly kiss him in *To Catch a Thief,* like a judge hired to award marks to a skater. His elegance was so underplayed it could seem introverted. He reached pathos in *Penny Serenade* and *None but the Lonely Heart.* He was acrobatic in *Holiday,* hilarious in *Bringing Up Baby* and *The Awful Truth,* and plain old perfect "Cary Grant" in *North by Northwest,* where he has giddy erotic scenes with Eva Marie Saint, if you recognize that talking can be as sensual as touching. He enlarged our sense of what a gentleman might be, and surely that involved an understanding of femininity.

Despite his ambiguity, most Grant plots settled on his good nature and happy-ever-after prospects. But in one film we are shaken by his unreliability. Hitchcock's *Suspicion* (1941) was meant to be the story of Lina (Joan Fontaine), an heiress wooed and then murdered by a scoundrel con named Johnnie Aysgarth who will eventually ascend the staircase to her room bearing a glass of milk glowing with poison.

That great shot remains, but Hitch had to drop the ending for reasons of commercial reassurance, telling us instead that Lina's suspicion had come from mere misunderstanding. (Hitch thought this escape clause was "deadly.") Johnny and Lina are going to be "all right." Fontaine won an Oscar, but Grant was far more deserving: fiendish, gleeful, mercilessly cold, perpetually dishonest—almost for its own sake—and curiously attached to an English idiot chum (played by Nigel Bruce). You don't have to be too alert to see that Johnny is horrified by women. He's not obviously gay, but Grant comes close to the devil. Hitchcock quietly exploited the fact that Grant did not like Joan Fontaine—we feel it. His Johnny cries out for a full film beyond Hitchcock's cautious pact between box-office and bourgeois restraint. Still, Grant makes Aysgarth the most disturbing man Hitch ever put on film, and good old Cary understood the part.

There was more in Grant than Scotty Bowers noticed. Who knows where future biographies of the man will go or how much more evidence there can be? And who can deny but that, as a screen actor, he reassessed the entire possibility of what an attractive man might be. I knew an old lady once who assessed some men as "dead attractive"—that was Grant. There was something fatal in him.

I doubt he was ever simply happy—except perhaps when he saw Jennifer watching him. I talked to Grant a little near the end of his life and I was surprised to discover how uneasy or anxious he was. He was afraid of not getting the point, like a lot of eighty-year-olds. My guess is that a crucial part of his development was in his time with Betsy Drake, the least mentioned of his marriages, though it was the one that lasted longest.

Betsy Drake was born in Paris in 1923 to a wealthy family: her grandfather had founded the Drake Hotel in Chicago. She met Grant in 1947. They fell in love as fellow passengers on the *Queen Mary* and acted together in two modest films, *Every Girl Should Be Married* (1948) and *Room for One More* (1952). She was seldom relaxed on screen. They were married in 1949 and seem to have been happy for several years, until he had an affair with Sophia Loren during the making of *The Pride and the Passion* (a 1957 film that might have had no other purpose). But that came just as Drake had written a script for Grant's next film, *Houseboat,* in which she thought she was set to play the lead. Grant then dropped Drake from the project, ordered a new script, and cast Loren instead—though she soon went off and married the producer Carlo Ponti, who would star her in *Two Women,* for which she won the Best Actress Oscar.

That bitter episode exposed some selfishness or spite in Grant. The couple were only divorced in 1962. She later laughed at the suggestion that he had been bisexual. They were having sex so much, she said, there was no time to consider whether he was gay. That remark may have been meant as wit and fun, and it meets both tests. But it can have a deeper meaning: that all across the nation there are mixed couples, married or not, who make love as a way of warding off awkward and insoluble questions about who they are, or might be.

Who are we, and who do we want to be? We have been raised to assume that straight sex is an urge and an instinct, a birthright and an identity. But it could be a safety net, a kind of Bunbury for those of us with uncertainties. Doing that, the thing, doing it, vigorously, happily, regularly, may be a way of denying critical thought or the capacity for other things, for anything.

After divorcing Grant, Drake studied at the UCLA Neuropsychiatric Institute and got a degree in education from Harvard, and she wrote a novel. She may have been the most valuable companion in his life, until his daughter arrived. Grant would say the LSD excursions she encouraged cleared up several of his emotional problems. People want to believe in such "healing": they say they are cured or better or whole, while being on their way to disintegration and death. Equally, we have passed through the grotesque era in which sane and benevolent practitioners believed in aversion therapy, hypnosis, or simple castration as ways of "curing" homosexual tendencies. By now, we know that it's that "benevolence" that needs to be treated.

When I talked to Cary Grant he was a slipstream of eighty-year-old ease and sophistication, on stage. He still looked like "Cary Grant." But in person he was consumed in unease and anxiety. I suspect he had always acted to escape that panic and in the process he carried so many of us closer to imaginary comfort. We should thank him.

Betsy Drake died in 2015. I don't know whether she left any writing about Grant, but who in his life had a better chance of clarifying his unease? Not that that would have settled every question in his gaze or his rueful, edgy presence. But those things amount to art and they are still there for anyone ready to enjoy his films and their uncertainty.

It doesn't matter whether Grant was gay or not. That is the mixed signal or recommendation he left for history. The films are more valuable than the question; they are even an answer to surpass the question. The other day, Scott Eyman, who is setting out on a Grant biography, asked me, "Would a gay man really marry five times?" It's a fair point: whatever else, Grant had great hopes for marriage—who can claim more than that? The historian in me admits "not proven," but the film watcher feels the answer is transparent. That uncertainty over Grant's nature may become a verdict on more and more of us.

Five marriages, or more? Is that being crazy for wives or a dread of loneliness? The longer I look at Grant, the more I realize that "good looking" requires our closest attention. It seems he was ready to be anyone, and that's where the life of an actor educates our efforts to live up to the new roles change has made available for us. That sounds exciting, but it may be intimidating: a part of us still feels acting up is being dishonest or "not true to oneself."

12

Indecency, Gross or Mass Market?

Dirk Bogarde and James Fox in *The Servant* (1963), a film that honors a good
manservant's respect for décor and accessories. There's no screen like home.

IMAGINE IT IS 1963, and think of Rock Hudson watching Dirk Bogarde in *The Servant*.

In 1963, Hudson had opened in a miserable film called *A Gathering of Eagles,* where he plays Colonel Jim Caldwell of Strategic Air Command, put in charge of a failing unit in the service to bring it up to scratch. Hollywood has always liked stories about men taking charge and some people feel an orgasm coming at words like "Strategic Air Command." Jim has to act tough with his fliers, and he risks losing the love of his wife. But everything turns out okay in the end: the marriage and the skies stay safe. There's no inadvertent nuclear explosion, and Jim does not fall in love with a fellow officer or a shy mechanic.

Those times were tense. *A Gathering of Eagles* would have been conceived around October 1962 when the Cuban Missile Crisis had made the world sick with fear while clinging to the hope that strong American men would keep us safe. Because of that, General Curtis LeMay, chief of staff of the Air Force, had given his blessing to *Gathering of Eagles* and called in SAC's assistance. So the film is solid on military authenticity. Otherwise, it's rubbish, and the thirty-eight-year-old Hudson must have foreseen that as he grew older his chance of getting more worthwhile parts in films was receding. Would he do *Death in Venice* or *Ice Station Zebra*?

Dirk Bogarde was only four years older than Rock, and their careers had followed a similar arc. Both were gay and anxious to spare the public that knowledge—they were "idols" and successes with rich careers. Bogarde had served in the war, directing bomber raids, and he had been present at the relief of Belsen concentration camp, an experience that never left his pessimistic intelligence.

He had been the bland apple of the audience's eye in Britain throughout the 1950s. His presence promised that everything would be all right. In several "Doctor" films he had played Simon Sparrow, a young doctor who scrapes through the escapades of the medical profession and has a reliable or saucy girlfriend (Muriel Pavlow or Brigitte Bardot). Sparrow was good-looking, modest, funny, and likeable; the films proved big hits and were the basis for a career during which

Bogarde also played plucky war heroes (*The Sea Shall Not Have Them, The Password Is Courage*) and romantic figures (*So Long at the Fair, A Tale of Two Cities, Campbell's Kingdom*). He was one of the biggest box-office attractions in Britain and an eligible bachelor. Few in his public guessed he was gay, and the press did not break his secret. He had a steady companion, Anthony Forwood, whom Bogarde did not acknowledge in public.

Bogarde was a smart man and a conscientious actor looking for better opportunities. In 1961 he agreed to play the hero in *Victim*. This was the story of a barrister who comes to the aid of several gay men who are being blackmailed; homosexual acts were illegal then in Britain. But the lawyer is himself gay and he must emerge from the closet and reveal himself to his wife (played by Sylvia Syms). The film was praised as groundbreaking, and it is a decently made melodrama in which Bogarde took a risk, though he played the barrister as he would have done a wing commander handling the Battle of Britain.

We like to think we honor courage, and movies made a cult of it that forgot the ways people really behave. Real bravery can go unnoticed for decades. *Victim* was reckoned a landmark while few remembered *South,* a TV play broadcast in London in November 1959. It was adapted by Gerald Savory from a play, *Sud,* by Julien Green, an American who lived in Paris and wrote in French. Set on the eve of the American Civil War, it concerns a Polish military officer in the South who has gay yearnings. That role was taken by Peter Wyngarde, ridiculously handsome, mysterious in his origins and uninhibitedly gay. *South* was received in bewilderment and horror. One reviewer summed it up: "I do NOT see anything attractive in the agonies and ecstasies of a pervert, especially in close-up in my living room. This is not prudishness. There are some indecencies in life that are best left covered up."

Until they demand to be noticed, at which point "indecency" may burn off in the light of ordinary behavior.

Wyngarde died in 2018. His career had been blighted by his reputation as a vivid "perv," at best an amusement, at worst an outrage, and convicted of "gross indecency" in 1975. The charge seemed full of dread, yet the fine was only £75.

He did his best with a career. He was the face of Peter Quint in Jack

Clayton's *The Innocents* as well as an ultra camp spy in the TV series *Department S* and *Jason King.* He was also one of Alan Bates's lovers. Bates had a wife and children and several discreet gay affairs. He could be a very good actor—as Guy Burgess in *An Englishman Abroad,* in *The Go-Between, The Caretaker,* and *The Fixer,* but above all on stage in Simon Gray's *Butley* (1971), playing a scabrously witty university don whose life is falling apart, and whose profuse talk is a diatribe against everything he has held dear.

Ben Butley is an archetype for the wounded eloquence of humanism and hidden gayness, and there is so much in its angry energy that is bisexual or opposed to conventional theories of what is straight in our crooked lives. It is a play about hopeless outrage, and it was directed in its premiere by Harold Pinter, a master of intimidation and leashed malice. *Butley* was Bates's most extrovert moment, though Dirk Bogarde (who was in *The Fixer* with him) was catty enough to say that Bates was "as sexual as a packet of Kleenex."

Bates was knighted and got a CBE—well deserved. Wyngarde was regarded as a flamboyant wreck—equally on his merits. Wyngarde (real name, apparently, Cyril Goldbert) might have been a magical role for Bogarde, knighted in 1992. ("All nonsense, I suppose," wrote Sir Dirk about his honor, "but people in the street seem to like it." He was the inside's outsider.)

Victim seemed current, but it had doubters everywhere. Bogarde recalled that "the lawyers who had to read it for libel declared that there was no problem but that they wished that they could wash their mouths out: they found it so distasteful!"

Perhaps lawyers believed they were saved. In 1954, there were over a thousand men in prison in Britain for homosexual offenses. In the 1950s there had been several cases of upper-class men being charged and convicted and these cases got press coverage. John Gielgud was arrested for importuning in 1953; for a moment he thought his career was over. Alan Turing had been convicted in 1952, chemically castrated, and then in 1954 he seemed to kill himself. Turing would have been another role for Bogarde. (It was 2014 before he reached the screen in *The Imitation Game,* played by Benedict Cumberbatch.) In 1957, a government inquiry led by John Wolfenden had recommended the decriminaliz-

ing of homosexual acts in Britain, but it was 1967 before that sentiment became law.

It was not that the movies or Bogarde could be relied on in the
crusade. The actor delivered another film early in 1963, *The Mind
Benders,* made by the team that had done *Victim.* This is not a distinguished work; except in the garish self-importance of its poster: "PER-
VERTED . . . SOULLESS! The most dangerous and different motion
picture ever brought to the screen!"

The Mind Benders concerns a psychological research unit conducting experiments in sensory deprivation. A senior professor on the project has committed suicide under the stress. It is suggested that he was a
Communist giving away state secrets. Dr. Henry Longman (Bogarde)
wants to repair the older man's reputation. He volunteers to repeat the
isolation experiments himself, just to prove they are a threat to stability. His loving wife, Oonagh (Mary Ure), knows he's doing the
right thing—because Henry always does that, and because we are in
a scheme where lovely, unoccupied wives are imprisoned in that faith.

Longman puts on a diver's suit and is immersed in a pool without
sight or sound. He's very shaky when pulled out of the pool, but a stern
police figure wants to establish that Henry's sense of reality is truly broken. So he threatens to return Longman to the pool and then whispers
poison in his ear about the slut his wife is.

Longman cracks. When he comes around after this third-degree,
his wife is not only just as lovely as Mary Ure could manage (that was
her thing, her one thing) but also pregnant with their first child. So
she's wide-eyed happy until the shattered Longman starts slagging her
off . . . like a cruel, bitchy gay stereotype. The character's predicament
could have been played straight, with Longman as a damaged man.
Instead, he releases a pent-up gay spite as stagy as it is shrill. Bogarde is
suddenly awful, but had he tapped into his own distaste over years of
covering up?

A few months later, Bogarde agreed to play Barrett in *The Servant,*
a character and a malign force that film had seldom seen before. That
picture was made by an American, Joseph Losey, in a cultural climate
where upper-class privilege was under mounting attack. Losey had
done some brilliant films in Hollywood (*The Prowler, M*) before he

left the country—earlier Communist allegiances were going to get him blacklisted. He and Bogarde had made one film together in England, in 1954, *The Sleeping Tiger,* where the actor had played a killer, and done it well. The writer entrusted with *The Servant* was Harold Pinter, an assassin to British superiority and privilege (until they came his way).

The challenge in *The Servant* was social and sexual. Barrett is a manservant hired by Tony (he never has a surname) to look after him. But Barrett (he has no first name) takes over the Chelsea house and becomes a degrading force in the life of his supposed master. It is a film about class, the decadent vulnerability of useless gentlemen, and the Iago-like intelligence of this servant. Barrett is never identified as being homosexual, but his listless sensuality hangs over the sadomasochistic setup and Bogarde plays the servant as an insolent and vicious usurper. It was a startling performance that may have taught the public who Bogarde was, but for the most part they said, well, that's all right, so Bogarde moved from being a misleading idol to a very good actor.

I saw some of *The Servant* being shot. It was a film about three characters in a house (the claustrophobic sensibility came from Pinter's screenplay and the production design by Richard Macdonald). The several rooms of the Chelsea house were all gathered in a spidery line on a Shepperton sound stage and Losey was moving the camera to make them feel as connected as sites in a sinister labyrinth.

The other two roles were Tony (James Fox), the wealthy and indolent young man, and Barrett's alleged sister, Vera, the seductress who starts Tony's fall. Vera was played by the young Sarah Miles. At that time Fox and Miles were having an affair, and this was palpable on the set and sometimes disruptive. For the seduction scene, Losey dressed Tony in a kimono and fur boots. When Miles saw this, she yelled out at Fox:

"Oh, you great stinking queer, you think I'm going to play the scene with you in that grotesque costume, you're crazy. This is a love scene and I'm not going to play any fucking love scene with you in that costume!"

Actors don't have to understand what they're doing—they only need to do it with grace. Losey was sometimes at a loss with the unruly and inexperienced young actors caught between their real and fictitious feelings—he did alter that costume. But Bogarde was playing a tactful role with naughty children, encouraging them to behave and do their work. As a good-natured, amused manager he was like the actor who had played Simon Sparrow—decent, amiable, well-mannered. Yet in a few moments, on the call for "action," he would become the obnoxious, insinuating, lower-class, and indecent Barrett. It was acting, of course, but it was breathtaking in its slithery speed.

It was an odd English occasion in the calm village of Shepperton. There were people playing bowls on lawns that led to the Thames; others gardened or tended allotments. Yet a discreet bomb was being readied in the studio. There was a canteen lunch for everyone, with Fox and Miles sneaking away for whatever while Bogarde rolled his eyes. We looked at rushes: they were stunning—Bogarde was a genius. Then Losey picked me out, came over, shook my hand, and said he was glad I was there. Why was he so nervous? He had no idea who I was. It was the first film set I had ever seen and still the best.

When the British public saw *The Servant* enough of them knew they were seeing "a queer," and could handle it. Maybe there was too much of the vicious Waldo Lydecker (from *Laura*) in Barrett—he was doing a menacing portrait of gayness. That was excusable because the gayness was not spelled out. Instead, we were watching the best screen portrait done so far of a kind of acidic homosexual marriage. It was disturbing, but it was understandable. If Rock Hudson had seen the film he might have groaned to think that such bold things were being done only a few thousand miles away, but without him.

By 1970 Bogarde was playing Aschenbach in Luchino Visconti's *Death in Venice,* while Hudson was Major William Larrabee in the box-office flop *Darling Lili,* before getting embedded in *McMillan & Wife* on TV. The contrast in opportunity and ambition is clear, even if Hudson was never going to be as subtle an actor as Bogarde.

Bogarde was liberated: you can feel it in the letters he wrote to friends. He was a gossip there, candid and flighty, though in interviews he stayed formal and closeted. (Fellow actor John Fraser regretted Bogarde's austere public silence about his sexuality.) But in playing Aschenbach, he went farther than he had ever been, into makeup, pathos, and exaggerated sensitivity. I think it's a bad performance in a painful movie, but *Death in Venice* was important in 1970—as a land-mark in the spreading prestige of gay ideas; and for Bogarde it was an exciting if not gleeful adventure. Here he is writing to Joe Losey about working with Visconti (from his collected letters *Ever, Dirk*):

> ... we are shooting in Panavision which has added millions to the slender budget.... I have 18 changes ... and we shoot also in the Tyrol and in Munich ... because the TRUE story of DIV was that Mann, an old friend of Visconti's, was travelling on a train from Venice to Munich in 1910 ... and in the compartment was a strange being in full slap ... desperately unhappy, his died, dyed, hair streaky ... his false eyelashes coming off in his tears. They spoke.... It was Gustave [sic] Mahler ... and he had just fallen in hopeless love with a child of thirteen in Venice.... And so from there it went. So, although we are not telling anyone, I am in fact playing Mahler ... and look rather like him with the putty nose-job and the rimless Lennon-glasses.... Long hair ... oh! dear I am a sight at the moment....

Part of Bogarde's amusement there is that of a gay actor enjoying the sport in pretending to be gay. In Britain, more than in America, the community of acting takes some delight in acting gay when that is not always the real situation. It's part of the camaraderie and bravado in a dangerous life: some British films on the Second World War and its hallowed teamwork are rife with inadvertent gay tenderness. This spirit led to the term "luvvies" in Britain; that does not refer to sexual choice but to an ongoing swish charade. It means actors who are pretending to be actors. When you're out of work, it is the only way to go. In his splendid, louche letters, you can always hear Bogarde's sly, insinuating voice.

Of course, Visconti himself was gay, as was Fernando Scarfiotti, who was in charge of production design on *Death in Venice*. Bogarde and Visconti were both miffed when their film did not take the Palme d'Or at Cannes—it lost to *The Go-Between,* directed by Joseph Losey.

The 1960s soon believed that theirs was an age of liberation, but not too much of that was evident in movies—the medium and the business was attached more to order than disruption. In 1969, Stanley Donen directed *Staircase* (taken from a Charles Dyer play) in which Rex Harrison and Richard Burton were uncomfortable playing a couple of queer hairdressers. Burton observed that as the shoot progressed, "Rex is a bit worrying latterly. He's become much less queer. In fact he's hardly queer at all—he's almost professor Higgins." The film is bad, and it made people uneasy: Roger Ebert called it "an unpleasant exercise in bad taste."

But what right do critics have to lament "bad taste" at the movies? Hasn't that always been part of the deal? There's another Bogarde film that deserves examination under this heading. *The Night Porter* (1974) was written off as rubbish by top American critics. In *The New York Times,* Vincent Canby called it "romantic pornography." It meant much more in the postwar Europe familiar with German occupation. Charlotte Rampling plays a former concentration camp victim and Bogarde is the SS officer who once possessed and tortured her. They are reunited in a rundown Viennese hotel where they re-enact their tryst to the point of death. It's the key Rampling picture: she is as blank as a slave, absentmindedly naked, and perversely arousing, yet as calm and untouchable as a sleepwalker.

As a project, written and directed by Liliana Cavani, *The Night Porter* relied on the trust between Bogarde and Rampling and on his caring for her in so exposing a role. It was he who got her into the picture. She would say, "Dirk became my soulmate . . . we had the same sensitive form of intelligence, let's say, and the same way of feeling things." She was about to become a corrupted icon, very provocative, and consenting to her enslavement. She had just had a baby. Rampling was not a subtle actress, but she had a unique fallen-angel presence. To commit to this venture, she said, she hardly thought about the sadomasochism. She told herself, "Dirk wants me to do this and I know I have to do it." The bond between the characters imitated the pact between the actors. As for Bogarde, he cherished Rampling and felt she "is too full of angles. She has no curves. . . . Charlotte is also very male." Years later, he treasured the impact of the scene where Rampling had straddled him in a sexual act.

Bad taste? Of course. But *The Night Porter* lives in my mind more vividly than classier films, like John Schlesinger's *Sunday Bloody Sunday* (1971), where Murray Head and Peter Finch share a big kiss. That was nominated for four Oscars and very well received. Schlesinger's previous film, *Midnight Cowboy* (veiled in its homosexual relationship), had been made in America, and it won Best Picture. But it was unlikely that the quiet openness of *Sunday* could have played in an American setting. Even in Britain the project had awkward moments. Alan Bates was unavailable; Paul Scofield declined the Peter Finch role; Ian Bannen was cast and then dropped; and when it came to that big kiss being filmed, Schlesinger recalled hesitations:

> It was in the original script but written so that it tried to make light of it, tried to make it almost disappear, as if it wasn't happening. Penelope Gilliatt, who wrote the screenplay, and I basically disagreed about this. I didn't think that it should be portrayed with any kind of apology. She wanted it done in a long shot, with the two of them kissing in silhouette and all that kind of thing. I wanted the doctor to greet his lover, as if it were the normal thing to do. I said that if we started putting it in silhouette and long shot, it's special pleading and coy. I wanted them to be absolutely overt about it and unembarrassed. And they did, and they did it beautifully.

There were distinctions. In *Victim*, the barrister's wife is horrified on discovering her husband's sexual nature. She is going to leave him, but then she relents and thinks perhaps they can work it out. That attempt might make an interesting picture, but still it leaves the Bogarde character prepared to struggle on. There is a suggestion that he can "conquer" his gay feelings—that misguided hope was still active in society. One year later, Otto Preminger made *Advise & Consent*, an inside-Washington story in which a senator (from Utah), played by Don Murray, is stricken when his brief gay past is exposed. So he kills himself. Both these films were pledged to the orthodoxy that while gayness might be recognized and sympathized with, still it was aberrational and likely to end badly. So the audience did not have to feel implicated in its acceptance.

The business of movies had no doubt over what relaxing censorship meant. At long last, naked women might be seen. You wondered if that freedom would extend to men. We could see men enjoying women on screen, but not entering them with erect penises. That sacred member is still not admitted in mainstream American movies, except as pornography (which is a river next to that main stream). But female cries of orgasmic joy have been with us for years. The expectations of virile men were unassailable. In the supposedly central *Last Tango in Paris,* Maria Schneider was naked a lot of the time while Marlon Brando was excused that openness. The dominant male gaze let some men be more private or more ethereal. They were photographed as gods, the way women had often been idolized. They needed no explanation.

Still, something had happened two years before *Advise & Consent* that made a travesty of its earnest approach to sexual variety. *Some Like It Hot* suggested that in America if you wanted to deal with a difficult subject you should abandon dramatic solemnity for wild comedy. It might help if you didn't quite know what you were doing.

So I don't think Billy Wilder was intent on pulling the carpet out from under the feet of sexual stolidity. He wanted to make a funny movie and a hit, and the gimmick he saw was that of two guys dressing up as girls. Great inroads might be achieved in the guise of farce or what was once called "screwball," so long as you noticed that the two parts of that word had definite erotic connotations.

Some Like It Hot was one of the new films more about movies than life. So it takes the hallowed set-piece of the St. Valentine's Day Massacre, Chicago, and gangsters and says: suppose two desperate musicians had seen the shootout, and been seen seeing it, so they had to find cover? They join an all-girl band, Sweet Sue's Society Syncopators. No, it's not credible, but credibility is out the window, thrown out by surreal insight.

Curiously, Billy Wilder had some reputation for being homophobic—or was it more misanthropic, in that he didn't warm to anyone? There were signs of that in the film's singer, Sugar Kane, and the way she was rendered is now a matter of cultural regret. Sugar was played by Marilyn Monroe, either very voluptuous or beginning to be out of movie shape. She is lovely, nearly falling out of her dress as she sings "I Want to Be Loved by You," and very funny. But that is because Sugar is treated as an idiot: she mindlessly obliges the project of kissing Joe/Josephine (Tony Curtis) to restore his manhood. You can almost tell that Wilder deplored Marilyn's lack of professionalism: many of the guys on the film had bad things to say about her. The audience was set up to laugh at Sugar behind her ample back.

If you wanted to watch intelligent women in the movie, you turned to Josephine and Daphne. They had to be smart to survive because they were Jack Lemmon and Tony Curtis in drag. That was a hoot and a conundrum. Lemmon plays Daphne like a white-faced clown, desperate and nearly out of control. It's difficult to think anyone would fall for her. But Tony Curtis has worked hard to be feminine, and he does seem more like a transwoman, or a great drag artist. You might fall for him. Curtis did not find this easy, so it helped him to have his Joe scenes where he could be Sugar's unscrupulous macho exploiter, with every vestige of audience lust backing him up. In its day, it was a source of glee; now that drag scene is far less comfortable.

Daphne the misfit has a stranger joy. She is noticed by an addled millionaire, Osgood Fielding III, wonderfully played by Joe E. Brown. When the film reaches the breathless point of needing to end, Osgood has a motorboat to sweep everyone away. He regards Daphne by then as his significant other so she feels she has to make it clear that her relationship with Osgood can only be limited. At last he takes off the wig and can blurt it out. "I'm a man." To which Osgood responds, "Well, nobody's perfect," with the aplomb of an elderly fellow who'll take what he can get and a premonition that strong or surviving men need not be immaculate.

That is a famous line still, nearly sixty years later, and it produced immediate delight and uproar as a get-off line. But it is richer than it seems on its first hearing. It suggests that Osgood had seen every prospect of a solid (if ridiculous) relationship. Had he guessed Daphne was a man? Was there a chance that Lemmon's wry wreck of a guy would trade "dignity" for the right prenuptial agreement?

Beyond that, the line amounted to a heresy in American movies—that nobody really was, or needed to be, perfect. That disrupts the tranquil order of films being perfectly cast and totally emblematic. That's how Garbo could be the ideal, sweet, and tragic courtesan in *Camille* instead of an aging, sick woman who slept with anyone who could afford her (and who wore camellias in the novel to signal whether she was menstruating or available for sex).

I doubt Wilder meant for this ending, or the whole film, to be a stink bomb thrown at a coronation procession. He wanted to make a sensational comedy, not a sexual revolution. But sometimes it doesn't matter what you intend. Films can be like aircraft carriers: huge, expensive, ponderous, and taking so long to arrive. At other times they are sharks in the sea. So *Some Like It Hot* has survived as one of the most influential of our movies. Through lurid improbability it intuited what might be about to happen.

Cultural ideas were changing quickly. Civil rights were being spread across the board, but the movies only made tame gestures to that: *The Defiant Ones, Lilies of the Field, Guess Who's Coming to Dinner,* complacent and conservative pictures that had no idea how little they knew of black experience. "Women's Lib" was being talked about, so women could take off more of their clothes on screen. The greatest beneficiary of abandoned censorship was young men acting out their urges. Clyde Barrow of *Bonnie and Clyde* was a new kind of hero who could shoot common people without losing our support. Better yet, in the end, Clyde would get what had proved so elusive for him: the chance to take up Bonnie's perpetual invitation.

Unexpected pressures were crowding in on movie sex. Censorship was fading away: in 1966 there was a flash of female pubic hair in Michelangelo Antonioni's *Blow-Up,* as cute as the hula hoop. That was a witty but respectable art-house film in which it was a little easier to get away with nudity. Gorgeous breasts were coming in like fruit in its prime: remember Apollonia (Simonetta Stefanelli), Michael's first, brief, bride in *The Godfather*—or Jane Fonda in *Klute.* But the thing that would be called pornography was not far away: in 1972 *Deep Throat* earned $100 million according to FBI estimates—they were interested because the picture had underworld backing. Pornography, or skin movies, were as old as Hollywood. There had always been some instinct for regarding filmed sex as more thrilling than the real thing. But *Deep Throat* played in art-house theaters; it was a social event for educated young people. In the age of home video, beginning in the late 1970s, there were tapes that some of us played as foreplay to our own sex or which we tried to imitate. The technologies of video were just preparation for a time when children could summon up spectacular porn on their iPad. The educational value of this was profound, but perhaps the excitement of the original thing—or its connection to desire—was being muffled or bypassed.

Soon enough it was possible to see gay porn nearly as easily as the straight version. That might induce horror in some viewers, but the history of horror teaches us that shock wears off. The supposed spearhead role of the mainstream American movie was being usurped by what might be amateur film footage showing entirely new things.

There had been arty, experimental films about sex going back to the late twenties. They had been made for their own sake and shown at colleges, film societies, or at polite orgies for people interested to see sex in fresh ways. (Libertines are always ready for technical instruction on what goes where.) There was a marked homosexual fascination in the work of Jack Smith, Kenneth Anger, and many others. Their imagery was often beautiful and usually pretentious, but the filmmakers were paying for their own films (or getting the cash from a patron), so why not? So many mainstream films have been crippled by the creative debt to Other People's Money. These personal works had their roots in avant-garde European films, the work of Luis Buñuel (*Un Chien Andalou, L'Age d'Or*), Jean Vigo (*Zéro de Conduite, L'Atalante*), and Jean Cocteau (*Le Sang d'un Poète*), who favored gay liberation along with the freeing of any other artistic impulse he could think of.

Un Chien Andalou, just seventeen minutes long, is the essential movie poem on pansexuality. It was the result of Buñuel and Salvador Dalí comparing dreams. They tried to film them, with the proviso that there be "no idea or image that might lend itself to a rational explanation of any kind." The film was funded by Buñuel's mother and shot on 35 mm in 1928. When the money ran out, Buñuel cut it by hand in his kitchen.

The film is a reverie entered through a compliant female eye that in the opening sequence is slit open by a razor. Thereafter, it observes the desperate gestures at straight and gay sex as if studying scorpions or the private lives of medieval popes. The imagery is ecstatic and "dirty" yet impersonal. It is ninety years old now, but it feels as if it was thrown together last night—if we had geniuses as casual and piercing as Buñuel. In one simple dissolve, instinct's hands take a woman's breasts and the squeezing turns them into buttocks.

I showed the film once to a class at Stanford, asking the students to let the film into their subconscious. When the film ended, there was a hush as if I had horrified the young. I hope that was so—what do they expect from school? Make no mistake: some films are toxic and disruptive as well as sublime. You could play *Un Chien Andalou* with David Lynch's *Blue Velvet*. Everything useful about the emotional-sexual ardor of adolescence is in that double bill.

It was in that tradition that America discovered a bland but single-minded gay filmmaker, Andy Warhol, and pushed him toward the mainstream. He was a creative force who had reached the point where he could ennoble a soup can by signing it or noticing it. He worked in a variety of graphic arts, but he was fascinated by movie, by Hollywood and celebrity, and by the way untalented people might imitate or wish to be outlaw celebrities. At first, his movies were observational and about duration: he would turn on a fixed camera, go away, and come back later to find he had a banal movie that entranced young audiences.

As if in insolent imitation of the old movie studios, Warhol established his Factory as a gathering place for artists, filmmakers, pickups, or available young lookers who were ready to be used. Some of them were open to sexual exhibitionism, to gay and straight activity, capable of anything and fazed by nothing. They became underground celebrities and mockeries of real, old-regime stars—Viva, Joe D'Alessandro, Edie Sedgwick, Candy Darling, Holly Woodlawn, and many others. With the aid of Paul Morrissey—because Andy was often too bored to do the work after he had seen the null concept—the Factory produced an array of films, some of which got an art-house release or were banned and sent to the underworld of fashion. The Factory was a meeting place for sexual pickups, and some lives there were damaged or destroyed—but that had always been true of Hollywood, too. In some ways Warhol was satirizing mainstream cinema and its humbug romanticism. But some of the results were deadpan landmarks in sexual cinema.

Blue Movie was shown in 1969, created by Warhol and Morrissey and their two players, Viva and Louis Waldon, who lie around talking about Vietnam and sex and sometimes doing it, the real thing, there in rough black and white on 16 mm. The sunlight on the bodies and the rambling improvised talk are sometimes ravishing. The film was 105 minutes long and said to have cost $3,000. But why so much? It was the kind of film "anyone" could make, and young people were soon obsessed with filming their own sexual attempts until they began to see that sex might be comic, boring, and empty if seen from the outside. Here was an astonishing problem: the liberty suddenly available to film only taught us that sexual experience might not be accessible to cinema.

Warhol had no faith in anything, no matter that he was a conceptual genius. He wanted to be uninvolved; he aspired to boredom; and sexual action—gay, straight, any way you looked—was a perfect demonstration of this. His revolution depended on an age of people disenchanted with revolutionary purpose. In works like *Trash, Heat, Chelsea Girls, Lonesome Cowboys,* and *Blue Movie* the commercial mystique of sex fell away and sometimes the essential mystery stared back at us like a tiger from its cage. Or a cat in a bag.

As never before, the pansexual nature of all film, its horniness, and its detachment from such value systems as "love" were on display, and the result could be dismaying. Liberation had disclosed a new prison. But homosexuality was out there as part of the disconsolate orgy, and only bigots believed it was different from straight sex. Hollywood was over as a burning light in our imagination and a guide to our lives, and we have not yet found a wonder to replace its captivation.

Andy Warhol spoiled some lives. He had had a lover, a young executive at Paramount, who later died of AIDS. In 1968, just as *Blue Movie* was being made, one of his people, Valerie Solanas, shot him. He recovered, but recovery was not really his thing any more than he believed in any agenda of enlightenment or humanist progress. He is a strange absent presence in his own work: he says artists are impostors or stand-ins. But his irony edges into nihilism and a refutation of the cozy idea that art is good for us—like Ovaltine or yoga.

Indecency rarely lasts long. If it is close enough to serving our desires in the dark (whether or not we would admit them in the light) it evolves into being a business, and in business or the making of money we have our fewest scruples.

In the fall of 2017, as male sexual confidence in America came under attack, a striking new show began to play on HBO. It was *The Deuce,* created by David Simon and George Pelicanos. The setting was New York in the early 1970s, and "the deuce" was a slang name for Forty-Second Street, where sex became a new media commodity. Indecency was too lucrative to stay casual or secret. Prostitution was common if also illegal on the neon streets and in the shabby stripped-down buildings where rooms could be hired for as long as it took. And then it occurred to us that purchased sex—the hurried, clumsy transaction—could be industrialized as a leisure pursuit that was sweet to watch and that could be rerun. Compared to regular movies, like *Klute* (about a failing actress who becomes a call girl), porn was another hideaway.

The Deuce was intended to be "gritty." From Simon and Pelicanos to Michelle McLaren, the director of the pilot, that duty was nearly sacred so the streetlife was offered undoctored—though the prettiness of its women exceeded Forty-Second Street averages—while the photography, by Pepe Avila del Pino, was little short of "beautiful." "Gritty" as a movie style is a riddle: neon, scum, and darkness can be radiant in film's shining. And our sofa, in our home, is less gritty than safely removed. You can tell yourself *The Deuce* is very real, but you don't smell the disinfectant, the stale perfume, the sweat, the cum, or the vomit of the reality.

The makers tried to show the sex as matter-of-fact, sordid, and brutal—or even erotic as a spectacle for voyeurs. There was a gentle passage where a mature hooker (Maggie Gyllenhaal) gave a birthday present to a high school kid, putting on his condom with her mouth.

Gyllenhaal's character was often naked above the waist, with no CGI cover for her forty-year-old breasts. It was acute casting, for Gyllenhaal is a respected actress, seldom given to glamour or personality projection. You felt the need to take her seriously—but with humor. In one scene her character is involved in shooting a porn movie where she realizes that the alleged cum being squirted on her face is actually cold potato soup. This was probably funnier on the plasma screen than if you had been that woman without an umbrella.

Early on, a changing of the ways dawned as Gyllenhaal's character, Candy, a mother whose child is looked after by the grandmother, saw the light. She was an independent operator, without a pimp. To help a friend, she took a date that turned into that porno shoot. She went home with a stolen reel and projected it. It was then that she saw a fresh angle for a jaded business. She would become an entrepreneur in porn flicks. As well as acting, Gyllenhaal was a producer on *The Deuce*. Her Candy was an unsentimental visionary who saw that a hooker's routine trick could be a coup played on the world's screen, making far more money than a prostitute dreamed of. Sex was all very well. People desired it. But the real thing could be awkward, embarrassing, dangerous, and demeaning, whereas on screen it attained a strange cute serenity.

The Deuce enjoyed rising numbers: by the end of the first season it was getting two million viewers per episode. A second season was ordered. I suppose it stood comparison with the realism of *Boogie Nights,* though it lacked the fantasy element in that movie. At the same time, it was an entertainment surely aimed at guys in which the male characters were pimps or small-time crooks, dressing and acting like refugees from *The Godfather,* snarling their dialogue, abusing women, and brandishing wads of cash. You could see how guys got off on the show—the way they had been digesting movies all their life. As for the women, they showed off their bodies and their acting aplomb without protest. Like so much in American screen life, this disparity was something you went along with, just as people knew more or less what Harvey Weinstein was and didn't bother to mention it.

The Deuce was on our screens just when the storm of revelation broke on male misbehavior in the business. The TV show had been conceived at least a year earlier, but if it had been in development in 2017 would it have been proceeded with? As a commodity it was loyal to ancient ideas of how women could be exploited and to the poker-faced come-on: Let me show you some really shocking, indecent things.

Then the dragnet of accusation picked up James Franco, an executive producer on the show, a sometime writer and director, and an actor playing twins in a dynamic story arc. It was said that he had behaved inappropriately with several women in the business. Days after he'd won a Golden Globe for his acting in *The Disaster Artist,* some shadow of rebuke came over him and people started asking what should happen to James Franco. In turn that involved a survey of what he had said about sex on screen and in life.

Franco had seemed heterosexual in his work, but he was smart and brave. In an interview, he said that it was how an actor was on screen that defined his sexuality. It was a matter of "how you acted and not by whom you slept with. . . . I like to think that I'm gay in my art and straight in my life." A similar air of enigma hung over Kristen Stewart.

All of this was in the age of a president who had boasted of far more indecent behavior and who might have had his lawyer make a six-figure payoff to a porn movie actress working as "Stormy Daniels." Of course, our president was only acting his role, while watching screens to see how he did. If that seems grotesque, recognize how far the double act has tested most of us in the last fifty years. We may be straight, but it's not straightforward.

Dirk Bogarde was a pioneer in acting and in deception; he was also a very funny, smart man in a life crowded with friends or pals. But he felt little reliable companionship. That plight can affect straight actors, too, for they may recognize how far they rely on the kindness of strangers. If you're wooing strangers (audiences), you may not master the range for intimacy. He had become a dedicated and hard-working author—with a string of old-fashioned novels and memoirs. That brought fresh success as he stopped acting.

He ended sadly. His onetime manager, companion, and lover, Anthony Forwood, died in 1988. Bogarde had by then given up his treasured house in the South of France. He withdrew to a flat in Cadogan Gardens, close to Harrods. His health declined as loneliness set in. He stayed wry in his letters, but there was a dismay, too, that he could not come out of his official closet, no matter that hardly anyone believed in it by the time he died, in 1999, aged seventy-eight. He had published seven volumes of autobiography and never acknowledged the core of his being. Was he ashamed or had he been conditioned by secrecy?

There is a fine documentary film, *The Private Dirk Bogarde* (2001), produced for Arena by Anthony Wall and directed by Adam Low. It seems sadder and more resonant now than *Death in Venice.*

13

The Male Gaze

James Dean and Nicholas Ray preparing for *Rebel Without a Cause* (1955).
Film is at its peak with desires that cannot be attained.

BY 2018, A LOT OF US were aware of, and ashamed over, the dominating male gaze in our movies. That phrase had been used in film theory for thirty years; now it was something the public were chanting. But hadn't it been there all along as a force that men and women thought too profound to be shaken? Not that the gaze is simply sexual or a power play turned into a marketing strategy. It is a codification of human desire that guided our narrative habits. It is a point of view that extends to race and poverty, courage and caution, and the story of America. Dealing with it will shape our destiny? Nothing is going to be harder. America the beautiful has to be feminized. Miss America giving up bikinis will only go so far.

Natalia Nikolaevna Zakharenko was sixteen in 1954, and she had called herself Natalie Wood since childhood. She felt many of the insecurities of being sixteen but she was trying to school them into the energy and the needy look to win the role of Judy in what would become *Rebel Without a Cause.*

She was a young beauty, already famous for her eyes, her spontaneity, and her grown-up laugh. But Los Angeles had been loaded with that sort for decades. It was where such women went, looking for the light and a tender camera angle. In parts of that city, it is possible to believe that the young women are all slim, poised, and bright-eyed wonders. They can feel beautiful yet somehow body-snatched—they are so anxious to please. Talk to these women and some do seem knocked out. For decades, men saw this hope and prettiness coming, daring and seemingly unafraid, and so their notion of the ideal women in pictures hardened into a type that scared real women. We needed plain women, but looking makes that hard.

To be a knockout of the moment, male or female, is like being heavyweight champion of the world, or president. The pinnacle is short-lived and vulnerable to scathing reappraisal: a young beauty fading out can be as sad as a hitter who has lost his timing. But Natalie Wood had her season, until it was inescapable that she was forty-three. Her moment was captured by Dominick Dunne in his book *The Way We Lived Then,* a fond observer of passing glory, and a passionate hanger-on:

> Natalie had real glamour. When she went out to a party or a premiere, she always looked like a million bucks, with her great diamond drop earrings flashing.... Natalie used to stand behind the bar, mixing drinks, looking great, with a cigarette in a holder hanging out of the corner of her mouth, always having a good time. She was fun and she was funny, and she always knew the latest Hollywood dish, and I loved to listen to dish. My scrapbooks are full of her pictures. She had a wonderful habit of putting on her lipstick after dinner, using the blade of her knife as a mirror.

That was a habit guys loved: it suggested that Natalie was up for danger and sharp in self-awareness. Hollywood cherishes the clash of bold-type names and intriguing rumors—*have you heard about* **Natalie Wood**? She attracted many men and slipped in and out of marriages and alliances—she would marry Robert Wagner twice without quite settling the relationship. No one was more steadfast as a source of affection and trust for her than Mart Crowley. He was gay and she had sponsored Mart in his writing of *The Boys in the Band,* a 1968 play about a group of homosexuals edging out of the closet. In return, he was her solace, her confidant, and her beard. Young knockouts need safe counselors. When she died, Crowley took pains to enlist Hollywood craftsmen (like hairdresser Sydney Guilaroff) to keep her a knockout still for her funeral. That knife she had brandished was her portable screen. But was she studying herself or saying look at me?

In 1954, Wood was doing all she could to get the attention of Nicholas Ray. He was forty-three, tall, prematurely gray, handsome and moody, and as hesitant as the male star of *Rebel,* James Dean. No one was ever certain which of them—Ray or Dean—was most drawn to imitating the other. Ray would direct *Rebel,* he would cast the picture, and he was a mentor in the eyes of the kids hovering for parts. He should have known better, you may say—he could be arrested now. But Nick Ray was as volatile or as unsteady as many teenagers. That's a reason why *Rebel* turned out so well.

He had directed ten pictures by 1954. Natalie had acted in twenty. She was in the running for the role of Judy. She had a script; she had been hanging out at Warners where the film would be made, and at Ray's personal bungalow at the Chateau Marmont on Sunset Blvd. He was based there while in preproduction on *Rebel*. Ray had had two marriages and two divorces: the first to Jean Evans, a journalist (1936–42); the second to the actress Gloria Grahame (1948–52). Grahame had starred in Ray's movie *In a Lonely Place* (1950), but that marriage was at its end already by then. One factor in its breakdown— not the only one—was that Ray had caught Grahame in bed with his thirteen-year-old son from the Jean Evans marriage. (She married the son later.)

So Natalie wanted to be noticed by this powerful and attractive man, and all she had going for her were her amazing eyes, her bursting need, and being sixteen. She was desperate to be liked and to have that admiration or affection turn into casting—so she had a script life to work on, sufficient to distract her from the incompleteness of her own. There are few occupations closer to insecurity than acting, where an aspirant must go before strangers, do a speech, a walk, and a look, and may be rejected on the spot for being inept, homely, uncool, or not hot. Not hot is the American curse.

It's not that Natalie Wood was necessarily virginal (except when a part required it). She had been active sexually as a kid with boys her own age and with older men. Her mother—who was very anxious for Natalie's career—enabled her to have an affair with Frank Sinatra. It had meant a lot to both of them.

Nick Ray noticed her—he had some sense of her work as a child actress in *Miracle on 34th Street, No Sad Songs for Me*, and *The Star*. So he asked her out to dinner and then took her back to the Chateau, and there it happened.

You need to consider how you want to have this described: He made love to her or with her? He seduced her? Did he more or less rape her or take advantage of her? He fucked her—they fucked together? He came and maybe she did, too? She got the part of Judy, and she is terrific in the film. I can easily believe she is better than the actress Warners had had in mind—Debbie Reynolds (who was twenty-three). There were other contestants for the part, one of them Jayne Mansfield, who at twenty-one hadn't made a film yet. Mansfield doesn't seem right for high-school Judy in *Rebel;* her voluptuous body looked more mature than twenty-one. But Ray was sleeping with her, too, and she had shot a test for him. Nick was also considering Carroll Baker and Lee Remick for the part. That doesn't mean he was also screwing them; he was busy seeing Shelley Winters, too, while pretty sure that she was not right as Judy. There was a lot in the erotic air.

Casting and suitability are not the same thing: you may tonight, on impulse, go to bed with someone and be delighted, without ever contemplating a longer life with him or her, let alone your future. It is a part of our romantic life (and our romantic sense of ourselves) that we treasure our impulses while guarding long-term plans. In any consideration of sexuality in the movies, you are going to have to determine how much you are shocked or surprised, or how fully you understand and accept that seminal line from *Chinatown* uttered by Noah Cross (John Huston), "See, Mr. Gittes, most people never have to face the fact that at the right time and right place, they're capable of anything."

If *Rebel* was being made now, and word got out about Ray's behavior, I think his career would be over. The exploitation would seem clear. But Ray was not a cruel man or a natural monster of power. So what was he doing? That question is at the heart of the male empire in filmmaking. He was acting that way because he could, and because that assertion of power assisted his need for creative authority. In the climate of the work pretty women understood a need to be attractive and pliant. Directors take advantage of actresses, but there are actresses who need to give themselves over to the male vision and the wish to do good work. Some sexual affairs are working arrangements. Some marriages have similar strategies.

Actors and characters are guinea pigs in a large experiment about ourselves, and movies have made erotic fantasy a sport and a pastime to offset our dull anonymity. Most of us lead lives of limitation, hardship, disappointment, and a lack of glory. So sex can be our relief and release—we feel it's what we deserve and even the best time we will ever have. We have glorified it as a flag of freedom.

One other thing: at the time of *Rebel* (with its poignant male bonding between Jim and Plato) Nicholas Ray was also thinking of male lovers. Not all film directors are so versatile or scattered, but if you're going to make a film like *Rebel Without a Cause,* in which everyone (beneath a certain age) seems desirable and giddy with desire, then you have to know how to photograph boys as well as girls as if you could love them.

Some time around the production of *Rebel,* Natalie Wood was raped. There is no suggestion that the offender was Nick Ray or anyone else involved on *Rebel.* But Suzanne Finstad in her book, *Natasha: The Biography of Natalie Wood,* says that it was a famous actor-producer, a "Mr. Hollywood." Finstad's book is thoughtful, sympathetic, and well-researched: it has sixty pages of source notes. The author had the story from several people who knew Wood, and she admits that different people placed the rape in a room or in a car.

Nothing was officially reported: the rapist was so well established that a claim against him might have ruined a novice career. Such charges have seldom been successful in Hollywood history. In 1921, Roscoe "Fatty" Arbuckle was charged with raping Virginia Rappe, who had died as a result of a party at the St. Francis Hotel in San Francisco. He had two hung juries and then an acquittal, but his career was stopped in its tracks: being "Fatty" was a clue to wickedness.

Finstad's book was published in 2001, and it never names the rapist. That suggests the man was still alive and litigious in 2001. But Finstad says he was more than twenty years older than Wood—in which case he would have been in his eighties at the time of publication. I do not know who the villain was. Sixteen years later (the man could be one hundred now) I don't think Ms. Finstad has filled in the blank.

So consider these possibilities:

1. Natalie Wood was deeply imaginative, or "hysterically" so. (Society still nurses the superstition that that wildness can overtake females—though it neglects the way some men inhabit extremes of macho overconfidence.) Uncertain incidents gathered around Wood like admirers. We will likely never know just how she died, but most of us "know" her foreboding over dark water, because we treasure her

character's frightening encounter with dangerous water in Elia Kazan's *Splendor in the Grass*.

2. We all know the way in which real actions—things that happened to us—can be enlarged in the creep of self-dramatization that owes a lot to our experience of movies and filmed stories and their urging that we deserve more than ordinariness. This is not always "lying," though lies are more allowed now than once was the case—we have learned to have such a faith in our imagination that facts have turned rubbery.

3. It is in the nature of books about movie stars that authors are vulnerable to the idea of the sensational. Publishers do not like to believe stars lead dull or empty lives; they may ask for a list of hot bullet points to share with the media. I do not know Ms. Finstad; I admire her book and I think it is very understanding of an actress who might be Natalie Wood. I do not seek to question Ms. Finstad's integrity. But it is possible that such an author—with such a star—might polish the germ of a story, not just to make a book lively but because in several true senses the incident captured the atmosphere in which a teenage actress had gone along with male power (and charm) and who had even orgasmed on cue—because that seemed helpful to becoming known— but who then later shrank back into the privacy of regret and horror. Good actors have to believe that stories are happening to them. It is how they get ready.

It's another part of this atmosphere that Ms. Finstad suggests Wood's mother would have hushed up the incident and even been gratified by her daughter's getting it on with a celebrity and a powerbroker. She seems to have had no qualms over Nicholas Ray being her daughter's lover or seducer.

Here is another incident. Early in 1956, Gavin Lambert had been at a party in London. He was in his early thirties, a film critic and the editor of *Sight & Sound*. A few years earlier, when Nick Ray's debut film, *They Live by Night,* opened in London, Lambert had written a perceptive review of it. Now, in 1956, Lambert noticed a man across the room who he guessed was Ray: "a man with powerful shoulders, a leonine head, and graying blond hair, very handsome but gloomy, stood alone. By choice I felt. He seemed to create a circle of isolation around himself."

Ray and Lambert became friends. Nick was less articulate than Gavin, so it was a treat for a director to hear such smart praise. Lambert gave up London and *Sight & Sound*. He went to Hollywood to be Nick's assistant on a few films, and in that process one night they became lovers. "He [Ray] put his arms around me and kissed me on the mouth. An hour or so later he said that he wasn't really homosexual, not really even bisexual, as he'd been to bed with a great many women in his life, but only two or three men."

Their affair did not surprise Lambert, though it was the first unequivocal sign of Ray's bisexuality. He also discovered that Nick was reliant on drugs and alcohol. In his memoir, *Front and Center,* John Houseman (who had produced *They Live by Night* and *On Dangerous Ground* for Ray) gave a shrewd account of Ray's romantic personality:

> He was a handsome, complicated man whose sentimentality and apparent softness covered deep layers of resilience and strength. Reared in Wisconsin in a household dominated by women, he was a potential homosexual with a deep, passionate and constant need for female love in his life. This made him attractive to women, for whom the chance to save him from his own self-destructive habits proved an irresistible attraction of which Nick took full advantage and for which he rarely forgave them. He left a trail of damaged lives behind him—not as a seducer, but as a husband, lover and father.

An intelligent observer might have deduced some of this from the films alone. Ray had favored good-looking young men: Farley Granger in *They Live by Night* and John Derek in *Knock on Any Door* and *Run for Cover* were pretty to an extent not plausible in the rough kids they were meant to be playing. Granger was admittedly bisexual; Derek was not. Ray had a good-looking nephew, Sumner Williams, who had roles in six of his pictures. Then, in *Rebel Without a Cause*, Ray made a definitive portrait of immature romantic longing in one young man for another, with his treatment of Plato watching Jim.

How often did Ray's homosexual nature show through? At the University of Chicago, a professor had tried to seduce him, and the two were undressed in a car with Nick not able to come. So he was torn about his split personality—what are such splits for, and what prompts the steady anguish in Ray's films? In *Bitter Victory,* two officers are locked in rivalry, supposedly over the same woman. The two officers (Richard Burton and Curt Jürgens) hate and fear each other, but no one else means as much to them as they do to each other. As the woman they are both supposed to desire, Ruth Roman looks like someone invited to the wrong party. In *Wind Across the Everglades,* a young game warden (Christopher Plummer) is enraptured by the Everglades bandit-monarch (Burl Ives), who slaughters wildlife. The attraction can exist in enmity as easily as in love.

I saw Ray enough at the end of his life to be aware of his contradictions. Time and again, his films oppose a sensitive hero and a circle of male hostility. It's as if he followed that shape without thinking. It was his own story, of course, just as he dramatized the struggle between Hollywood's system and a valiant but disaster-prone maverick or would-be genius. He believed his films were about him, in a way earlier generations would not have dared to think.

Houseman's suggestion and Lambert's personal account appeared in 1983 and 2000, well after Ray's death. In his lifetime Nick Ray was adored by film critics as a heroic figure who made films in which the inner life and existential yearnings were expressed in adventure, action, and what passed for manliness. Jean-Luc Godard, when he still loved American movies, had declared: "And the cinema is Nicholas Ray." Do not doubt the place of hero worship in film criticism, or the way once upon a time, young men felt that François Truffaut looked like them.

Ray made *The Lusty Men* in which Robert Mitchum and Arthur Kennedy play rodeo riders like fraternal rivals. That mood is there in *They Live by Night, Rebel Without a Cause,* and *Bitter Victory,* all of which could be synopsized without any mention of gay feeling but cannot be watched with the same detachment. That leads to an examination of movie subtext or suggestion. Ray was cherished—by Godard and Truffaut in France as much as by Gavin Lambert and *Movie* magazine in Britain. None of those celebrations mentioned the gay instinct, just as Hollywood refused to think its code of male prowess had hidden meanings.

Still, the famously male directors—like Howard Hawks and John Ford—are worth scrutiny. Ford was a stranger and more unsettled man than his films suggest. He was Catholic, yet at twenty-six he married a divorced non-Catholic. He would celebrate male companionship on screen over decades, yet he was famously sadistic toward the men who worked with him and loved him. No one was treated worse than John Wayne.

Ford worships women, mothers, and obedient beauties, but that can be a warning sign. In defending Judge Roy Moore, President Trump told us that "women are very special." That solemn adoration may be a clue to sexual bigotry. Women are not special. They are as ordinary as men. Yet we helplessly agree that they are "beautiful" without applying that word to males.

For decades (prompted by Kieran Hickey) I found some of Ford's studies in male friendship creepy and bogus. I do not admire his cavalry pictures or his code of silent male alliances. Maureen O'Hara (a key Ford actress in five films) was once astonished to find "Jack" kissing a famous male star—it was surely Tyrone Power. An experiment? An escape? A truth? Some Ford enthusiasts say that O'Hara was making mischief because she was jealous of Ford's feeling for Kate Hepburn. Maybe. But perhaps it is time to believe women and to wonder why their testimony is often disparaged.

So many women in Ford films are detached from reality by their special or madonna status. He seldom looks at a woman on screen with desire, yet he eroticizes Wayne's harsh solitude in *The Searchers* and has a taste for whining bullies like Victor McLaglen.

Howard Hawks had several wives and many affairs and was not caught kissing an actor. He was in the habit of using his status as movie director to gather and promote women. There have been directors who feel unfulfilled if they are not in love or in bed with their actresses. But Hawks's case is stranger.

His films cultivate witty and outspoken women—this trend goes from Carole Lombard in *Twentieth Century,* Katharine Hepburn in

Bringing Up Baby, and Rosalind Russell in *His Girl Friday* to Lauren Bacall in *To Have and Have Not,* Joanne Dru in *Red River,* and Angie Dickinson in *Rio Bravo.* These are some of the most piquant, brave, and witty female performances on American film—and in *The Big Sleep,* Hawks throws in women with the energy of a great fielder getting to fly balls. That film has Dorothy Malone in the Acme bookstore, Martha Vickers sliding down the stairs, and Lauren Bacall playing phone-tag—not to mention a handful of eye-catching cabbies, waitresses, and librarians. Wherever he looks, Hawks finds a pretty girl. And yet those "independent" women, with great lines, tour-de-force scenes, and moments where they trash and tame men, all eventually cave in and do as their men want. The insolent Marie in the Martinique of *To Have and Have Not* gives up teasing Harry Morgan, grabs his arm in delight, and shimmies away into the night with her guy, as his doll. That can be read as obedience to Hollywood's business needs, but it is also Hawks's ultimate admission about his own expectations—feelings that were seldom met for long in life. He was an inspired fantasist and no great shakes in bed according to his wife, the real Slim. Many womanizers leave women dissatisfied. They tend to come in their own minds.

Some Hawksians will flinch at this because they have made a cult of guys who can shoot straight, land a plane on a small mountain plateau, and swap lines with articulate women. It is preposterous to suggest that Hawks was gay or that he didn't dote on women. Still, he celebrated the close understanding of men who did business together: the deepest love in *Red River* is between Clift and John Wayne; the comradeship on films like *Air Force* and *Only Angels Have Wings* has an air of how women get in the way. In the paradise jailhouse of *Rio Bravo,* under siege, where the guys sing songs and kick alcohol, they do not invite Angie Dickinson to their house, not even to make a more fragrant stew than Walter Brennan's Stumpy might know about.

The ending of *Red River* is one of the most ambiguous scenes in Hawks's films. As a study in rivalry, the picture deserves a fatal confrontation between Tom Dunson and Matthew Garth—the rancher who abandoned the woman who loved him, and the adopted son. In other words, Tom has had a son by a kind of immaculate conception.

Dunson needs to drive his herd of cattle from Texas to a railhead in Kansas, but it's on that epic journey that he becomes such a tyrant that Garth takes the herd from him, aware that Dunson will follow in implacable pursuit. This tension reaches its climax in the streets of Abilene, where the herd has been delivered to the railway. Dunson arrives; he advances on Garth and challenges him to use his gun; but Garth declines to be so violent.

Hawks was famous as a man's man or a womanizer; Wayne was monumentally straight; Montgomery Clift was gay; Hawks was too astute not to exploit that gulf. So Garth lets himself be beaten at first and only gradually joins in a fistfight. This comes after Dunson has fired at him and nicked his cheek.

As they are wrestling, Garth's girl takes charge and tells the men that anyone can see they love each other. They stop and she storms off. Dunson tells Garth he should marry that girl; Garth frets at being ordered around. He will marry her—he knows it. But the girl does not come back again. The film closes with a fond two-shot of the two men as they plan a new branding iron for their ranch.

Not everyone was happy with that scene. Borden Chase wrote the book for *Red River* and he wanted decisive violence, with Dunson dying in the end. He hated Hawks's revision of his ending and lamented the way the woman taught the men to behave. The argument goes on among Hawksians, but it's hard to deny the gay subtext that Hawks introduced. Only one writer, to my knowledge, got to the heart of the scene. That was Parker Tyler. He was writing about another film, *The Outlaw* (a bizarre Western shot in 1941 but not properly released until 1946), credited to Howard Hughes but actually started by Hawks. It involves a mythic standoff between Billy the Kid and Doc Holliday (two men who never met in life, but life has its shortcomings):

> As the rivals face each other for the duel, and the clock gives the signal to shoot, Billy's guns remain hanging in his holsters. As Doc taunts Billy for cowardice, the former artistically nicks each of his ears with bullets. Psychologically Billy's inert passivity needs explanation; everything, including manly honor, is at stake. Realistically speaking, something *unconscious* must restrain him.

What can this be—if not subconscious homosexuality—but the shadow of the Oedipus guilt falling on the trigger finger?

There are other directors quite able to photograph women and enjoy them. Alfred Hitchcock drew fine work out of many actresses, especially when their characters were being grilled, mistrusted, or put under stress—think of Ingrid Bergman in *Notorious,* succumbing to poisoned coffee and afflicted by Cary Grant's disapproval; of Grace Kelly's boldness taking her up to the Thorwald apartment in *Rear Window* and the dread of being discovered there; and of Janet Leigh in *Psycho,* hounded, stripped, and given the third degree for forty minutes before brief respite leads to slaughter.

At the same time, Hitchcock was very torn over sex, and for decades he was shy of touching the actresses he might ravish with the camera. Along that way, he did a number of films that have a thread of gayness. In *Rope,* John Dall and Farley Granger are brothers in an experimental murder. In *Strangers on a Train* Guy Haines (Granger again) seems heterosexual—his fiancée is Ruth Roman—but he is fascinated by Bruno Anthony (Robert Walker), the least impeded homosexual in a mainstream American movie up until 1951.

Strangers on a Train was a novel by Patricia Highsmith, who is a significant figure in this story. I met her in Toronto in 1992 and was impressed by her gray-rock demeanor, her curious kindness (it declined to be ingratiating), and what felt like a leashed intelligence, as if it frightened her a little.

I asked her what she felt was the best movie version of her work. She did not hesitate: it was Robert Walker as Bruno. But I'm sure Tom Ripley was on her mind, and he is as chilling a figure as Marion Faye in Norman Mailer's novel *The Deer Park. The Talented Mr. Ripley* came from a novel Highsmith published in 1955. That book had been a success, but it was characterized as "a psychological thriller," which does not satisfy its sinister intimations. It was the first of several books that used the character of Tom Ripley as an amoral, indeterminately sexed opportunist, a man who seemed to be writing his life as both a screenplay and a book by Dostoyevsky.

Highsmith felt she could not be open about being a lesbian, so she made Ripley a man—she took the name from the *Ripley's Believe It or Not* cartoon. In her notes for the novel, she liked the idea of his being untrustworthy. He was "a young American, half homosexual . . . a harmless attractive-to-some, repellent-to-others kind of young man, he becomes a murderer, a killer for pleasure . . . he must never be quite queer—merely capable of playing the part."

In the novel, Tom Ripley is an uneasy, impoverished loner hired to look after a wealthy young man named Dickie Greenleaf (that name tells you how good Highsmith is). Dickie's father asks Ripley to bring his son home from the Italian resort town where he is idling his life away and to devote himself to the Greenleaf shipping business.

Ripley makes the trip to Mongibello (an invented place—the movie used Positano). He meets Dickie and Dickie's girlfriend, Marge, and insinuates himself into their lazy, hedonistic life. This troubles Marge because she feels Tom is imitating Dickie and even trying to acquire his personality. She warns Dickie that Tom could be gay. That so disgusts Dickie he dismisses Tom as "a mooche"—whereupon Tom murders Dickie and takes over his life. He begins to pass himself off as Dickie. In the novel, Tom has to ward off the suspicions of Marge and Mr. Greenleaf, of Tom's friend Freddie Miles, and even the police—after Tom has been compelled to murder Freddie. But he manages it all. He comes through, free and rich—he has picked up Greenleaf money. But as the book closes he feels a vague anxiety that will not leave him. He fears exposure. He is perfect yet flawed, a Henry James American in Europe.

I have recounted the plot of the book because Anthony Minghella's film of *The Talented Mr. Ripley* departs from it. Minghella told me he saw the project as the story of a pained, lonely outsider who yearns to be accepted. "Ant" regarded himself as such a figure: he was the son of an ice cream salesman and café proprietor, born and raised in Ryde on the Isle of Wight, a mediocre seaside resort far from the center of British life. He had attended the University of Hull, another outlier to cultural importance. But he had risen by virtue of talent. He was not conventionally handsome, but he was appealing because of his talk and his vision, though I doubt he was ever convinced by that. Filmmakers often fantasize over their films as much as we do.

His movie of the novel has a different ending, and you can say that was Ant's wish to pin down the vague paranoia that is so effective on Highsmith's page. But his change was also an inspired grasping of the novel's gayness. Tom finds another friend, Peter, and he allows this gentle man to feel that Tom is attracted to him. That cunning helps Tom evade how really he might be in love with Peter. This is set against two female characters, Marge (Gwyneth Paltrow) and Meredith (Cate Blanchett), who are more plot functionaries than attractive beings. They are almost overlooked because *The Talented Mr. Ripley* is more interested in male ties.

Thus Jude Law gives his most charismatic performance as Dickie, enough to help us share Tom's infatuation—and to make it clear that, in killing Dickie, Tom (Matt Damon) is beset by conflicted feelings. Equally, Tom kills Freddie—an intimidating bully-boy performance from Philip Seymour Hoffman—and then he kills Peter, who is presented as a passive and uncritical partner for Tom. As if Tom could ever be so calm or happy.

When the film opened, Jude Law won a lot of critical praise for his Dickie. That was deserved, but seeing the film again I am more impressed by Damon's Tom. The actor lost weight for the part so he seems boyish and unreliable. This is a look he initiated as the kid soldier wasted by drugs and deceit in *Courage Under Fire*.

There is a passage in *Ripley* where Tom and Dickie play jazz together on a hot Italian night. They duet on "Tu Vuo' Fa L'Americano" and then Damon croons "My Funny Valentine." It is a love scene cloaked in the doomy spirit of Chet Baker. The sultry rhapsody reminds us of that self-destructive player, once known as the Montgomery Clift of the trumpet before his life collapsed and the teeth fell out of his slack mouth.

The more I looked at *The Talented Mr. Ripley*, the clearer it was that Minghella's own need to be recognized and accepted had meshed with Tom's urge to be an immaculate lost soul. The scenes with Damon and Law are tense with suggestions of appropriation. In the book *Minghella on Minghella*, Ant gives this account of how the production filmed the key scene where Tom murders Dickie on the boat:

There was a wonderful transition to the next scene, for which I had this almost sexual image in mind of Ripley sleeping with Dickie once he's dead. It's as if the only way he can finally embrace Dickie is to kill him first.

Minghella turned the novel from contemplation to pathos. Highsmith does not take sides over Tom Ripley. She observes the murderer and the opportunist as if watching one wild animal prey on others. She does not feel obliged to moralize over the situation. But Minghella made the decision to care for his Tom; instead of settling for scrutiny and coolness, he sees Tom as lonely or needy. He places Matt Damon's character as being in "the most defeating and unendurable prison of being alone with yourself and having to account for yourself and having distanced yourself from any possibility of intimacy."

This had a big impact on marketing the final film. There were disagreements over whether the ending was "right," or useful. As Minghella put it, "I was very aware when . . . we started previewing the film of how uncomfortable the audiences felt with the homoerotic elements of the movie, which for me, were of no consequence whatsoever."

There was a money issue (the film would struggle to get into profit), and Harvey Weinstein was its distributor, taking his usual forceful interest. He sometimes imposed himself on actresses, but he interfered with edits and numbers, too. I think Ant was trying to stress that he was not gay, just as *The Talented Mr. Ripley* was not promoted as a gay picture—like *Brokeback Mountain,* say, the unequivocal story of two male lovers in an unsympathetic world. Ripley was a thriller, its ads proclaimed, but that label was as inadequate as the same word applied to the Highsmith novel. More than a murder story, this is a reflection on loneliness yearning for attention. Minghella was straight, but as he gazed at this story he surely saw the shapes of gay romance.

You can decide that the mainstream of American film concentrated on guys because film stories always tended that way. Brave men faced danger and ordeal and won the women as a reward. Thousands of films follow that pattern, and for decades the screen permitted little more than a heterosexual gaze and a kiss. There are prolonged, symphonic kisses, and Hawks and Hitchcock were virtuosos with that music: think of lingering embraces in *Notorious* and *North by Northwest* that take over the action, or remember Bogart and Bacall getting acquainted. It was not feasible yet for actors and actresses to get naked or down-and-dirty. But the medium could be more seductive because of that restraint. So some great films and directors settled into looking at how men managed together.

No director insisted on daring or independence as much as Orson Welles, who ostentatiously diverged from Hollywood patterns and presented himself as an outsider. He never convinced Hollywood or himself that he was part of its seasoned male club. But he tried. As a young man he had been precocious sexually. He had three wives—one of them, Rita Hayworth, famous as an international love goddess— and he had many affairs, with agile ballerinas as well as with Judy Garland and Lena Horne. Yet the sixteen-year-old Welles—very beautiful, but still baby-faced—got his break in show business by talking his way into the Gate Theatre in Dublin when it was run by two flamboyant queens, Hilton Edwards and Micheál Mac Liammóir. They had been entranced by this looming boy genius and by the lies he uttered with such sincerity. It was the start of a lifelong friendship. Mac Liammóir would later be a superb, insidious Iago to Welles's Othello in a film that is far less interested in its Desdemona. Had something happened there in Dublin? No one is sure.

Even great admirers admit Welles's relative indifference to women in his films. One never feels that the middle-aged Kane has the hots for Susan Alexander (Dorothy Comingore)—it's more that he means to impose her on the world as a singer. In *The Lady from Shanghai,* with Rita Hayworth, and made as their marriage was on the cusp, he is in awe of her iconic status and half afraid of her. There is little sense of warmth or infatuation. In *Touch of Evil,* the camera roams over Janet Leigh in her underwear, but she never gets her honeymoon with Charlton Heston. That film is etched in sexual frustration, as when Tanya (Marlene Dietrich) hardly recognizes her old flame Hank Quinlan (Welles himself dressed up in padding and makeup to be excruciatingly unattractive). Welles had deep divisions in himself, torn between vanity and self-loathing.

By 1960 or so, Welles was very large, and would get fatter still over time; yet he was only forty-five. As the years accumulated, one had to wonder what he did sexually or how he did it. There are ways, of course, but screen heroes have to live by the screen's potential. Jeanne Moreau is briefly naked in *The Immortal Story* and very touching. Welles's own mistress, Oja Kodar, is ogled (too much, I think) in *F for Fake*. The long-unfinished *The Other Side of the Wind* has Welles's most directly erotic and arousing scene—but it seems Kodar directed it, and she is its odalisque. The sequence feels at odds with Welles's own taste, as if he might have withdrawn from it.

Near the end of his life, Welles had a project from his own script, *The Big Brass Ring,* about a homosexual relationship between a promising politician and his elderly mentor. He asked a bunch of stars of 1980 to be in this film and they all turned him down. That may have been because of money and some fear that Welles would never complete the film. But were Beatty, Nicholson, Redford, Burt Reynolds, and Clint Eastwood ready to play a gay man? Or was Welles quite prepared to hint at that part of himself?

It's more instructive to note how steadily his work deals with betrayal between male associates: above all, there's Kane and Leland; George and Eugene in *Ambersons;* Michael O'Hara and Bannister in *The Lady from Shanghai;* Mr. Arkadin and the man he hires to investigate his own past; Othello and Iago; Quinlan and his old sidekick Pete Menzies in *Touch of Evil;* Hal and Falstaff in *Chimes at Midnight.* Those ties and their loss preoccupy Welles. Women are seldom as important. In addition, don't forget Welles and Joseph Cotten (Harry Lime and Holly Martins) in *The Third Man,* or his very fruitful, then violently destroyed, bond with John Houseman. In his memoir, *Run-Through,* Houseman sounds like someone in love with Orson and trying to manage him in the great Mercury years.

Hawks, Ford, Hitchcock, and Welles are dead. So let's wonder about Francis Coppola, Martin Scorsese, and Quentin Tarantino. *The Godfather* and *The Godfather Part II* are seminal films still, not just compelling entertainments (and people watch them regularly over the years), not just seductive indulgence for our secret love of violence and crime, not just the best family films of their time, but tributes to the undying loyalty and reward of male society. Connie is a steadfast family member who learns obedience to the cause. Kay is the one outsider in the films and she could have been an outraged critic of the Corleone way. So she is excluded from the circle as unworthy, and the first film ends on the woeful face of Diane Keaton's Kay being shut out of the room and the world.

The men in the films do not have sex together, though sometimes they're driven to murder (which can be a carnal festival in cinema). But the mood is heavy with the respect or honor they obsess over. Nothing disputes the archaic, sentimental, and horrendous self-attitudinizing of these guys. Fredo (John Cazale) is the one who might be gay—he's a dope with women—but Coppola never wants to go that far. The men kiss Michael's hand, but no other part of him. They would die for one another but generally regard females as offering a hole to screw and a means of securing male heirs. You can say this is Italian, but the code is American and what the kingdom of the movies always wanted. There are entourages in Hollywood still—agents, executives, and lawyers who riff on the lines and the self-importance from *The Godfather* and who keep a restricting gaze on what women can and should do.

Martin Scorsese's high genius lasted just a few years but he is one of the great American directors as well as a model for so many others. Let me dismiss the least chance of innuendo: in about thirty years, Scorsese has had five wives (there have been three children) and there were affairs to go with them, including a hectic romance with Liza Minnelli at the time of *New York, New York,* his most rueful study of the attempt by a man and a woman to be together, also known as marriage.

Marty is not gay, but a homosexual sensibility or acuity seeps through his work because his men are more interested in each other than they ever manage to be with women. This amounts to a passion, and it is the only thing with a chance of overcoming the existential solitude that is the moral weather in his films. It is also preoccupied with violence, as if that could smother uncertainty. In the ritualist *The Departed,* male associates compete to off one another. The first gang came with *Mean*

Streets, a film that has a wounded madonna (she is epileptic) who is
no match for the men who are in peril of betraying one another. The
rapport in that film between Harvey Keitel and Robert De Niro led
to *Taxi Driver* (written by Paul Schrader), in which the chronic isolation of Travis Bickle makes him desperate to gain an unsuitable girlfriend (Cybill Shepherd) before settling on a fanciful effort to save a
child whore/madonna (Jodie Foster). She is Travis's ideal because her
innocence keeps her out of reach. Travis would sooner exist in helpless
incoherence with guys or turn upon them in slaughter. The violence in
Scorsese (and it applies to other directors of his era) is a substitute for
the impossible sexual attraction that cannot be owned up to.

Scorsese is too self-aware not to recognize this obsessiveness, even if
he worships obsession. So there are a few films in which he strives to
lean the other way: *Alice Doesn't Live Here Anymore* is a gesture to fem-
inism for which Ellen Burstyn won an Oscar. In *The Age of Innocence,*
Scorsese honors Edith Wharton by showing two women in a romantic triangle, but their situation does not spring to life. In *The Departed,*
Vera Farmiga is inserted like a bay leaf in the male stew playing an
unlikely shrink who is trying to diagnose and heal male fury (like a
good professional, she has sex with two of her patients).

There is only one woman in Scorsese's work who struts like the men
and who is radiant with gangster panache and sly sex: that's Ginger
(Sharon Stone) in *Casino.* She is a wanton, an utter and proud loner,
the embodiment of greed who defeats her husband (De Niro) in every
aspect: she cuckolds him, she ruins his business and steals his money,
she smashes up his car, and she obliterates his sense of order. She makes
Casino Scorsese's late masterpiece. Nowhere else has he accorded a
woman his highest tribute: she can be self-destructive—and make that
a dance like LaMotta in the ring. The pensive and calculating De Niro
gazes at her with envy and bitterness in *Casino;* the result is a triumph
and an unexpected comedy, which is not Scorsese's habit.

Another seething layer of *Casino* is the rivalry between Ace and
Nicky (De Niro and Joe Pesci). Like Ginger, Nicky undermines Ace's
smooth game in Las Vegas; he is the dark id that will not let the ego
live in peace. This is the third part of the De Niro–Pesci triptych that

started with them playing brothers in *Raging Bull* and carried on as two of the *GoodFellas*. It is also the most frightening and hilarious, for *Casino* is *The Odd Couple* fought to the death.

For Scorsese, Pesci is the demon outlaw, a fearsome, unpredictable force of danger—the way he exults in going over the top in *GoodFellas* is the scary engine of that film. His temper is never under control. He is capable of shooting the toes off an onlooker for sport or on an impulse to scorn boredom. Yet in *Raging Bull* he is the mere and humble brother, the second to Jake LaMotta, the groomsman to the bull. He is an adoring figure who has to be repudiated, exiled, and cast into the horror of separated brotherhood.

Jake has two wives in that film, and the second—the iconic Vickie (played by Cathy Moriarty)—is the closest Scorsese ever let himself come to direct sexuality, as a folksy, dumb blonde in burning white who goads and torments the bull's erection as he contemplates having her while desperate to harbor his strength and bodily fluids in training. Their scenes together are poignant yet filled with a horror at eroticism (Scorsese was once set to be a priest, and in *Silence* he concentrated on two Jesuits). These scenes are vital to explaining the thrall of conspiracy that hangs over the film.

LaMotta is a champion and a man who will not go down. But his valor and his prowess are sapped by the coterie of scumbags and neo-gangsters (the stealthiest of gangs), the guys who watch over his career and fix a fight here or there, betrayers of his integrity. He is a bull, but he is afraid he may be a steer.

As led by Nicholas Colasanto and Frank Vincent (a recurring face in Scorsese's world—knowing, treacherous, pulpy, and insidious), these boys constitute an ultramale underworld (they seldom keep women around worth speaking to) who idolize Jake yet seek to ruin him. They support the fight with Tony Janiro, a pretty-boy fighter and an opponent Jake deliberately disfigures in a warped need to deny attraction. "I don't know whether to fight him or fuck him," he says. *Raging Bull* is a movie of genius and is more fascinated by gay iconography than the films of Warhol, Pasolini, or Almodóvar, because Scorsese feels it is taboo. Together, Jake LaMotta and Michael Corleone make a male assertion that has been central and problematic in American cinema:

Women? Who needs them? Who trusts them? So screw them! (As a description of sex, "screw"—with its suggestions of fraud and actually impaling someone—is full of hostility.)

Quentin Tarantino is the emblematic example of the smart macho kid who has been raised on a legend of male-oriented films and who constantly turns to the grail of a group of wild guys who use women, with warmth sometimes, but rather in the way they would handle guns. You hold it, you aim it, you pull the trigger. Then you dump it—the way Michael Corleone discards his gun at the Italian restaurant after he has executed Sollozzo and McCluskey.

There are vivid women in Tarantino's work: the snarly, aggrieved Amanda Plummer in *Pulp Fiction,* the very competent Pam Greer in *Jackie Brown,* Melanie Laurent in *Inglourious Basterds.* But there are cuties who are window dressing, crazed tomboys, or punching bags—Uma Thurman in the *Kill Bill* pictures (and in *Pulp Fiction*), Jennifer Jason Leigh in *The Hateful Eight.* Nothing challenges the orthodoxy of male intelligence or attitudinizing. The core Tarantino film is still *Reservoir Dogs,* his first, where the world is only guys, given the names of the spectrum (Mr. Pink—the hangdog Steve Buscemi—thinks his title is horribly unfair). Those men grind on each other and are forever poised in diagram compositions of several males all pointing their guns at one another. Tarantino might dismiss this inner meaning spelled out. But he is limited as an artist by his gridlock of males trying to stare each other down. In 2018 he admitted that he had known too much about Harvey Weinstein to have stayed silent (and Harvey was his patron for two decades).

These brief career estimates cover much of the best of American cinema—and they remind us of how steadily the glory of such pictures longs to transcend the plain reality of life in America. So why should a talent like Scorsese stay infatuated with a dream of gangsters? And how can we now fail to see that the same fantasy has inflated Donald Trump?

14

Perverse

Rita Hayworth and George Macready posing on the set of *Gilda* (1946).
Sometimes a production still will alert you to a scene that is missing from a film.

DOES IT EVER OCCUR TO US that men and women need to dislike each other? Is their bond locked up in the atmosphere of contest? Does the mythic embrace we aspire to sometimes resemble wrestling? Were decades of pursued screen happiness as oppressive as TV commercials that promise everything will be all right if we just purchase this product or that? Was there a premonition that love doesn't last, so blow on its embers of hostility and regret?

In their golden age, only a few movies could be so perverse as to nurture that antagonism. Cary Grant seemed a nice guy until you felt his cold malice in *Suspicion* and even in *His Girl Friday,* a worthy contender for the best film ever made. It earned not a single nomination in 1941, but you cannot trust the Academy: in the space of a few years, *The Shop Around the Corner, His Girl Friday,* and *The Lady Eve* earned just one Oscar nomination among them (original story on *Eve*), while pompous fluff like *How Green Was My Valley* and *Mrs. Miniver* carried off Best Picture and enough nominations for bowling allies. *Mrs. Miniver* had ten nominations and six wins; *Valley* had ten nominations and three wins.

Mrs. Miniver claimed to be addressing "the war." It was said the film made people eager to join that cause. Were we really such idiots? A better tribute to that Hollywood is how often it preferred to follow the lasting war, the one between the sexes. Walter (Cary Grant) in *His Girl Friday* is the editor of a big-city newspaper. Hildy (Rosalind Russell) was his star reporter. They were also married once, and I daresay some observers gossiped about Hildy having slept with Walter to get better assignments. Why not? The danger to marriage is less infidelity than boredom. Somehow we have to sustain the hope that we're sleeping with a stranger—with still more to come.

In *His Girl Friday* Walter and Hildy are divorced at the outset. It's easy to imagine why: Walter is a self-confessed stinker. Like his creator, Howard Hawks, he may have eyed copy girls, stenographers, and waitresses. Perhaps he screwed some of them—nothing personal—when he had twenty minutes. Far graver, he had the habit of ordering Hildy around, talking her down, and taking the air she needed to breathe. Until she'd had enough and opted out. Then a freed Hildy took up with Bruce, an insurance man (from Albany!) who lived with his mother. She needs her mind tested, but she thinks she wants a decent, dull guy—even the stooge that Ralph Bellamy generously provides as Bruce.

When Walter hears about this, he kicks into higher gear. It's not that he's in love with Hildy or that he falls for her again. It's that he can't bear to be bested in a contest; he won't risk failure or stability—so many men in movies are warped by that perseverance. And he and Hildy do function together at newspapering like a great double-play team. Doing the job is their honeymoon.

There was a further level of sublime aberration in *His Girl Friday*. It had turned its own origins inside out. For it had started life as a play, *The Front Page*, written by Ben Hecht and Charles MacArthur, that was a hit in 1928. At that time, Hildy and Walter had both been men, played by Lee Tracy and Osgood Perkins on stage, and then by Pat O'Brien and Adolphe Menjou in the rather tame 1931 picture.

But it was the restless Hawks who had wondered, why not make Hildy a woman—and Walter's ex-wife. One evening, he set up a reading of the play: he had "a girl who was there" to read Hildy while he played Walter himself. "My Lord," he realized, "it's better with a girl reading it than the way it was." This was the difference between routine aplomb and genius, but who was that "girl"? It could have been Nancy Gross, the "Slim"-to-be, who had caught Howard's eye and ear in 1938.

In all the film's comic furore, is Rosalind Russell quite "attractive"? I hope her ghost can forgive this: she was good-looking, smart, quick, funny, and easily amused; she had so much, except that I never want to go for her. And we are talking about a Howard Hawks picture from 1941 when he was at his seductive height, with his new wife, a famous beauty and wit twenty years his junior. Howard was as much a model for what Hollywood guys wanted to be as Michael Corleone would become thirty years later.

Russell has a bourgeois, common-sense edge—she seems as if born married. Slim was always free or wild. Russell also has a brisk, sensible superiority to the film's latent voyeurism. Her Hildy truly wants to get up to Albany, have dogs and children, and make chicken pot pie for Bruce. Walter will rescue her from that in what Stanley Cavell called a comedy of remarriage—and a sublimely frenzied movie. It is also an unimpeded enactment of male supremacy. Hildy and Walter will remarry, but then soon enough he'll flirt with a masseuse and ask for a little more private work on his tight shoulders. The dance will begin again: separation and divorce seem vital if wooing and remarriage are to stay vibrant. Hildy *is* his Girl Friday—a second-class citizen.

Are we even sure that Walter likes Hildy—or notices her? He enjoys scooping rival newspapers with her; he admires her skills and her wit—that's why he wisecracks for her, though that often entails oblique disparagement. Does he actually desire her, for her sake? Or does he hate the thought of losing her? This odd detachment has to do with her respectability, and his wry distancing—or with the gay side in Grant. But the best chance desire can hope for is being thwarted, divorced, and disdained. Those things are its oxygen.

If 1940–41 was Hollywood's peak (it had many glories), was it because a film exploded the homilies of romance in favor of flirtation and the joyful cynicism of journalism without much faith in its supposed grail, the Truth? *His Girl Friday* taunts that ideal, just as it elevates love and sex in brilliant, frenzied laughter. If the screen will turn actual sexual congress into a laborious sham, then perhaps conversation is as hot as we will ever get? This brings to mind the razor-fight sexual talk in *Closer* (a Patrick Marber play that Mike Nichols filmed in 2004). That film has a scene between Clive Owen and Julia Roberts, talking about sex, that is more woundingly erotic than a hundred *Pretty Women*.

Such thoughts gathered after the revelations and accusations in the fall of 2017 that a range of men from Harvey Weinstein to James Toback were behaving badly or as if they hated women. They were using their status as gatekeepers to the screen to take advantage of female supplicants. Toback was said to have approached strangers on the street and suggested they might be in a movie. Some of those women responded, despite being comfortable enough in finance, medicine, engineering, or unemployment, because they nursed an irrational desire about being discovered for a picture that presumably came from a lifetime in that fraudulent culture.

I do not question the charges brought against Weinstein and others or dispute those men's brutality. But these offenses were not new. Since it began, the movie business was founded on men being superior voyeurs who cast women. That tradition covers Griffith, Chaplin, Sternberg, Hitchcock, and Hawks—among others. The profession and the art systematized sexual exploitation in which women bartered their bodies and their intimacy for a chance to be on screen.

Don't just blame the businessmen. Males in the dark in movie theaters were spying on women in a similar way and enlisting them in their fantasies. It was a licensed promiscuity with new skin every week. If you are shy of listing your names, I'll offer mine: Yvonne De Carlo, Rhonda Fleming, Maureen O'Hara, Linda Darnell, Jean Simmons, Donna Reed, Elizabeth Taylor, Kim Novak, Grace Kelly. I cut out their pictures and masturbated over them. I don't think I was alone, though there was a feeling of loneliness. The movies persuaded me that desire required secrecy.

There is no defense for the behavior of Weinstein et al., but there can be regret over denial of their work. Louis C.K. confessed to his sins, and lost every contract overnight. He deserved rebuke, but his last film, *I Love You, Daddy,* which was withdrawn, is appealing just because it is voluntarily self-destructive, from a man confused over his own sexual feelings. Toback's film *The Private Life of a Modern Woman* may not be released, and that will deprive us of Charles Grodin's moving performance. As a predatory homosexual, Kevin Spacey was erased from *All the Money in the World,* yet the trailer suggested that his brief appearance might be among his most impressive performances. Spacey has been extraordinary: he has two Oscars and many other awards. He dominated a hit series for Netflix, *House of Cards.* He was not the first fine actor you wouldn't want to share an elevator with.

Will Harvey Weinstein be punished? Will a vigilante mood wreak havoc with his backlist? Are we at risk of seeing no more of *My Week with Marilyn, The Reader, Gangs of New York, The English Patient, Pulp Fiction, sex, lies and videotape, The Crying Game,* or *Scandal*? Those are films he "saved" or enabled; they are adventurous entertainment; and they are all "sexy" from a time when that was still a come-on for audiences. Are we ready to abandon movies that urge us to be sexy? Is that day coming?

Will the film business acquire decency if every sensible reform and legal safeguard is imposed? Will it alter if women achieve a fair stake as camera people, directors, company executives, and studio owners? It's pretty to think so, but movies have a poor track record at being fair and decent. Too much about the medium depends on the inequality of dark and light, of display and voyeurism.

The presentation of the Golden Globes in January 2018 had heartfelt speeches by women protesting exploitation. There was applause and plainly some comfort. But no one quite noticed that the telecast included a lavish promotion for *Fifty Shades Freed* as well as many ads trading on the beauty, the half-dressed allure, and the desirability of women. The reformist drive needs to go further than it has thought of yet—it may need to rid our airwaves of advertising. That is said to be impossible, but the possibility is worth pursuing. After all, no one likes advertising, and many of us feel it has corrupted imagery, discourse, and television itself.

I have trouble believing in a sanitized picture business. Moreover, for the better part of two decades already erotic excitement has been ebbing out of mainstream American movies, a sign that the old thrill may be going stale—a natural evolution in which we are less impressed by sexual bliss than we were a hundred years ago, and more alert to hostility between the sexes. There have been habits in our history that had to be eliminated, like slavery, and film fans should not close their eyes to a kind of slavery in cinema, its way of shaping social expectations. Can voyeurism go to rehab? Or is it intrinsically unfair and shadowed now by the cultural force of pornography?

Porn is full of male hatred of women, and it intimidates the mainstream attempt to convey sexual experience. Something like Jane Campion's *In the Cut* is very brave (it was widely abused). It includes female nudity and abandon (it is Meg Ryan's triumph) and even a glimpse of the honorable cock of Mark Ruffalo. But it does not attempt steady sexual intercourse between the characters played by Ryan and Ruffalo because . . . well, because it would seem improper to ask movie stars to do that, to do *it,* and because such a film would never get a rating or do business (competing with all the porn where pretty people do what they do in anonymity). In pornography there is often a fascination with the perverse: not just "abnormal" sexual pairings or orgiastic situations; not just bestiality or even snuff; but the implicit awareness of men dominating women and listening for their pain or servitude to register. It is a masturbatory code, ingratiating itself with many male customers. There are porn actresses who could not carry a line but have an interminable repertoire of moans and screams.

"Perverse" sounds like a warning; it suggests the willful departure from good norms. Take care with that thinking. Watching characters who do not know they are being watched is itself a kind of perversity, and it's in the essence of moviegoing. Perversity, and a hatred it masks, have been going on for a long time.

Decades after they were made, some films are hard to explain. It's as if Hollywood assumed it could do anything and did not need to think ahead. So how did *Gilda* (1946) arise in the postwar euphoria? That year, the real Rita Hayworth was upset when her name and picture were put on an atom bomb being tested at Bikini Atoll in the Pacific. But she was a publicity bombshell and thriving on it in our innocent imagination.

Gilda is set in Buenos Aires, where the shabby gambler Johnny Farrell (Glenn Ford) is saved from a vengeful gang by Ballin Mundson (George Macready), a supercilious gentleman who carries a sword stick and has a flashy scar on his cheek. An unlikely friendship develops, like a gay sophisticate picking up rough trade on the street. They have an unspecified bond, in which Johnny works at Ballin's casino. Then Mundson goes off on a trip, leaving Johnny to run the place. As Ballin returns, Johnny is deeply moved and anticipatory—it's startling to see the look of joy on Ford's drab face. But he is soon cast down, for Ballin has a new wife, Gilda (Hayworth), ravishing and flagrant in black-and-white, and like a new sword stick to prick at Johnny. Johnny and Gilda were once lovers; that ended badly and now they fall into mutual contempt, in the course of which Gilda does a taunting song, "Put the Blame on Mame," easily read as an attack on Johnny's compromised manhood.

Gilda has a happy ending, but I cannot remember it. In my mind, the film stays a scathing portrait of dislike between two movie-star leads, with the undercurrent of a ménage à trois that dare not speak its name. Does Johnny want Gilda or Ballin? That question is the more intriguing because Glenn Ford was generally a no-nonsense, second-grade icon, steady and passively upright; but in *Gilda* he is down-at-heel, furtive—it's as if the part was only half-written and left to the actor's sleaze factor.

Who made this film or felt its toxic edge? Ford and Hayworth were straight. So was director Charles Vidor and the boss at Columbia, Harry Cohn. But the film was produced and largely written by Virginia Van Upp—she was close to Hayworth and married, but did she have a gay edge? Was Macready gay? He is in the line of Clifton Webb in *Laura,* stingingly eloquent and brined in disdain. Macready was married with children, but he was a partner with Vincent Price in an art gallery in Beverly Hills, and Price was bisexual.

It is glaring and modern now, but in 1946 no one mentioned the gay subtext. They referred to *Gilda* as a good, sexy thriller, as if Rita's voluptuousness solved everything else. Some movies are made in a code that no one seeks to explore. Film seems full of show-and-tell, but mystery thrives there too and lasts better than obvious things. Perversity is in the bogus Buenos Aires light. Mundson says, "Hate is a very exciting emotion. Hate is the only thing that ever warmed me." A coyote is roaming through the film.

Is that point about Rita Hayworth and the bomb simply incidental? Or was there something in the postwar mood that helped explain the buried unease in *Gilda?* It was a heady time, if that's what you wanted to think. The war was won, America was the world's champ, and audiences went to the movies in record numbers. But two experimental shots had been injected into that cheery bloodstream, call them Auschwitz and Hiroshima, and there was a new ambivalent alertness over sex. Wars spur faithlessness and endorse power. Torture was in the air. The song in *Gilda,* "Put the Blame on Mame," is no masterwork, but it has a striking idea. The beautiful woman singing the song (it was Anita Ellis's voice—Rita was not a singer) volunteers for the blame. What blame? Anything you can think of, when the "you" is "us" out there gazing at dames and ready to put them down—or worse. The song refers to the San Francisco earthquake of 1906, and talks about Mother Nature being responsible for it. But the singer—isn't she Mame?—knows better:

> One night she started to shimmy-shake
> That brought on the Frisco quake.

In other words, is a woman's sexual disturbance, her orgasm (not widely recognized in 1946), a source of mayhem in the world, for which women, even beauties, need to take the blame? The silly lyric hints at the anima as a vengeful force that becomes more and more suggestive in films. Do men envy the female orgasm because it seems unhindered and emotional?

Meg Ryan was a rom-com favorite in the anodyne *Sleepless in Seattle* and *You've Got Mail* and was then mocked for the naked feeling of *In the Cut*. But perversity is a liquid that slips beneath closed doors. The femme fatale seemed to be a stock character once, dangerous for eighty minutes and killed off in the last ten. But some films discarded that safety net. In Joseph Losey's *Eva*—a signal box-office failure—Jeanne Moreau is imperiously erotic and a harsh monster. She overrides and ruins her male target, Stanley Baker, as a dishonest writer and a feeble man. And she is not punished.

Elsewhere, in Truffaut's neglected *Mississippi Mermaid*, male desire is turned into a fatal theorem of submission. Jean-Paul Belmondo is a wealthy tobacco farmer on the island of Réunion (in the Indian Ocean, east of Madagascar). Lonesome, he writes away for a mail-order bride. He corresponds with a woman who will fill that role: she seems decent and plain-looking. But when he goes to the harbor to meet her, she has become Catherine Deneuve. He ignores this disparity, she is so perfectly desirable.

They marry; they have an idyll; but she flees by boat with most of his money. He pursues her in vengeance and hires a private detective to help. Then he finds her as a cabaret singer in France, in Antibes. She begs forgiveness and tells a tall story about what life did to her. He buys it (Belmondo is so dry there is no hint that he believes it). They are reunited. But the detective appears—so Belmondo murders him. We suddenly realize how *amour* has turned *fou*.

Then the couple retreat into a wintry countryside and privation. Their money is ebbing away. They are in a hut in the snow, and he suspects she is poisoning him. He tells her he knows what she's doing, and she breaks down. Oh no, she cries, I love you. It is all he needs to hear or can tolerate. The film ends leaving us to wonder about their fate. Desire feeds on dissatisfaction and anxiety.

Cultural authorities tend to pigeonhole deranged or unwholesome obsessions like *l'amour fou,* and that can comfort Americans into thinking such pacts are foreign. But *Eve* was made by an exiled American, and *Mississippi Mermaid* comes from a novel, *Waltz into Darkness* (1947), by America's William Irish, a poet of perversity, a fearful homosexual, and a mama's boy who had little to live for once she died. It can seem un-American to say this, but our greatest nation's view of sex is often crippled.

Mulholland Dr. (for drive and dream) is by David Lynch, who has scant faith in straight-marriage or happy-ending insurance schemes. *Mulholland* is a warped fable about Hollywood and a sweet blonde, Betty, who comes to L.A. from an Albany-like hinterland to be the next Harlow or Monroe. She meets Rita, a sultry brunette amnesiac who has lifted her name from a poster for *Gilda*. The men in the film are all sketchy, dishonest, or loathsome—it's as if the kid in Lynch feels threatened by men. So the erotic heart of the film—and Lynch breathes furtive anticipation like a boy edging into the dark—fixes on Naomi Watts and Laura Elena Harring, movie dolls of standard American manufacture. (Harring was a former Miss USA who had been married to the great-great-grandson of Bismarck; this is not made up.)

Born in 1946, Lynch was raised in the last age of movie dolls, and he tends to see women as nice girls or disguised whores. He is not gay, but in *Mulholland* he is more interested in watching two beautiful women get it on than in bothering to show heterosexual sex. He believes in perversity to a point where it becomes normal. That paradox comes directly from surrealism, but *Mulholland Dr.* trusts an old movie principle, that watching sex can be nicer or less fatiguing than doing it. So in *Blue Velvet* there was a persistent feeling that we should be asked to see such things.

Louis Malle's *Damage* (1992) turns on a disastrous pact of self-destruction. This is taken from a Josephine Hart novel adapted for the screen by David Hare. Stephen (Jeremy Irons) is a government minister with an apparently happy family. He seems warm, rational, and benign (like the kind of person we try to be), but he is poised for madness and so he notices Anna (Juliette Binoche), girlfriend to his grown son. She is driven by a compulsion in which she seems to have no will or interest—she is a little like Charlotte Rampling in *The Night Porter*. When we watch their "illicit" coupling we are voyeurs who always want more; movies steadily undermine our moral strength. Do we want these people to be saved—to put on their clothes and stop doing it? I don't think so. Voyeurism is a fatalistic or doomed preoccupation. As moviegoers we would be let down if the couple acted sensibly. We are always eager to see disaster. The film's title has no doubt or room for hope.

David Hare recalls that "Binoche found playing the part of Anna extremely difficult because she wanted a psychological explanation for her behavior, and of course there is none, or none that's readily available in a self-help manual. Her basic point was that you can write a person as a mystery, but it's very hard for an actor to play one. . . . Anna is both hooked on sexual love and aware, from her past, of its deep, deep dangers."

We feel a shadow of cultural betrayal—that romance was a perverse trick—and it weighs heavily on filmmakers just because the movies were such ads for the pursuit of happiness. Anna tells Stephen that her brother committed suicide rather than yield to an incestuous relationship with her. This young woman is like the mythological Lilith, a passive force who believes love always leads to damage. Nothing less than the hopes for humanism are being threatened here in a story of emotional apocalypse. The Irons character loses his lofty position in government, his marriage, his son, his lover, and his self-respect. But that fragile dignity can be the first casualty in overwhelming passion.

These are films where the female is untrustworthy, dangerous, or even nihilistic. You could say the women are alienated from discourse with males; and that reflects a widespread female frustration in society. Be prepared for more of these fathomless, vengeful women on screen—take a second look at Isabelle Huppert in Michael Haneke's *The Piano Teacher,* an exemplary but cruel teacher and a frozen presence in whom sexual perversion struggles with exquisite music.

Some men may feel harassed by these blank-faced angels. But be assured, fellows, there are far more films in which men visit serial malice on women. That is the slasher genre after relaxed censorship encouraged violence (and aggression toward women) more than any chance of women's pleasure. Much of that was commercially stimulated by *Psycho*'s hounding and slaughtering of Janet Leigh—it was a film about her bra and a knife. That seemed to liberate Hitchcock from being a repressed watcher. It was soon after the success of *Psycho* that he physically urged himself on Tippi Hedren. But his urge had been clear a few years earlier, in *Vertigo:* Hitchcock was afraid of women enough to kill them, not once but twice.

The cinema has had a habit of adoring women before ripping them apart that comes from our ill-deserved safety in the dark and our urge to support male characters who may be in need of therapy. In *Vertigo,* at the age of fifty, James Stewart's Scottie seems virginal or untouched. Has this ex-cop known any women before? Has he slept with Midge (Barbara Bel Geddes), his dogged and fond friend? It doesn't feel like it. So Midge's work designing brassieres is a surreal comment on his innocence. Does he then see Madeleine (Kim Novak), the incarnation of voyeurist desire, as the first woman on his island? From the outset, Scottie is a deep stairwell of self-pity.

There is a tender edge of frustration or perversion in Hitchcock. Norman Bates seems like the kindest person in his film, and Hitchcock chose the gay Anthony Perkins to play him—the first casting decision on the picture. In *Rebecca* . . . there is no Rebecca! In *Vertigo* there is one Novak too many. In *Suspicion,* we await a murder, only to be denied. Think of Robert Donat and Madeleine Carroll handcuffed together in *The 39 Steps.* (This woman does not exist in the John Buchan novel.) In that enforced proximity, his hands come so close to her erotic zones. But how can a man and a woman handcuffed make love without feeling crippled? In *Rear Window,* the Stewart character lusts after Grace Kelly's character, but he is encumbered by the derisory hard-on of his vast plaster cast. In *Marnie,* the man has to rape his wife. In *Notorious* and *North by Northwest* there are rapturous kissing scenes that precede the man's fear of being betrayed. Is it possible that Roger and Eve in the latter will ever find a settled life to match the erotic interaction of their talk on the train? Do lovers need to keep remeeting instead of going steady? Hitchcock was both prurient and guilty: that tension seldom leaves him and it directed his personal life.

Like any voyeur Hitchcock knew that looking is the most ardent male condition—yet he understood that it depends on never being satisfied. It was his blessing that he was usually restrained by censorship. The one time he was in the clear, on *Frenzy* (1972), he made a hash of its big sexual scenes. But Hitchcock still haunts male-gaze cinema, thirty-eight years after his death. He looks at women as lovely slaves in his harem; he can be cruel with them, but he knows watching is its own prison.

Does that help explain the difficulty we have now in making (or watching) great love stories? Younger audiences are reluctant to commit to old-fashioned romances, and that may be because actual sexual release is so much more available in their lives than it was in the 1940s and 1950s. So movie romance has to adjust—and it needs to abandon the hysterical male pact in films as good as David Fincher's *Fight Club,* where a wrecked but sexual woman (Helena Bonham Carter) provides uncritical rag-doll comfort for the guys. It's time to forgo films in which men abuse women, take them for granted, and keep them around as wasted Girl Fridays. That funny phrase does not conceal its slavery.

Phantom Thread (2017) shows a way ahead, as one of the most absorbing perverse love stories ever put on screen. It is possible that some people who saw the film and felt lost with it may be surprised to hear it talked about as a love story where eroticism is spurred by 1950s restrictions.

Phantom Thread concerns an esteemed society couturier in London of the early 1950s: he is Reynolds Woodcock, and he is Daniel

Day-Lewis—the mastery of the actor is inseparable from Woodcock's obsession with perfection as a dressmaker. He lives guarded by his sister Cyril (Lesley Manville), not creative, but an indefatigable manager without any apparent life of her own. Then at a country hotel, while ordering a sumptuous breakfast, Reynolds meets Alma (Vicky Krieps), who takes his order, feels an immediate rapport with him, and will agree to be his muse and companion while beginning a campaign in which she resists the ordering of this immaculate authority figure.

Do they have sex? It is implied that Woodcock has had a line of female models whom he dresses for shows and undresses for himself. One by one, Cyril gets rid of these women as he tires of them. He is not so far from a movie mogul of the 1950s, giving a chance to waiting women and using them for pleasure. They are vital to his work, and he is a predator. But Paul Thomas Anderson films *Phantom Thread* in an arousingly chaste manner. Woodcock puts clothes on Alma; he takes great pains in measuring her for dressmaking, finding that she has meager breasts, though her nipples are prominent beneath her silk slip. They do go giggling into Reynolds's bedroom sometimes, but the film shows no lovemaking, as if Anderson has grown weary of erotic cinema or because he seeks something deeper. This couple do not sleep together, but they are in a shared dream.

At the end of the picture there is a flash-forward in Alma's voice in which it is suggested that the couple have had a child. But the pram being walked is never revealed as containing a real baby. It is possible to watch the film while believing the pram is empty. After all, Reynolds and Alma are each other's child and each other's parent. The movies have always been a medium for adolescents—at seventy-seven, I admit it. Any air of shame would be mere acting.

What interests Anderson is the struggle between the characters. Alma is so much younger and more naive than Reynolds. She stumbles when she first meets him, suggesting a physical awkwardness that is far from Reynolds's insistent grace. But Alma has a maternal wisdom that surpasses education or experience. She looks at Reynolds and tells him not to get into a staring match with her because he'll lose. That spine of resistance begins to nag at the master. He is horrified at her disobedience and the noise she makes with her toast at breakfast. She is a disturbance in his life that he never anticipated. He complains about her, but she only smiles at this and abides.

She has mischief in her along with saintliness. She becomes like a lost princess (or a novice witch) as if protected by some magical rite. But she has to school the selfish loneliness in Reynolds, his silly habit of having things his own way and making them fusspot perfect. To do that she has to checkmate Cyril and then, finally, she cooks for Woodcock and . . .

I won't say what follows, so you should see the film and let its story work. But the movie develops into a trial of arms as demanding as, say, the epic battles in *El Cid* or your favorite film about men in armor with swords the size of dreams. Movies tend to worship artists, but here is an ironic exposé of creative self-absorption.

Phantom Thread is one of those films—there will be many more—in which a woman has to be perverse to show a man how to behave. It seems parochial—London in the 1950s, with antique dresses, two sacred, hideaway houses, and a cult of protocol—but it is the most radical and acidic love story made so far in the twenty-first century.

The scheme of our happy endings was for blessed couples coming together at last, ready to go home and to purchase the inventory of American goods. It was as TV took over from movies that we had to see our narratives embedded in economic plans. But the children of advertising are never satisfied. It's in their bitterness that perversity looms as something mercifully un-American.

15

Burning Man

James Toback and the Eiffel Tower during the shooting of *Exposed* (1983)

JUST A FEW MONTHS BEFORE *Phantom Thread* opened, on Sunday, October 22, 2017, I was working on this book and so I didn't discover until the next day that the *Los Angeles Times* had run a story claiming that James Toback—one of my best friends—had sexually harassed or inappropriately approached thirty-eight women with suggestions that he might put them in a movie in return for sexual favors. Within forty-eight hours that figure had reached more than two hundred. Jim had never been as famous before.

I began to see how a book originally aiming to be an account of gayness in movies had to lead to something larger and more threatening. This might be a book to undermine the most fearsome Kong on Skull or Manhattan islands—the legend of American male supremacy.

I first encountered Jim in March 1978. I was teaching film at Dartmouth College in New Hampshire, but I was also film critic for the *Real Paper* in Boston. Those two jobs were not as compatible as they might have seemed: they required a two-and-a-half-hour drive from Hanover, New Hampshire, to Boston that could be very testing in winter, a season that might last from late October to early May. So watching films became caught up with mad driving. Sometimes I would drive down with Lucy, my lover (she is the author's wife now). We saw a film; grabbed something to eat; then we drove back north and I wrote a review in the car that Lucy would phone in to the paper (to Pat McGilligan, the arts editor) the next morning while I tried to teach Orson Welles or whatever. The car and the phone were about as far as technology had gotten then.

But it was on a Saturday morning that we drove down to see *Fingers,* the first film made by James Toback. A friend had told me it was unusual, scary, and very sexual. Ever since *Psycho,* that combination had been respectable for serious film commentary. I believe now as I said then in the *Real Paper* that *Fingers* was one of the great debuts in American film. Like most movies, it did its helpless best to claim reality, but it was a psychic fable about origins warping maturity, and about an existential ego in panic over its confusion. It seemed to take place in Manhattan, but it was actually Metropolis.

Jimmy Angelelli (Harvey Keitel) is an enforcer for his racketeer father (Michael V. Gazzo). Yet he is an aspiring concert pianist, too. That impossible or abstract clash of ambitions is spelled out in his parents: the rowdy, Italian, rascal gangster lit up by Gazzo's bravura sleaze; and the austere, forbidding, and insane Jewish mother, played by Marian Seldes. (These parents never appear together in the film—they could not exist in the same frame.) Jimmy is the child made out of their war, torn by contrary personalities but held in place by fairy-tale certainty. He is as addicted to "Summertime, Summertime" by the Jamies as he is to Bach's Toccata in E Minor. We know, and he knows, that he will fail, and that explains the dread that hangs over Keitel's pale anguish.

Jimmy sees a girl on the street, Carol (Tisa Farrow), and he wants her in a complete yet impersonal way. She is wan, undecided, and she acts "desirable" in the meek way of so many female characters in films. She is a slave to Dreems, a commanding or mythic black figure (played by former football hero Jim Brown). Jimmy is also made anxious when three gay men in a restaurant seem to be watching him and gossiping about him in a knowing way. They are from his nearly smothered subconscious.

His attempt to audition at Carnegie Hall, to win Carol or to have her, to survive the intimidating menace of Dreems, while also being the agent of his father's racketeering, lead to appalling violence. This is a deeply disturbing film coming from a cultivated mind determined to surrender to the compulsions of his subconscious. I still think it is a great movie, though I lacked company in that opinion. By the time my rave review appeared in the *Real Paper*, *Fingers* had been closed out of its first run.

Days after the review ran, Jim Toback reached me by phone in Vermont where we lived. He was grateful for the review (there had not been too many), and he was very friendly. Film reviewers get such calls when directors are building careers, but Jim also said we should meet. That was unusual because most film directors know reviewers are somewhere between boring and pathetic and cut off from the existential hazard in being a creator. Jim was encouraging and equal, and he offered friendship—perhaps I was as doomed as he was and yet riding on the same exhilaration. Apart from Lucy, he was the most exciting American I had met.

Jim and I have been friends ever since, though sometimes a year has passed without our meeting or talking on the phone. Then we would resume as if the gap had been half an hour: Jim may have spent a greater part of his life on the phone than anyone else I know. I wrote an essay about him that appeared in a book, *Overexposures* (1981); I heard later that he had copies of it that he passed out as a testimonial, especially to women he was pursuing. What are critics for in the medium made for desire?

The first time we met, he invited me to lunch at the Harvard Club in Manhattan. This was way out of my social league, and wonderfully impressive. We talked for hours over oysters and champagne. He came up to Dartmouth with a girlfriend, Etan Merrick. He spoke at a screening of *Fingers* and enraged or alarmed some of the audience. We played baseball in the garden of the house in Norwich, Vermont, where Lucy and I lived. He played hard. He was as enthusiastic about sports as I was, and he would talk about Dostoyevsky and basketball's Bill Russell in the same sentence. He was a gambler: he had written the screenplay for the 1974 film *The Gambler*. I heard him place college basketball bets over the phone a few times, and he said in his dark, grinning way that some of his debts had earned the attention of Mob enforcers.

I was never sure how much of this talk was an act aimed at someone who might write about him. I was not a gambler—though I was fascinated by its crazy peril. Along with talk of women and violence, I put a lot of the gambling tales down to a movie-mad hustler who made up stories to keep in practice—to be alive, to be on the brink of scenario. That's an imbalance in which movie people live. I've been there much of my life, and it can pass as rational.

Then one night Jim and I had dinner at a Chinese restaurant in New York in the East Thirties. Jim was living in a Manhattan residential hotel at that time, and he needed to shop for a few supplies afterward. So we went on to a market. It was ten or eleven at night. Suddenly he panicked. He had left something at the restaurant. We ran back the several blocks and found the place on the point of closing. But there under our table, where he had forgotten it, was a black leather money belt. I had never seen such a thing before, nor had I ever seen the new banknotes packed inside it. There they were—not Monopoly money. Jim said it was $50,000 and he needed it for a payment. He laughed about it. How was he so cheerful while on the edge of peril? How are any of us? He talked about risk and death as if they were girls he might pick up.

He helped me get a modest screenwriting deal for a picture that was never made. When Tom Luddy and I edited volume 4 of John Boorman's series of books, *Projections*, we got Jim to write a journal for it, a jazzy, thinking-out-loud stream of conscience-free consciousness about being in the movie jungle. He wrote with utter freedom—he was always as good a writer as filmmaker. A book of mine, *In Nevada* (1999), was dedicated to Jim. He and I did a conversation one evening in the Oak Room at the Algonquin Hotel. I introduced him when he received the Kanbar Award for storytelling at the San Francisco Film Festival.

I was on the set of his *Love and Money* in the San Fernando Valley, and then later had dinner with Jim and Klaus Kinski. (He cast Kinski after wanting Johnny Carson in the part.) On Riverside Drive I saw some of *Exposed* being filmed, with Rudolf Nureyev not sure whether he was offended or amused that Jim hardly bothered to direct him. But he did direct the film's other star, Nastassja Kinski, in a phone booth once. As a result, the two of them, Nureyev and Kinski, looked gorgeous but abandoned in *Exposed*. At his best, Jim presented people as inexplicable marvels—and I think that was his dream for himself. He had a real, muddled life, but he longed to rise above it.

As time went on, I realized that Jim was three years younger than me. This seemed unlikely: he knew so much more about a level of life that I was in awe of—he knew how to order oysters and which champagne to pick; he was an insider at the Harvard Club; in a matter of moments he could roll out famous names—people he knew or had known—Aaron Copland, Norman Mailer, Frank Costello (a gangster), and some South American prince of money he had roomed with at Harvard. Some of those dudes were real; and for some of them Jim had chapter and verse, with dialogue. Then there were the movie people he knew. And all the time, in the surge of his talk, he was very funny, human, and generous. He was showing off, for sure, but he seemed to guess that might be good for me. I was new in America, and in a love affair for which I had given up a wife and three children. I must have seemed wild and crazy, too—though I generally hid that from myself.

We were both only children. My mother had died too young, in 1976. Jim's mother, Selma, was a diffident celebrity. She had been president of the League of Women Voters. I met her. She seemed a forlorn New York lady, born and married into wealth, who'd become a widow who had fallen on harder times—and one of the hardest crosses she had to bear was Jim. Her sad eyes guessed he was doomed and a danger to himself, but they loved him to distraction. She even asked me and Lucy to do whatever we could to take care of him. This was disconcerting, since we felt he was showing us the world.

Whenever Lucy wasn't there, a bolder Jim appeared. He was driving us once on Santa Monica Boulevard when he stopped at a light and noticed a woman three or four cars back. So he left me in the car at the light and strolled back to talk to her, to pick her up. That was for the sake of a chance meeting and possible sex—and this woman did show up with him a day later—but I felt it was also a way of asking what I was going to do in a pulsing convertible when the light turned green. It was a scene, and many movie-minded people believe that the best way of containing experience is in scenes. If you were bored, or trapped, you cut away to another scene.

In traffic, Jim indicated that if I wanted to ride along with him after women in L.A. I was very welcome. You couldn't really be in that city then without noticing young, slim, attractive women and their aptitude for being approached. And photographed. It was part of movies, I suppose, and few people then worried over the air of exploitation. In *Fingers*, there had been a startling scene where Danny Aiello takes a gangster's girl (Tanya Roberts), in passing, and then drops her. It was as if to say, look, this is what happens in movieland—and isn't that what the audience is expecting?

By the late 1970s, no movie audience could escape its own condition, that of sitting still in the dark for unprecedented things, often a fusion of sex and violence. That scene with Tanya Roberts was such an example: not only was she taken, she was treated with contempt.

I declined every offer to be Jim's companion in sexual adventure, and he was generous enough not to laugh or set me up as a prude or a hypocrite. I loved Lucy, and I loved the idea of being loyal to her, because I had a bad record in that respect and I was in horror at myself. That may have impressed Jim or placed me as a Dostoevskian brother torn over desire and guilt. We interested each other. I think we still do, no matter that the horror has been filled in lately with a vengeance.

For me, Jim was a mentor and an inspiration as well as a means of access. He was authentically smart and lyrically stupid—and I felt like his brother in that weird compact. His younger brother. I daresay I bored him, but he didn't let that show, and I think sometimes my reading of *Fingers* pierced him. I saw it as a fairy story in which Keitel's Jimmy, always fussing at his hair, losing his way in talk and at the piano, was an inept child longing to be in a man's world. That nervous energy still drives the film, and offers a psychic cockpit that Jim has never reentered.

I knew I was hero-worshipping Jim and I understood that my own upbringing prompted that. My father had left my mother and me when I was born, and I was always looking for male friends. Jim had had and quit on a wife already, and it was plain that he kept several girlfriends at a time so as to avoid committing to any one. So we made a pair of brothers, as unalike but as committed as, say, Dmitri and Alyosha Karamazov.

I don't think we were ever physically attracted to each other, yet that possibility was there like a ghost in the room. I had never had a homosexual life. Jim, I think, had once had a few encounters with older men who were impressed with his youth, his precocity, and his sheer cheek. The two of us were consumed by women on screen, but we were so into movies that I now see how far those male gangs in American films may go in great fear of actually being examined and talked to by women, instead of having them as obedient icons who were there to be possessed. This is hindsight to a great extent. And this book is much concerned with how the movies taught us to see the intricacies of desire and the often terrible relations between men and women.

But for a while I rode along with Jim, knowing he was a show-off, a bad example, and dangerous company but loving him for many of those reasons. It's thanks to Jim that I learned something about the existential tumult of young American filmmakers. As such, I sometimes tried to advise Jim (as a critic!; I told you I was stupid). He seemed a very good listener. He nodded eagerly as I tried to explain him to himself with a view to new film projects. He agreed; he admired my insights, he said. And he ignored them. Jim does only what he has thought of. On his second movie, *Love and Money* (1982), he survived not just my recommendations but the more substantial influence of Pauline Kael, who had persuaded herself to go to Los Angeles to be his credited producer on that film. Jim shrugged off both of us with ease and aplomb. The film was terrible, one of the worst he has ever made. He admits this now in a voice of triumph.

There is another Jim in this story. I mean the Jim Brown who played Dreems in *Fingers* and who had retired from the Cleveland Browns in 1965, after rushing for 12,312 yards and making 106 touchdowns. He was one of the greatest running backs ever, and so handsome and well-spoken that he had gone into the movies as an actor (with so much more presence than O. J. Simpson, who came along later). In 1968, Toback went to Brown's house in the hills above Sunset. He had been hired by *Esquire* to write a profile on the great man and ended up living in Brown's house in Los Angeles and being a kind of brother to him. This had resulted in a book, not long but radiantly starstruck, *Jim: The Author's Self-Centered Memoir on the Great Jim Brown* (1971).

It is a book about brotherhood, about a white Jew's infatuation with a black legend, and it describes the orgy that seemed to offer itself in the late 1960s. It is also another version of the Karamazov bond, taut yet supple, suggestive but uncertain. When I read the book it was clear to me that Toback had been drawn to Brown in the way I felt drawn to Jim.

At Jim Brown's house, Toback was part of an entourage with seven black guys who got into matter-of-fact orgies with maybe twice that number of women of all races. I don't mean to suggest that feeling and affection were not involved sometimes, but the sex seemed as vigorous as tennis or pick-up basketball. It was a spree in which the women were pliant instruments: I daresay many of them were models and would-be actresses on the edge of getting into pictures as well as athlete groupies. Some of them must have gone away damaged and in despair. Here is part of Toback's elegiac account that captures the literary ethos of 1970 and his attempt to say that what must have been tough contact and blunt usage was also a kind of ideal situation:

Jim feels that call makes the mood; mumbling, leads us all into his room. Jim and his, I and mine, tandem. Isaac Hayes singing about his two women, a dark low room, a wide low long bed; all of us on it, naked. Mixed doubles. Mounting, I serve first, feel good, loose; sense no time passed, no disconnection, from the other night; sense her feeling the same. Feel the rhythm picked up on the other side, single to our double, double to our triple. The bed sways, swings, bounces, springs. Two become one, four become two, then four one; blending, melding. Black and white, female, male. I hold her, press her, taking her beat, giving her mine; throw ours to them, receive theirs. For the first time ever, as though in the beginning, discovering it, creating a form to be followed for ages, by ourselves again, by others after we are gone.

This is a man interested in writing who is delivering high-flown pulp. And that says a lot about the war between writing and movies, as well as the toxic stew of sex, race, and any effort to deny our loneliness.

Cut forward more than forty years. In New York, in the spring and summer of 2017, I saw Jim several times. He showed Lucy and me a rough cut of his latest film, *The Private Life of a Modern Woman*, starring Sienna Miller. It had some of the best scenes he'd ever done, notably those involving Charles Grodin as a grandfather facing dementia. But Lucy and I felt the film did not work: it lacked a dramatic shape; we did not care enough for Miller's lead character; it had ponderous scenes—in one of which Jim acts; it was very short (seventy-one minutes) yet it seemed smothered in a sauce of Shostakovich and scenes from a Bosch painting. Jim thought the film was feminist, but that seemed absurd in an age of Shonda Rhimes and the impact of the women's march in Washington that followed Trump's inauguration.

The film needed so much work to have a chance of being released, let alone liked. We all talked at length about what that reworking might be. He listened and agreed. He said he was getting a lot of valuable ideas. But I'm not sure they had any effect on the film. Later, I heard that Jim was telling people I was "over the moon" about the picture. It opened at the Venice Film Festival to mixed reviews and failed to find a distributor.

This is a long way from the Jim of 1978. He is older, of course, though still capable of wild humor, great smartness, and spinning stories. But his health has suffered. He has had diabetes for a couple of decades. He gave up alcohol and was never quite as vivid again; in the last dozen years, he has developed arthritic knees that need replacement. He knows that but he refuses the operation because he is afraid of the pain. Restricted in his movement, he had put on weight. He was over three hundred pounds. So he was taking pain medication beyond the prescribed dose. We had breakfast one day in September 2017, when he lined up a dozen pills to go with pastries and diet soda. He read the opening passage of his memoir to me.

The memoir is a project of several years. As it began, I had introduced Jim to my publisher and he had gone in and pitched the book and his stories. Knopf declined that book proposal, but another publisher took it on with a sizeable advance. Jim spent that money and wrote maybe two hundred pages, well short of a whole book. The publisher asked for delivery, and when it never came they requested a return of the advance. Jim no longer had it. The publisher threatened to sue. In turn, Jim planned to take the book to another publisher for a much larger advance (he was contemplating that at our breakfast). He read me his draft account of how at Harvard in the 1960s he had gone on an LSD binge with extraordinary hallucinations (these are re-created luridly in his film *Harvard Man*). That experience, Jim had always said—and I have heard him tell this story many times—erased his fear of death.

The passage he read was well written—if writing is a script for acting or performance. But it was a melodrama of self-glorification, short on humor or self-criticism, and enough to make a listener suspicious. I suggested that it needed more work and human context and I offered to be a reader if that would help him. Make it a confession more than a boast, I suggested. Jim said that would be great and he promised to send me a chunk of the book. It has never come—but other things have intervened.

Apart from his difficulty in finding a distributor for *The Private Life of a Modern Woman,* his publishing predicament, and his health problems, Jim was in another trap. Always a gambler, he had one big win in the past (a seven-figure sum) and then the showman in him had allowed the casino to take a picture of him packing the money in a bag. Somehow that photograph had reached tax authorities, who asked for their share of the winnings. Jim had told them that he had just as rapidly lost the money, and anyone fond of him would find that scenario very likely. But they believed he had squirreled a chunk of it away in secret. They offered a settlement sum that was beyond Jim's means.

This pressure was building just a few weeks before the *Los Angeles Times* story on October 22, the one in which thirty-eight women made harassment charges against him covering a period of decades. Jim denied these claims. He pointed out inconsistencies and factual errors in them. He even said there was a conspiracy against him. But there were a lot of claims and they did resemble pick-up techniques evident in some of Jim's films, like *The Pick-Up Artist* and the rueful *Two Girls and a Guy,* one of the best movies about male liberty going crazy.

That same summer of 2017, over brunch at the Harvard Club, Jim talked about the sexual action at Jim Brown's house nearly forty years earlier in rougher language than he had used in *Jim.* His memoir could be one of the great books about the delusions of the film business and the way they have poisoned relations between men and women. But that would require a simple candor that goes against his dreamy grain.

For centuries, sex was an instinct, an imperative, an expression of power, and the engine of reproduction. Then we began to imagine that it was tied to ideals like pleasure and love, and we started thinking about it to a point where the old drive could be stilled or put in doubt.

We came to see that sexuality was a part of something better called desire, an urge that reached beyond the physical to imagination and soul.

But what disturbs me, and what has impressed society at large, is the way movies blessed desire and predatoriness, made them beautiful, even. The voyeur in the audience had learned to sense his power and how cruel it might be, as well as the way it cut us off from reality and touching, the things we thought had meant so much to us. The world of film woke howling in the fall of 2017; the dream was broken. That affects Harvey Weinstein—as well as you and me.

Jim and I talked amid the splash of news stories, when he had little to do or hope for except his memoir. The chance of its being published seemed remote, though Jim said there was an agent promising him a lot of money for the book. We cannot resist the sound of what we hope to hear.

But he was in a tight corner now. Jim had a routine when I first met him. "I'll not live past forty," he promised. He was thirty-four then and the other day he was seventy-three. His plan was decisive and existential: he would destroy himself so no one else would have the satisfaction. Growing older and less fully himself daunted him. "I'm absolutely unafraid of dying," he said. If I argue that he was terrified of dying, that is a measure of the ordinary good-natured man who lived in the back room of his gaudy scenario.

As he aged, his storyline built: just before his own suicide, he would dispose of a hit list of people he deemed unworthy. He never named names. But he went so far as to set up a TV series on the idea—a dying man who seeks to save the world from monsters. That series has never happened. Besieged and broke, Jim exists on the phone, spinning scary yarns about himself. He has been a creep sometimes, but he understands flying.

Talking to him had become harder. He would not admit to any merit in the complaints against him. Instead he was angry about being charged, and foul-mouthed in his denial. He said it was all the result of mass cowardice and a suppression of human nature. He did not appreciate the widespread awakening of power for women or the exposure of arrogance and brutality in some men. At one point I told him to consider getting treatment. He didn't like that, but something in the idea intrigued him. He had always loved talking about himself, and he played hopscotch with confession and boasting.

But the complaints against him were consistent, they seemed to describe the same man, and they were depressing. Time and again, they depicted episodes of masturbation and intimidation instead of sex. It is curious how many of these Hollywood stories do turn on masturbation, with its landscape of solitude or remoteness. There seemed to be no relationships, just the need to ejaculate. That's like a lot of pornography where intercourse concludes with the guy jerking off on the woman's face.

Jim said the world was ending, and not just his part of it. His humor had eroded. Talking to him was suddenly disturbing, because it exposed foolish illusions I had held for years. So he said I was no longer a friend—though he maintained his friendly, laughing manner. I told him his memoir might be a great book if he wrote the truth and trusted it to be plain and not a movie. And if there was a publisher brave enough to touch it.

He waited apprehensively, in fear of legal proceedings. But then in April 2018 the Los Angeles district attorney said he would take no action against Jim. The hundreds of accusers had faded away to a handful. Some charges were beyond the statute of limitations, and one complainant failed to materialize. Jim was jubilant: his story seemed vindicated. His atmosphere was harder to recover, but I felt relieved: it was easier to telephone him in liberty; and his incarceration could have reduced any earnest prison to merry chaos.

He was writing with zest. He said he had done six hundred pages by June 2018 (and he had dropped sixty pounds). There might be another movie on the horizon. He sent me a hundred or so pages of the book and they were vivid, and funny, and unmistakably Jim. I doubt if any Hollywood figure of the last forty years has had more experiences, or has Jim's ability and need to tell this story. It could be his great work.

It has to be.

16

Gigolo

The poster for *American Gigolo* (1980). It's close
to the point and far from an attack to say that Paul Schrader's
film aspires to the mood of a knockout poster.

LUCY AND I began to live in San Francisco in 1981. We came from Vermont and teaching at Dartmouth. It was a larger decision than we appreciated at the time because we took it for granted that, sooner or later, we'd gravitate to Los Angeles—we felt we were movie people, for reasons of possible employment but also as a matter of sensibility. We saw life as the ripe ground where movies would flower. Things that happened to us reminded us of movies or of ones that might yet be made. We looked—we saw, we framed the process. Maybe life got too little appreciation in our melodramatic gaze. As a way of seeing life, the movies have been a terrible dead end.

Instead of going to L.A., we became caught up in a city about to be engaged in an epic of homosexual experience. By the time that turmoil was passing, the movies had changed so much that they had lost the glamour that once drew people to L.A. Did movies still have the passion we had felt in moving west, and that had directed my life since the age of four? A lot of that glamour had consisted of very fixed, adolescent attitudes to the roles of men and women.

In 1981, life was delicately poised in San Francisco: It was only three years since the convulsions of Jonestown, when the Peoples Temple had gone away to the jungle of Guyana and been led into its suicidal rapture. Ten days after that shock, Mayor George Moscone and Supervisor Harvey Milk were killed by Supervisor Dan White. That was a crisis in gay history and a skirmish in what would be a new cultural war. For homosexual America, a conflict and a revelation were occurring in the city. By 1990, there were 100,000 deaths from AIDS in America, getting on for twice the number lost in the Vietnam War.

A movie person could feel the potential in all this turbulence. The scenario might take lurid forms: there were those who believed AIDS was God's punishment for evil or unnatural homosexuals. My daughter Kate found out she had HIV in that time, and became the bravest person I know in working for women in the same predicament. She also stayed alive. There had to be movies about this "problem," even if it was hardly thinkable that the mainstream, commercial screen would detail anal sexual intercourse or an obsession with heroin. It was no surprise that there would be a documentary about Harvey Milk or that Gus Van Sant would one day make *Milk* (2008), in which Sean Penn won an Oscar playing Milk and Josh Brolin was nominated as Dan White.

So consider those two men in November 1978, when White sneaked into City Hall and shot Moscone and Milk. Milk was charismatic, endearing, open in his enthusiasms and his confusions—he was fresh and inspiring, untidy, alive. He was sometimes confused or silly: he had been an awed admirer of Jim Jones and the Peoples Temple once, well before that Guyana massacre when 918 people died.

By contrast, White was stoic or repressed—he was closer to dead. Gay activist Cleve Jones noted a markedly "childish" aspect to White. You can say he was a bigot, alarmed at homosexuality and at so many challenges to his scheme of American order. He can seem like a man repressing feeling, but no doubt he felt overwhelmed by emotions he could not describe. He had served in Vietnam in the 101st Airborne Division; he had been a cop and a firefighter; he was a Catholic and a family man; when seen at the right angle he had the handsome, square-jawed look of a hero in a TV series or a comic book. He was like a movie guy from the 1950s: a cop, a cowboy, an oil rigger, a college football coach. I daresay he liked to believe he was reliable, and so he smothered forces in himself that were unpredictable and disorderly. Was he afraid of gayness out in the open? Why would an ex-cop shoot a gay supervisor? Shoot to kill: five shots, including two in the head after the body had fallen.

Milk was a muddle, a Jewish showman seeking progress in society. White was more problematic or mysterious but as interesting dramatically. Imagine Dan alone on screen, thoughtful, walking, pondering, in those moody moments of half-noir introspection that can soften any tough guy on screen. So why did White do what he did? What was he hoping for? Was he depressed? Are hope and depression twins in America?

Then wonder why his jury convicted him of voluntary manslaughter instead of murder. The facts seemed inescapable. Still, the jurors found a way to ameliorate what had occurred—gay people had been "excused" from the jury pool. The climate of the trial seemed liberal enough, but it was too blind to see its own prejudice. You feel that White the cop and conservative would have been disturbed by that verdict. This is not excusing White or dishonoring Milk. But in the history of sexuality in America Dan White is as instructive as the lively, brave Harvey Milk. If you want to comprehend the America of today and the cultural war building in the nation, then White also deserves a movie.

Thirty-three years later, my publisher was wondering about a book on how gays in Hollywood had meant so much for our movies and for our culture. I was interested to read that book, and sometimes if you want to read a book you have to write it yourself.

I felt a storm of questions gathered over the medium, the fun and the desire, the art and the business, that had done so much to direct our lives. And this was in advance of the astonishing outbreak—in the fall of 2017—of stories of how men in the picture business and the media had pressured, harassed, and exploited women. That was "breaking news," yet anyone close to movies had known these things, not only from gossip but also in the instinct for how a male gaze had always shaped the picture stories. What few appreciated was that if the rigid mythology in Hollywood films had broken down, how long would it be before the real feelings of the slaves to that system cried out? Movies had said women were special beauties, but now they insisted on being real.

If the crimes and the sins noted in 2017 were an accurate representation of power at work, then there was another fault in the system—that in watching our movies we had understood the structural crime and done nothing about it. Had movies made us helpless? Is that why we were sitting there in comfort, in the dark, without responsibility? We have to realize that in our intense request for watching, the screen has gently told us that we are powerless. The alleged "being in touch" with the world is a phantom. That's one reason why we believe our problems now are insoluble.

In 1982, actors Harry Hamlin and Michael Ontkean kissed cautiously in a film called *Making Love,* "A Provocative Tale of Hidden Desire" (as it advertised itself), which claimed to be the first mainstream picture to deal "honestly" with "it" but which is forgotten now because of its ponderous and timid departures. *Making Love* was decent in its intent, the work of a group of men, some of them gay, who had observed the increasing prominence of homosexuals in upwardly mobile American society and who had wanted to tell a story that spelled that out for a public who might be enlightened by the news. The filmmakers were Hollywood professionals, so they had hopes of making money on the picture, but they had a high-minded, educational purpose, too. In Hollywood, as in America, the idea of social reform while making a profit can be comfortable and attractive. Yet delusional.

The story for *Making Love* came from A. Scott Berg, the younger brother of a leading Hollywood agent, Jeff Berg. Barry Sandler wrote the script from that story, and Arthur Hiller directed—he was an accomplished journeyman with several hits to his name (*Love Story, Plaza Suite, Silver Streak*). The movie was released by Twentieth Century Fox, but the decisive person on the project was Daniel Melnick, who was producing for his IndieProd company. I knew Dan around that time.

Melnick was suave, sophisticated, a renowned poker player, an art collector, a connoisseur of sexual reputation, a little pretentious but entertainingly so, and good company. I stayed a weekend once at his lodge in Utah—rare food and wine, good stories, unexplained attractive women in the offing. I liked him and took high pleasure in the bathroom where everything was black: the tiles, the porcelain, the walls and the ceiling, the linen, the toilet paper. Only the water was not noir. The effect was hysterically cool.

Dan liked daring projects—he had been producer on Sam Peckinpah's *Straw Dogs* and Bob Fosse's *All That Jazz.* For a time he ran MGM; he was a major player and very social. He could have been a movie himself, and sometimes we talked about how such a project might work. I had an idea for him, about an impresario figure who becomes increasingly brilliant: he cannot say why, but he seems incapable of mistake. So he ascends, moving from show business to politics.

Then this knack or luck deserts him. Dan was tickled by the idea—we both knew it had to do with him, without mentioning it—but it was never done. Then, later, Dan's own wave collapsed. His career declined. He lost his money and died broke, an alarming victim of fickle destiny. But gamblers are not surprised by losing.

Melnick was emphatically heterosexual, but like anyone living and working in Hollywood he knew many gay people and was at ease with them. He had appreciated the risk in *Making Love* and taken it on with enthusiasm, but during the production itself he seemed to lose his nerve. Actually putting that story on screen and making it live as a film may have brought out his own fears about being thought gay, to say nothing of those of his actors.

So *Making Love* is carved in day-old aspic in which the shift from gelatin to concrete is occurring; it's genteel and like a plan for a film about people so ostensibly successful that they can experiment sexually as if sampling a new Sancerre. Zack (Michael Ontkean), an oncologist, is married to Claire (Kate Jackson, the "smart" one from *Charlie's Angels*), a television executive. They seem okay. They're childless, but why does a good marriage need children? Instead they delight in Gilbert and Sullivan and the poetry of Rupert Brooke. They are stable, decent, okay, boring people—like those of us who go to movies.

Then Zack meets a gay novelist, Bart (Harry Hamlin), and he is so attracted that he realizes he may be gay, too. His marriage to Claire ends. Zack and Bart have an affair, then they break up and Zack finds another stable male companion. Claire marries again. Zack and Claire meet once more after several years, and they smile and tell each other they are happy that they are both happy. Everything has worked out—have a nice rest of your life. I'm sure the outlines of this story mimic some L.A. relationships and many more all over America. Historically, it was notable that someone in Hollywood had attempted *Making Love*. But nothing could rescue its hushed trepidation. Self-censorship has always been more damaging in movies than that imposed by codes or guardians.

Making Love fell flat. Hollywood is avid for trends, though, and it felt that "the gay thing" might be warming up. So 1982 also delivered *Tootsie,* which tried to balance tricky gender issues without upsetting anyone. It's the story of an unemployed actor (Dustin Hoffman—small, opinionated, offbeat but unquestionably virile, safe) who pursues the role of a woman in a successful daytime soap opera. It's a drag escapade for confident, heterosexual audiences at a time when the word "trans" was unknown. It's also a clever, funny film: Sydney Pollack directed, Larry Gelbart and Elaine May were among the writers. Hoffman left no doubt about his frisky maleness, and the story had the accessible Jessica Lange as his eventual prize.

The picture was called daring, but it's no more advanced than *Charley's Aunt* (an 1892 stage hit). It's Hollywood diverting attention and hoping to seem hip. This worked: *Tootsie* grossed $177 million on a $21 million investment. It had ten Oscar nominations, though only one win, for Jessica Lange. It never risked being sexy, secret, or "dirty."

If its story was remade now, it would have the actor aware of his own unsteady gender in the course of the narrative. He might find himself gay or trans or even pansexual. He might have sex with everyone, as if he was the spirit of the movies. Doesn't the great light get at everyone? There had been such a film: in 1968, in Italy, Pier Paolo Pasolini had made *Teorema*. It was a fable in which an unexplained outcast, "the Visitor," comes to a bourgeois household and makes unequivocal love to everyone—the father, the mother, the son, the daughter, and the maid. This Visitor was Terence Stamp, in his most beautiful, blank state.

A subtler breakthrough had come two years earlier, in 1980, when Paul Schrader's *American Gigolo* slipped past the roadblock cautions against going homosexual. Under the adroit cloak of being "American," that film was made by a man intrigued by his own uncertain sexual feelings but aware that the movies had always been what Schrader himself called "pansexual." That term came from Parker Tyler's *Screening the Sexes: Homosexuality in the Movies,* published in 1972 (the year in which Schrader himself published *Transcendental Style in Film*).

The subtitle of that university press book pointed to its pioneering concentration on the works of Yasujiro Ozu, Carl Dreyer, and Robert Bresson. Those are lofty names in film history with a shared feeling for spiritual or inward identity, but their films were not much known to the audiences so shaken up by *Taxi Driver* (written by Schrader for Martin Scorsese). *Transcendental Style* was always meant for scholars and cinephiles, and Parker Tyler's book had some of the same readership, though while Schrader was earnest and wary of humor, Tyler was funny, wicked, bold, allusive, a louche but relaxed stylist, full of smart ideas and sliding connections. The wonder of *Screening the Sexes* is the ease with which it takes so much for granted while being so provocative; it slips along as easily as Julian Kaye (the American gigolo) strolls across an elegant room. It was a new kind of voice in film writing, as if to ask, Don't you realize the games we are playing in the dark? Tyler's opening paragraph ends with this: "Perhaps one ought simply to say that Miss [Mae] West's style as a woman fully qualifies her—as it always did—to be a Mother Superior of the Faggots."

Schrader was a film critic and a screenwriter let loose in the wild dark. As a kid raised Calvinist in Michigan and forbidden to see movies, he was captivated by the shock potential of the medium. Once he was liberated as a voyeur, his imagination began to revel in forbidden thrills.

Schrader couldn't take his eyes off Julian Kaye; and he infected us in the same way. Forgo the doctrinaire timidity of *Making Love* and feel your way into Julian's black Mercedes convertible riding the curves of the Pacific Coast Highway on a brilliant day. Julian's car is new, like his shirts. He does his own driving, but the innuendo of back projection nags at the streamlined affect. Could driving be the same dreamy abstraction as it is for Maria Wyeth in Joan Didion's novel *Play It As It Lays* (1970)? Maria's life is a wreck in the book and the movie (she's played by Tuesday Weld), but she finds peace or momentum in driving the freeways. That unnerving novel aspires to a trancelike condition in which reality is discounted or nullified. Maria has one friend, BZ (Anthony Perkins), who is gay, and who kills himself.

Then marry Julian's serene driving to a worshipful close-up of the serrated fin light on his car and the throb and swoon of Giorgio Moroder's score—full of bass notes deepened by electronic mixing arts until the music becomes a pulse. This is beauty, yet so ostentatious, so self-conscious, that it comes close to mocking itself. In *American Gig-*

olo the pent-up wit and elegance of film floods out—like hot butterscotch on vanilla bean ice cream.

It was part of Schrader's daring that Julian Kaye is an "impossible" hero for a mainstream film, a male prostitute and a sleek clotheshorse in moderne Los Angeles. Unlike *Making Love,* this movie adores L.A., its light and its freeway sheen, while knowing that the once and former movie kingdom was already history by 1980, as cosmeticized as a mummy soaked in preservative.

Schrader was a provincial and a puritan itching to break out: in his previous film, *Hard Core,* George C. Scott had been a businessman from Grand Rapids, Michigan, horrified by a depraved L.A. in which his "good" daughter had become a porn actress. So the Calvinist and transcendentalist in Schrader was won over by a new art that had grown up in the city in which everything was an inventory asset, from a car to its engraved invoice, or from a Barcelona chair to Julian himself perched on it. This unexpected and insolent movie sighed with deco desire and the rapture of a drawer of new shirts. Richard Gere's Julian was cool, detached, and creepy, a fatuous Apollo who outglamorized the dutiful female lead in the film (the worthy and lovely Lauren Hutton).

Julian drives his 450 SL from trick to trick. He is a freelancer with two agents offering his gentlemanly services. He specializes in older women of means, those coming to L.A. for a polite adventure or residents who are bored by their marriages. He is a male prostitute, a guy who can be chauffeur, translator, urbane reception escort, and stud for hire. Julian will screw them without taking off their fur coats. He knows the intricate folds of a clitoris as well as the scholarship of the Maine school of painting from the 1820s.

And there he is in 1980, ready to work for $1,000 a trick, on a 50–50 split with either Nina van Pallandt (Anne) or Bill Duke (Leon), his pimps. But don't get this Jules wrong: he is less actual or alive than the self-regard playing in his head. He has a vanity that is both spiritual and absurd. So Julian will give orgasms to fearful and sedate facelifts from out of town and flatter them, pocketing the folded tip (and passing part of it on to valet parking). All you have to do is call him, but he does *not* do fags. Julian yelps when he says this and a look of consternation flickers across what was still a baby face—Gere was just over thirty in 1980, and the actor knew this film was his break, albeit a risky opportunity. So don't forget, people, Julian is *straight*. If Julian did fags, this daring film would never have been made. Gere was ready to be an officer and a gentleman two years later.

His sour pimp, Leon, warns Julian about treading a fine line, because the ladies and their country clubs could drop him any day. Julian regards that freelance peril as freedom, and he knows Leon's spite comes from envy. The pimp wants to make Julian his own boy just as Ann recalls the time when she and Julie were lovers learning Swedish together in bed.

Other actors had avoided the Julian role and its dangerous fine line. Some people flinched from the entire concept: the young Meryl Streep was considered for the "love interest" (the Lauren Hutton part), but she disapproved of the picture's sordid tone—a promising sign? Christopher Reeve was wary of Julian, just as Schrader was nervous about having him. Superman might mean box office, but he wasn't slippery enough. John Travolta came close to doing it when he was hot because of *Saturday Night Fever* and *Grease*. One can see Travolta getting away with some of Julian, but he would have been so plaintive or pouty that the self-pity in Kaye could have turned excruciating. What Schrader got with Gere's reticence or distancing was that the clothes wore him. Gere was smarter than Travolta, more guarded or fatalistic, and far more possessed by the church of style. Gere looks at Julian's clothes as if he deserves them.

Julian dresses well because his clients expect it of him and because that gets him access to the L.A. Country Club and the Polo Lounge at the Beverly Hills Hotel. But it's also credible that he has become a gigolo because he loves to dress up. Being the gigolo, being "Julian Kaye" (you hope that name is fake), the clothes, the car, his place at the Westwood Apartment Hotel (where he never takes his women), are all signs of his need for acting or role-playing.

When Julian goes to Ann's beach house the casual toplessness of the pretty girls sunning themselves on the balcony is part of the film's offhand daring. Ann asks "Julie" (her name for him) if he won't stay a while with the other girls, but Julian disdains pretty girls. There are constant suggestions in his look, his clothes, and his glamour that he is a surrogate female.

After he has played chauffeur for one middle-aged duchess, a visitor from Charlottesville, he goes to the Polo Lounge and—deft touch—stops at the cloakroom to swap his dark chauffeur jacket for an Armani brown silk job that presumably is kept there in waiting. It's in that jacket that he first encounters Michelle Stratton (Hutton), a rich, neglected wife, alone in the bar, talking high school French and pretending to be waiting for someone.

Gere does this smooth routine very well (you realize that Travolta would not have understood its tone; his adolescent good nature would have killed Schrader's subtlety) but then Julian goes on an emergency mission for Leon—this takes him to Palm Springs with more luxurious driving and transporting views of the frosty-topped mountains on the way. California *is* a dream. The five-digit street address is the Rheiman house, an architected façade wedged into the desert, with only wealth to protect it against the deeper inner décor of desert. Julian finds himself with a rough trick this night. The husband, slender, in a pink sweater, vicious with self-loathing, tells Julian he has been hired to service his wife—while hubby watches. That seems pathetic and even cruel—but we're watching, too.

The wife is a voluptuous blonde in white and gray sheets who never says a word. She is like a doll in pornography. Her very soul has been Brazilian waxed. But as Julian murmurs to her with kisses and acquired arousal techniques, the husband in the doorway tells them "it" has to be done from behind. So the wife is turned over, like a corpse, and the husband orders, "Slap the cunt." Julian winces: he has a heart, and he doesn't do faggot stuff, though here is a mainstream movie treating sexual commerce with clerical aplomb.

Don't worry, or not too much, if you are picturing this blunt but beautiful film. (Those gray sheets are to die for with a platinum blonde and they pair with the line "Roll me in designer sheets" in the song "Call Me" by Blondie, a song that was so compelling in the picture and became a promotional point as it rose to number-one in record sales.) *American Gigolo* had an R rating, the one that says no one under seventeen can see the movie without being in the company of a parent or an adult guardian. So your five-year-old could see it with you, and it would be up to you to explain the point of turning Mrs. Rheiman's body over or the protocol for slapping the cunt.

Days later, Julian learns that this wife was murdered in a procedure that required handcuffs and violence. He is upset; he begins to lose his cool, because he's being framed—like other works of art. This frightens Julian, though there are also moments where Schrader is stifling laughter. When a detective comes to interview Kaye, it's Detective Sunday (a scruffy son of Joe Friday?), played by Hector Elizondo, and he's soon calling J. "Mr. K."

I'm being a little scathing of a film I'm offering as beautiful. That's not inconsistent; it's in the nature of a great deal of film commentary. It's also a reflection on the uncommon cultural status of the movies as it was emerging by 1980, when Hollywood was as near dead as Judy Rheiman in her final hours—which is to say, luscious, inert, available, and hopeless. Going to the movies has always had to face the question: Are we expected to take this seriously and write about it as if it were Henry James?

There is so much about *Gigolo* to hold your attention. Moroder's music was not yet cliché. John Bailey's photography is damp. Gere is very good. Lauren Hutton is better than her fragile part had any right to expect. Schrader had true brilliance and was jittery in his mixture of aestheticism and outrage. And then there was "Nando."

At the end of the movie, before the cast credits, there is a solo title: "Visual Consultant Ferdinando Scarfiotti." Scarfiotti was not credited for production design because he did not qualify under Los Angeles union rules. But the Italian was by then one of the most illustrious movie designers in the world. He had been a crucial contributor to lofty ventures like *The Conformist* (1970), *Death in Venice* (1971), *Avanti!* (1971), and *Last Tango in Paris* (1972). He was a visionary who liked to choose or approve every item in the frame and who regarded the human figures as elements of design as well as actors or characters. Schrader told me, "People used to say that Marty [Scorsese] would say, '*Taxi Driver* is really Paul's film.' Well, *Gigolo* is Nando's." He says he referred nearly every physical decision to Scarfiotti.

There was no hint that Scarfiotti was interested in creating whole films, but design can organize and direct a movie—especially if it believes the film's people are abstract, clothed forms going through certain motions. (These days, digital design of special effects aids this conceit.) Moreover, Schrader and Scarfiotti stayed close. They worked together again on *Cat People,* and *Mishima* was a film done under Scarfiotti's influence.

Scarfiotti was shy, amusing, civilized, and gay. He had collaborated with director Luchino Visconti on what is one of the declaratory gay films, *Death in Venice.* In fact, its self-conscious homoeroticism gets in the way of that project, smothers the adroit Dirk Bogarde, and sometimes tips the film over into unintended hilarity. Then for the heterosexualist Bernardo Bertolucci, Scarfiotti had done two impressive films. His design for both of them was revelatory in conveying emotion through décor. The apartment in *Last Tango* is a mix of desolation and carnal secrecy: it feels like flesh or a corpse; and its story comes down to anal intercourse. The notorious butter scene turns the unwilling girl into a boy.

The novelistic richness of *The Conformist* never loses sight of the displacement or effacement in the central character, a man defined by his insecurities. *The Conformist* also touches on a lesbian relationship and is at ease with bisexuality. As Parker Tyler put it, the protagonist (played by Jean-Louis Trintignant) is "as false a heterosexual as he is a homosexual," a remark that illuminates Julian Kaye and prefigures the odd status of men in many films of that era (think of Terence Stamp in *Teorema,* Alain Delon in *Purple Noon* and Melville's *Le Samourai,* and even Al Pacino in *The Godfather,* where women are shut out of the room and Michael Corleone's life).

Schrader called *The Conformist* an essential work in modern cinema. Then again, *Last Tango* offered up the idea of two people meeting for sex in an empty apartment and resolved to stay cut off from their own past. That is nearly quoted in the big love scene in *American Gigolo* where Julian Kaye will say nothing reliable about his past or why he has come to be a male prostitute.

But that much abstraction makes it easier to see that he is in quest of something beyond conventional male sexuality. Schrader had been married before, and he married his present wife, Mary Beth Hurt, in 1983. He had had love affairs with women (with Nastassja Kinski during the making of *Cat People*). This is not a book intent on outing people, but I would say that *American Gigolo* was the work of a talented man exploring serious uncertainty about the stability of his sexual orientation.

American Gigolo had a mixed press—it still has. Schrader admitted his own pretensions; he was proud of them, and he never hid from how the film's stilted ending was a quote from, or an homage to, the ending of Robert Bresson's *Pickpocket*—that terse, spiritual meditation in which an inveterate thief comes to redemption through his love for a good woman. As Schrader admitted: "I copied that ending in *American Gigolo*, which was sort of perverse, because *American Gigolo* is a very superficial film. I'm not rigorous enough to even attempt what he [Bresson] did."

Like many important films, it resists explanation. I feel the ending is a painful resolution of a situation that should be left open. It's pie-in-the-sky to believe in Julian Kaye and Michelle Stratton marrying, having children, and living a quiet life in the Valley. They click together in movie talk and in an abstract yet tender love scene, but they have no reality to build on. Julian is essentially unsettled; maybe the gayest thing about him is his disdain for domesticity or "getting ahead." But in the December 2017 *Sight & Sound*, Christina Newland extolled the film's ending as "a singularly moving moment of love and reassurance."

Not for me. Instead I think Schrader was making a film for Paramount, a new kind of movie, showing new, dangerous things—like Richard Gere, stark naked at the window of his apartment in a composition where the stippled shadows of Venetian blinds is . . . to die for. At the end, it had to work as a show, giving us a spurious vestige of comfort while the credits rolled. It worked: this strange, disconcerting, antiseptic movie, this disco spell, this iridescent trash (it *was* a Jerry Bruckheimer production), took in nearly $52 million having cost just $5 million. You wouldn't take your aunt from Charlottesville to see it, but it was a hit, and some aunts probably went on their own.

To this day, if you watch *American Gigolo* and go with it, you know you're being got at. It was the first secret gay film from America that knew the lifestyle could be seductive. An Armani snake had slipped into our drawing room.

Something was happening in those early 1980s that had to do with the expanding gay presence in society as a whole and the possibility of alternative sexual styles and stylishness. In 1981, Vito Russo published his book, *The Celluloid Closet,* a pioneering survey of homosexual careers and characters in movies. In 1984, *The Times of Harvey Milk* (made by Rob Epstein) won the Oscar for best documentary. Milk had worked to defeat the Briggs initiative, which proposed the mandatory firing of gay teachers in public schools; that measure lost by over a million votes, three weeks before Milk was killed. The result amazed many people. There were mounting claims by homosexuals for the right to be heard and recognized—which was still not legal standing. Following the Stonewall riots of 1969 in New York, gay pride marches occurred in other cities. A few hundred thousand came out to march in San Francisco in the mid-1970s, and the "normal" world acted astonished.

These shifts coincided with the slow dissolution of mainstream picture culture and public fatigue with old hero models who had as little irony over their nobility as John Wayne or Robert Redford. Those actors made some fine films, but they inspired the fallacy that good guys would carry the nation through any crisis. They told us and told themselves that they were icons and rocks. But as the business ideologies fell apart, movies had a chance to attempt awkward truths about life in America. That chance has yet to be fully taken. Much more would happen on television, where there were more and more sightings of gay characters, many of them presented with tender fairness as well as innovative humor.

It was also true that once people began dying in dreadful numbers from AIDS, homosexuals found the urgency to be more active or vocal. Rock Hudson became—at last—"an example," though this was late in his day (he died in 1985, soon after letting it be known that he had AIDS). Vito Russo died of AIDS in 1990, aged forty-four. In 1990, Tony Kushner's landmark play *Angels in America: A Gay Fantasia on National Themes* workshopped in Los Angeles. A year later it was performed at the Eureka Theatre in San Francisco. In 1992 it played in London (at the National Theatre) and one year after that it was deemed fit for Broadway.

But the embattled state of "national themes" goes on. The large collection of stories for the screen has produced, among others, *Brokeback Mountain, Will & Grace,* and *Transparent.* The laws guarding gay lives and rights in the nation have grown wider and more accurate. Same-sex marriage is now legal in a surprisingly rapid process of adaptation. Within fifteen years, the Defense of Marriage Act gave way to more than 60 percent of Americans reckoning that marriage was flexible and dull enough to accommodate gay couples. That haste does not mean it is universally accepted or that it would not be fiercely opposed in a crisis. Still, in less than a generation, gayness has gone from being against the law to a lifestyle lawyers live by. We have decided that Alan Turing was a hero, even if his uncommon service was rewarded with the offer of prison or chemical castration.

Laws can only do so much. They have established and protected many rights for black citizens and helped put them "everywhere" in America: not least in prison, in numbers that mirror black absence in good schools and nice neighborhoods. We have a black justice on the Supreme Court who is nearly silent on black opportunities such as he once benefited from; we have had a black president—and how he suffered for his innovative status. It may be some time yet before a gay candidate or a woman wins the presidency—though there is the consequent irony that asks, Well, who would want that job anyway? Maybe only a dumb straight boy would take it.

In the dark fields of the republic, blacks, gays, and women may be shunned, bullied, victimized, exploited, beaten up, and even killed. The hard core of all-American boys remains substantial, very hard, well armed, and resistant to persuasion. This is dressed up as being God-fearing (as if the home of the brave and free knew what fear could be). So we wonder how long we can put up with boys, guns, racism, rigid pride, religious instruction, and the confidence that links those elements to the delusion of American greatness. It is hard enough for a culture or an individual to be more or less decent, open, and benign; it is an aberration and a pretension to insist on greatness.

17

Doing It, Saying It

Seconds after the first coupling in *Last Tango in Paris* (1972)—
Marlon Brando and Maria Schneider, not asleep, but fixed as strangers

THERE HAVE BEEN MOMENTS in this book when I have hesitated over which words to use. And I have met people who admit to being uneasy with those words and with looking at movie scenes that seem to simulate sexual actions. Do people, do you, have "sexual intercourse"? Do we make love or sleep together—the formula I settled on for my title? Are we sleeping together or just side-by-side? So much of that language seems technical, too, or poetic. There was a film in 2017 where a husband and wife have sex—*Three Billboards Outside Ebbing, Missouri*. The couple are played by Woody Harrelson and Abbie Cornish (he is twenty-one years her senior). They do the scene tenderly, with fondness, in part because he is a dying man. We actually see nothing of their sex, but she tells him afterwards how much she likes his *cock*. In being touched by the scene, I felt that if she'd said "penis" the moment would have been undermined. Yet not so long ago the word "cock" would have been forbidden in a movie. Even in 2019, I'm sure some readers will flinch at it and wish to keep that word under wraps.

Do we "sleep together" when much of the point is in being awake? Would it be closer to the way we talk to ourselves to say "fuck"? Does that word date me? I recall when my mother slapped me for saying it, before I knew what it meant. The pressing word was part of the *Lady Chatterley* excitement, and the fuss that night (in 1965) when Kenneth Tynan said it live on British TV. For me in my time "fuck" was a romantic, idealistic word, reaching for a degree of candor or pleasure that had been smothered by caution. But the word has an undeniable male swagger that implies that women are "fucked"; it is done to them. That code stands up for erect, bold, decisive men and their leading role in an action men assume is consensual.

The word "fuck" has been as formative as the ways of showing it and doing it on screen—yet the action stays elusive: it has to do with fantasy and intellect as well as the discharge of endorphins and bodily fluids. Even now, saying "fuck" carries a tremor of magic in certain situations. The word itself can be arousing, or a Pavlovian bell. Could that change? Could some new words be coming along to relieve males of their supremacy? What word would women want to use?

But "fuck" and "fucked" now are common as intensifiers. "Damn it! Fucking hell!" or "I'm fucking angry!" with so many variants. I know a woman who uses such language. I have been married to her for nearly forty years, during which we have slept together so many times to mutual pleasure—or to private pleasures enjoyed at the same time. I put it that way because I think the heart of that sleeping is private or mental. It's secret, yet two people, spent, in one bed can feel they have done it together and done it well enough.

Does "fucking awful" have some residual, unexamined fear and loathing of our famous sex? Is there a hint here of the two sexes hating each other and the process that joins them? Is "penetration" bliss or violence? Let's say it's both. Well, not me, you say, not us—but listen to your passing language and ask whether desire is not troubled by its own enactment. Does desire rely on failure?

Is this talk troubling you? Surveys say "we" are having a lot of sex now, compared with 1950, and having it in ways hardly known then as things people could do. But do we talk about this wealth? Or do we still do it silently, in the dark, and without much reflection? Suppose it is so important that we need to talk about it and find some words. How important? Well, set aside pleasure—though sheer pleasure is hard to take. Suppose, in addition, that sex and its words and signs are very close to racism, to religious madness, to the yearning for guns, to power, poverty, and politics.

It is not just some intent lurking in particular movies; it's as if the whole medium has always been leaning toward this special intensity. It can even look back on history and bathe it in a modern, sexy light.

Cold Mountain is a rural settlement in North Carolina. As war comes in 1861, Inman (Jude Law) enlists, parting from his new beloved, Ada (Nicole Kidman). They have declared their feelings, but there has been no consummation. Ada is a virgin (we have to believe), even if Kidman's alert eyes and thirty-six years suggest a little more experience. We can't ask actresses to kill their own bankable eyes.

This turns into an epic story; the film of *Cold Mountain* (2003) is 154 minutes, and for most of that time Ada and Inman are separated.

They struggle to survive the war in a movie that takes pains over period authenticity and the severity of those harsh years. It was shot in Romania, but we trust its 1860s Carolina. The characters live near starvation and in perils; their nerves and their looks suffer. They are deprived of their beloveds. Then one day, Ada is out in the snow—she wears a nifty black coat in the film with a fetching black hat. She is looking to shoot wild turkey, something to eat, when she sees a lone figure coming down the trail. She hardly recognizes Inman. Back from the war, he is no longer young; he is haggard, with a rough beard.

We know what's coming; it's what we have been waiting for. In an ordeal story, don't *we* deserve some consolation, not just Ada and Inman? They talk; he shaves; but there is a hut available with a tasteful golden light from the fire. They are going to get it on, and the urge is so strong there's no time to consider what "it" is. What follows is a pretty scene, with a lot of amber skin, breasts and buttocks, the flawless slopes of Ada's stomach and beyond, period underwear and Kidman's head tipping back in ecstasy. *Can we do the ecstatic bit now, Nicole?* It is the sex scene, and it nearly ruins the picture.

Out of friendship, I was shown the film early by its writer-director, Anthony Minghella. I admired a lot of it, but the love scene felt out of joint with the rest of the picture. I seemed to be watching movie stars, not Carolinians from the Civil War; the film had the benefit of rich lighting, sleek flesh not dependent on roots and acorns or actorly attitudes. Minghella rather agreed. It was a necessary scene, he sighed. The movie would feel broken without it, for it fulfilled the logic of how Nicole Kidman looked, and the expectations its mogul, Harvey Weinstein, had for the enterprise. "We had to do it," said Ant, as if that payoff duty had smothered his natural wit and curiosity.

It occurred to me later—after Minghella had died, so young—that the romantic suspense in *Cold Mountain* was less interesting than the pathos in his earlier *Truly, Madly, Deeply* (1990), where Juliet Stevenson's longing for Alan Rickman is blocked but stimulated by his being dead, though his ghost still visits her screen. Sometimes, missing people means as much as being with them. And at the movies, the image is always beyond the window or out of reach.

For over sixty years, going to the pictures had been a matter of bringing our desires to a point of exquisite frustration. Would these beautiful stars ever do it? Cinema history had stepping-stone sequences of arousal, metaphor, and heady fade-outs to protect decorum. One might be Louise Brooks in *Pandora's Box,* discovered in a small room with a ponderous VIP collapsed in her lap as her breasts seemed ready to slip out of her sketchy dress. Another could be Deborah Kerr and Burt Lancaster, in decent bathing suits, rolling together in the salacious surf on a beach in Hawaii, and yearning for it in *From Here to Eternity.*

Those famous set pieces are tender in the memory, and the idea of Burt and Deborah continuing beyond a fade-out was more potent than anything two movie stars could have done in 1953. Fourteen years later, in the ending of *Bonnie and Clyde,* the shoot-out destruction of their bodies was a kind of orgy. But Warren and Faye had not done it.

What do we do in life—and what can people do on film? After all, film makes such a show-off about what we are going to see, you can forget feeling and the obdurate truth of damage. In Charles Frazier's novel of *Cold Mountain,* Inman and Ada are awkward, inexperienced people who have been numbed by separation. They do not leap on each other; they fumble toward mere touching. This takes time and the book lets that time elapse. They talk about their loss of years and fruitfulness. They are like battered virgins who at last slip into a togetherness that Frazier has earned by exploring the inward hurt of their desire. There are pages of this—written with mournful feeling and gathering urgency—before this:

> He had been living like a dead man and this was life before him, an offering within his reach. He leaned forward and pulled the clothes from her hands and drew her to him. He put the flats of his palms on her thigh fronts, and then he moved his hands up her flanks and rested his forearms on her hipbones and touched his fingertips to the swale at the small of her back. He moved his fingers up and touched one by one the knobs of her backbone. He touched the insides of her arms, ran his hands down her sides until they rested on the flare of her hips. He bowed his forehead to the soft of her stomach. Then he kissed her

there and she smelled like hickory smoke. He pulled her against him and held her and held her. She put a hand to the back of his neck and pulled him harder, and then she pressed her white arms around him as if forever.

That "forever" is reaching for the sublime. We do not expect Charles Frazier's rhythmic prose, his boned detail and precision, or his use of "swale" and "hickory smoke" to conclude with anticlimax—*But it really wasn't very good for either of them.* People in sex do sometimes get that result. For Frazier, the lovemaking is an elevation in the narrative. Inman will soon be dead, but the coition has left Ada pregnant. It is part of Frazier's preoccupation that he knows that while sexual action involves bones, hands, swales, and touching, there is so much about it that cannot be seen or uttered. The electronics of brain chemistry occur in the head, which is good for literature but a torment to cinema.

I have suggested that the movies arrived at a moment when they helped guide us from seeing sex as an obligation, a marital duty, victimization, or bad luck to a source of pleasure that might be the most intense we would ever find. It seems fatuous to regard that as anyone's design, but movies did coincide with a kind of mass romanticism—the wondering if we (as in *all* of us) could be happy—and that also overlapped with unhindered sensual pleasure (feeling good, satisfaction) and the delusion of pursuing happiness embodied in advertising.

For decades, our narrative movies were commercials for desire: they didn't just yearn for the object of the ordeal—like Ada being there for Inman—but they craved yearning itself as an engine of continued existence. In hindsight, therefore, it's easier to see the movies as a medium founded in desire's deferment than in its achievement: better to look at Valentino or Garbo in close-up, to want them, to dream about them, than to actually get to a point where Rudy and Greta could strip down, possess a rumpled bed in odd shafts of sunlight, and just talk and screw in their humdrum, blissful, untidy dream—the way Viva and Louis Waldon do in *Blue Movie*.

A crisis in this life of the imagination came when censorship gave up the ghost. Ironically, that seemed to be part of our wish to be grown up, mature, and free from humbug and hypocrisy. If we were looking at desire, why not have it visible? Well, maybe. Or was so much of the alleged liberation really a display of brutal sexism and the remorseless commercial exploitation on the part of the movie business?

No movie embodied this struggle of different desires more than *Last Tango in Paris* (1972). On the one hand, Bernardo Bertolucci's film was an appointed test site, and it quickly acquired an air of decisive drama, aided by Pauline Kael's *New Yorker* review with its references to the 1913 debut of Stravinsky's *Rite of Spring*. To read that review in 1972 was to be thrilled by Kael's anticipation of a sexual storm breaking, with characters and actors doing it on camera for a big or important picture—call it a masterpiece. Bertolucci and Brando seemed united in the feeling that sex deserved its delivery now, in 1972. You felt that Kael at least was getting it.

This was a project where the beautiful or the sordid, art and pornography, seemed to be screwing each other. It had two strangers insisting that immediate sex is more pressing than character, background, choice, or names. He meets Her in an uninhabited Parisian apartment and they couple in a sudden, unconsidered way. They have surrendered to immediacy, a denial of narrative. The physicality with which Maria Schneider's body spins away from her new lover, Marlon Brando, is as thrilling as any orgasms they have had. And parts of the film's beauty are the flesh-tone colors and the space or play of the empty flat—things conspired in by photographer Vittorio Storaro and designer Nando Scarfiotti. The action seems overwhelming and impulsive, but the look of it is loaded with art and myth. So when He turns Her over and brings butter to her anus, is he screwing a boy as well as outraging his nymph? Why is he drawn to anal intercourse and its air of mastery? Is that a feeling for raw power, a longing for perversion? Or is it some echo of homosexuality in the memory? These days, the "back door" figures a lot in our movies. It photographs well until you hear the Yale frat cry "No means yes, and yes means anal."

In 1981, a curiosity appeared: *The Quest for Fire,* by Jean-Jacques Annaud, derived from a novel published in Belgium in 1911. It was set about eighty thousand years ago, and its characters were Paleolithic, yet dudes like us. One element of the film had a radical female (Rae Dawn Chong), who civilizes a male by encouraging him to have sex with her in "the missionary position" as opposed to the rear-entry method that was orthodox then (and more observable in animals; we see chimps doing it that way in *Jane,* the 2017 documentary about Jane Goodall).

The assumption was that that new face-to-face position was more intimate or conciliatory. Didn't it involve the two looking into each other's eyes as they came? Wasn't that more loving? That term, "the missionary position," had been used by Alfred Kinsey in 1948 in *Sexual Behavior in the Human Male.* But he hardly knew where it came from or felt able to account for its religious undertone. Was it really what missionaries had recommended in colonial situations? Was it "better" than what had gone before? Was it more civilized? Or more likely to lead to pregnancy? Did it encourage the thought that sex was a sacrament in atheist times? Did the missionary have a gospel to share?

American audiences were intrigued by *The Quest for Fire*—it earned $55 million at the box office. Its fable helps us appreciate the sexual mythology in *Last Tango in Paris,* where a famous fading beauty (Brando was nearing fifty) was doing it with an unknown but voluptuous twenty-year-old. She seemed willing to be naked from any angle. She seemed to have sex; she seemed to be buggered. All by a man draped in a shit-brown coat whose private parts do not come into sight, whether flaccid or erect. Brando had said he would strip for the film, but he flinched at the last moment. He said he couldn't get it up. So he was excused or catered to. After all, he was being paid $250,000 compared with Maria Schneider's $4,000 (the film grossed $96 million). Later she said that she had been exploited, that Brando and Bertolucci had conspired against her in the anal sex scene. She felt raped.

Last Tango was first praised for its actuality, but a feeling of fraudulence soon crept in. The stars didn't do it in that Paris apartment—and once you thought about it you marveled that you had ever believed they would. After all, Marlon Brando was a movie star, and there was no tradition for such figures inserting an erect penis somewhere or other into some woman or some man. A primitive instinct in us said, No, *that* can't be done—*that* is sacrilege. In the TV series *The Crown,* Princess Margaret was shown during sex, but could a series show us the Queen having an orgasm?

From the late 1960s there was more sex in life than there had been ten years earlier. The pill was a generative technology. So there was more on the screen, too, as if candor had become obligatory. But there were problems or reservations. A number of actresses resisted the pressure to go naked. It wasn't that they weren't pretty enough or ready for two-faced movies full of "respect" yet fuller with dirty minds. There was even a film, in 1979, *The Seduction of Joe Tynan,* where you could see that Meryl Streep had breasts.

Of course, the men exposed nothing precious. They had been taking off their shirts since movies began; accordingly, they worked out and shaved their chests. But no one ever saw the dick of the great male icons.

There's another issue—technical, I suppose, but intriguing. Intercourse is hard to film or to see. When male and female bodies come together in the most obvious coital adjacency—the missionary position—there is not much room for a camera to squeeze in.

If you are Anthony Minghella directing the lovemaking sequence in *Cold Mountain* you realize that if Ada and Inman really get it on their bodies will be pushed tight together and you won't see what's happening. So you fragment the event (as Minghella does) into glimpses of caressing and foreplay; you stress how naked Ada is, as if her soul is open, too; you let the light warm the occasion; you guess you'll use music when you edit it, something rhapsodic (from Gabriel Yared)—and then you need just a few seconds of thrusting (Jude Law on top is a favorite) before you can go to your money shot, which is Kidman with her eyes closed, her head back, with a selection of tasteful sighs and groans.

I say tasteful because I doubt we're ready for grunts, snorts, roars, other elemental sounds, or even screams. (We do get them from David Lynch, but he hears so much.) *Cold Mountain* doesn't really want to suggest that Ada or Nicole are out of control—or to admit the primitivism in the spurt of coming. If you think about it, American film has been far more reluctant to show the guy coming or in a mix of glory and indignity. Pornography has a similar tight-lipped mood. Guys don't like to lose control—that screaming bit is something they induce in women. Their uncontrolled noise is the tribute to authority that guys expect.

So a shooting strategy evolved in sex scenes for mainstream movies. This mise-en-scène was as formal and precise as the way fistfights used to be shot. It amounted to a formula that seemed fake (or traditional) to audiences and felt like embarrassment and exploitation for the actors and actresses doing it. And in the larger world of film, those involved began to feel overshadowed or upstaged by the ribald frolic of Louis and Viva in *Blue Movie,* with his stiff penis in her incredulous but valiant mouth and with the spilling, uncomposed compositions in which they were on top of each other—and doing it? There was a revelation (teased by the title of the film) that sexual collisions could be foolish, clumsy, comic, and boring—until radiance struck. Sex felt ordinary—and that had always been a heretical idea in Hollywood.

Gay sex had advantages in this quagmire. It was easier to film: if one man buggered another, that allowed the camera to see both faces; it was a situation in which energy and satisfaction were more visible. The two bodies were more open than in the impacted missionary position. And if one person sucked another's penis, that was a tidy two-shot, as fundamental as shooting someone in the head.

There's a lot else: the narrative liberty in gay sex was freer than the straight merger—it did not have to live with the possibility of pregnancy, marital commitment, or contractual happiness. Apparently, gay people had sex because they enjoyed it. That was a bit closer to intercourse for its own sake. In gay sex, there was the chance that the whole performance could be for laughs or at least seen in an ironic light, in which two people (or more) could tell themselves, Well, we're just doing our Dionysian thing! instead of being drawn like Ada and Inman to the sacrament that had "true love" and "forever" in view.

Of course, gay sex scenes did not appear on mainstream screens. Not in *Sunday Bloody Sunday* or *Making Love,* not in *Brokeback Mountain* or any other brave arthouse treatment of gay life you might be able to name (it's not a long list). Now, you may be saying, again, Well, of course not. You can't do that. In which case you might recall or look at *Blue Is the Warmest Color* (2013). In that film, by Abdellatif Kechiche, two women are involved in a lesbian love affair with extended and luxuriant naked lovemaking scenes.

I was going to say it leaves no uncertainty about what women do—or what men could do for women. But then I looked again, and in the studiously composed shots of the two bodies at sex, down on each other, and with a sound track heavy with orgasm, I realized that vaginas and pubic hair were not actually in sight. If sex is raw and wild (*if* it is), then this vaunted film had stayed cool and collected.

In doing that, the two actresses—Léa Seydoux and Adèle Exarchopoulos—could not help but be implicated. They are both movie pretty and in very good shape. (We do not get our fair share of overweight lovers.) They were both apparently committed to the film—though there were stories later that they had felt exploited. To me, the film seems "very beautiful"—which means I liked looking at it—and I cannot separate that from my being turned on or aroused. A film of lesbian lovemaking has an easier ride at the box office than a film of male homosexuals at work. It's something men like to watch.

From the moment *Blue* premiered at Cannes (where it won the Palme d'Or in a unique decision that gave the award to the two actresses as well as the director), it was controversial. Some said it exploited lesbianism. Despite its length and its relative lack of regular action, the film did very well: on a cost of about $4 million, it earned nearly $20 million at the box office. A significant part of that came from male voyeurism in the audience, and it's possible to be disapproving of that. But then you have to accept that male voyeurism and female yearning have been locked together in what we used to call cinema. Did *Blue* promote or help explain lesbianism? Possibly. But many guys have been more understanding of that than they are of gay butt fucking.

"Gay butt fucking and fisting" is more or less accessible to readers now, and meekly acknowledged in pained, polite society even if in, say, 1960 the majority of people would not have known what the words meant. There has been an astonishing sexual education, though a conservative segment of America deplores the new knowledge and believes it has been a curse on decency and plans for American greatness. But we have lived through pornography, even if no one seems to have been responsible for it. Indeed, its tide seems as helpless as global warming or as helpless as we are in the face of it.

Pornography is a bad word, isn't it, and one that easily conjures up a sordid industry, ravaged by money, sexual exploitation, and unfairness to women. Just like Hollywood? Why not? A lot of pornography has been made in the suburbs of Los Angeles, with work for technicians and actors who find it harder to get hired on a big movie. But why is the word "pornography" bad, when the word "blue" is so enticing?

This is what pornography means in the dictionary: it is something—pictures, writing, actions—"that depict sex to arouse people to sexual activity." As if sexual activity is not pleasant, useful, and necessary if human life is to continue, and forgivable in the limited short-term (if you're dying in a cancer ward). The classification "pornography" is often assumed to be indecent or disgusting or commercially minded or wicked. But consider Charles Frazier's passage quoted earlier about how Ada and Inman at last reached carnal knowledge in *Cold Mountain*. Is that an objective description of what happened, or is it a self-sufficient expression of desire and sexuality that cannot be read or imagined without a level of sympathy that may be arousal?

Pornography is an old art or diversion. There are "dirty" pictures on walls that go back centuries, and some of them are officially priceless. But modern pornography is a manifestation of changing technology. There were blue movies before sound. Movies were, in their nature, things seen in the company of strangers. Implicitly the Production Code was a recognition of things that were fit to be seen in company, without loss of dignity or reputation. But in the late 1970s and the early 1980s, video changed our circumstances or our stance. It was a medium that could contain secret extremism that we could watch in privacy (or solitude). We did not have to be seen watching it. Our secret life found traction. Was it coincidence that this process took place just as the communal watching—going to the movies—made a more rapid decline than it had had in the decades since the arrival of television?

This would not have been possible without technological transformation. Within a few years we could rent tapes that were less stories than instructional records of carnal encounters. We could watch these in our own homes, with friends, lovers, spouses, and household pets— or alone. Film has moved from being a mass experience to an acceptance of solitude. We could use them as foreplay to masturbation, or they could be scenarios that we might imitate. We thought we were imitating sexual prowess, but weren't we also imitating imitation?

So it's not just naughty boys masturbating. It's not just lonely men and women getting closer to sexual release than they have managed in real life. It may be Supreme Court justices, ministers of religion, and accomplished psychiatrists using videotapes of sex to broaden their horizons.

Hadn't we been using entertainment movies in the same way for decades? All that had changed was the new privacy, the daring it might release, and the speed with which acts could be imitated. Yes, companies made a small fortune on these tapes, and young men and women may have been corrupted in the process; they may have killed themselves. But hadn't that been going on in movies?

Still, there is more to be said about pornography. It has many subgenres, but don't most of them cater to heterosexual male viewers? Is there porn made for heterosexual women? I don't think so, and I fear that signals a dominant male gaze that exists in nearly all cinema. We still know too little about the differences in male and female arousal in the process of watching. Are women voyeurs? Notice the assertion of power that rules pornography—and most mainstream movies. Aren't the women lying there to be filmed? Could it even be that the medium itself has embodied the sexual exploitation we realize we must disown?

I think the Frazier passage from *Cold Mountain* is equally arousing for men and women; take away the visual and the sexual imagination opens up. I believe that's what the author intended, in a generous spirit, and it is a measure of his writing that he makes us feel for Ada and Inman; he puts us on the cusp of fulfillment and tragedy. I would say much the same about the famous affirmative conclusion of James Joyce's *Ulysses*. This extends to Velazquez's *Rokeby Venus,* to nudes by Egon Schiele, and to many movies—*Pandora's Box, Belle de Jour, Blue Is the Warmest Color,* so much of Fassbinder, Almodóvar, and the way Margaret Sullavan feels anxious in *The Shop Around the Corner.* That film opens up so many mysteries, including the comedy of epistolary lovers who cannot abide each other at Matuschek's store in old Budapest. We trust they will be happy after "The End," but misunderstanding may be their heyday. The mythology of male authority has to be abandoned for these things to work.

It's in the many genres of filmed pornography that you can find a rich cavern of gay material. It involves young, thin, athletic pod-people, not necessarily beautiful but pretty in most cases, and as ready as soldiers who have had their fear operated on. The women (and many of the men) have shaved or waxed themselves because pornography regards pubic hair as an impediment to visibility. It is scraped away, and the camera becomes familiar with the folds of labia, the hood of clitoris, and the ways in which penetration can be accomplished.

These films are generally in the region of five to thirty minutes long. They are often very well shot and lit, though sophistication is not essential. There is no story, just the process, with a few abiding scenario outlines, like the young woman on the streets of some Eastern European city who timidly consents to be given a lift but turns out to be a nerveless sexual athlete. The sex is done without affection, responsibility, or consequence. There is seldom any conversation and little prospect of character or humor. The sex is straight-faced, merciless, like a workout.

You wonder if the availability of such material has stimulated indifference, or does it say, Look, you need to express yourself for the sake of your health. There are some people who don't have enough love or companionship, and feel miserable, but coming helps them get through poverty, loneliness, and rage without turning to suicide, murder, or acts of rape practiced on children. Would you prefer to have Father masturbate to *Boogie Nights* or be a functioning pederast?

Paul Thomas Anderson's *Boogie Nights* (1997) is so remarkable it's hard to pin down. It is a wild comedy where laughter treads on the pain of desperate and self-destructive people. Some are killed, some kill themselves. Real love is like the gay crush Philip Seymour Hoffman's boom operator has on Dirk Diggler—and that boom is a metaphor for mockery. The film has no more respect for sex than it might have for other hobbies and pastimes. It is also a portrait of an unscrupulous business with its own Oscar-like trophies and a bogus sense of being at the center of the universe. In Jack Horner (Burt Reynolds), the lethargic, bored impresario of all this sex, it has one of the most depressing American showmen in movies. (Several illustrious actors declined the role because they feared it would impair their dignity—then Reynolds got nominated for it.) In Julianne Moore and Heather Graham it takes

two attractive actresses, puts them through the drab motions of endless sex, and lets them be sweet, silly, vapid people mouthing platitudes.

Then there is Dirk Diggler, real name Eddie Adams (Mark Wahl-
berg, who has since disowned the film). He becomes a porn star, a
character based to some extent on the real John Holmes. Dirk and his
buddy Reed (John C. Reilly) are in the business of inserting themselves
into any indicated orifice. There is not a discriminating bone in their
puppy bodies. But they are fond chums in one of the most childish gay
relationships in American film. No, they don't have sex—but we know
them. Take that with the knockout revelation of Dirk's heroic member all done with plaster, merkins, and camera tricks—and you have
one of the funniest and most camp treatments of the heterosexual god-
head. The dick is a ridiculous show-off—something many women have
learned, but they go along with it in the spirit of compromise.

Only one other film is as revelatory as *Boogie Nights*. This other is
nice, sweet, crowd-pleasing, and deep-soaked in commercial compromise, but with one of the most famous scenes in American film. I am
thinking of the delicatessen scene in *When Harry Met Sally* (1989),
when Sally—Meg Ryan in her signature moment—shows Harry just
how much a girl can fake it in "coming" for a guy to keep him reassured.
As written by Nora Ephron and directed by Rob Reiner, it is a modern renewal of a construct from screwball comedy, that people make
bigger fools of themselves over sex than anything else. It also suggests
that a woman could manage on her own or with another interested
girl—don't forget that older woman in the delicatessen who observes
Sally's act and says, "I'll have what she's having." (That woman is Rob
Reiner's mother.)

You know the scene—and don't minimize the value of a movie scene
that "everyone" knows. The hope for an immense shared experience
still lives within the scope of movies. But such epiphanies are harder
now that the old romance of cinema—that we desired the thing shown
to us and would aspire to it—is tinged with irony, ridicule, or coldness.
What Ryan/Sally did in that scene was the introduction of a challeng-
ing future: that sex is pretense, an act, a masquerade, but one in which
we still long to believe. Do you see how far that simulated orgasm says,

Don't trust the old real, romantic thing. We can't do that anymore, just as we don't quite accept "love" as the proper or singular destiny of our stories. But maybe fake orgasms can be fun, too, and less tiring. We might be actors.

When Harry Met Sally is not a great film (I can recall little of the rest of it). It is not as good as *Some Like It Hot.* But is it more perceptive? The fake orgasm scene is like a second shoe falling after that passage in Billy Wilder's film where a bountiful yet abject Marilyn Monroe has to kiss Tony Curtis long and hard to dispel his impotence. In *Some Like It Hot* that "fun" glitters with cruelty and the exploitation of Sugar, whereas Sally is intelligent, amused, generous, and in charge. She may be giving away her own magic, but she seems to realize it's time her guy grew up. And she has an inkling that faking things could be a quest for humane kindness. In the decades of marriage ahead, not quite knowing if she's coming or pretending could be a lifesaver that commands respect and keeps Harry awake. That delicious misunderstanding is the bond that ties Alfred and Klara together in *The Shop Around the Corner.* Never settle for familiarity or comfort: they are death to desire.

18

An Open Door

Daniel Day-Lewis and Vicky Krieps in *Phantom Thread* (2017),
with clothes still an ultimate in movie erotica

DAN WHITE, the murderer, served just over five years in prison. On his release, he became a wanderer: he spent time in Los Angeles, by court order; he went to Ireland for several months; then he returned to San Francisco, and it was at his wife's home (they were separated by then) that he rigged a car so its exhaust would be directed back into the vehicle. I said "wanderer," and there's something sad or fictional in that word, as if to say a White movie could present him as a haunted outcast (Channing Tatum, perhaps?) instead of a deadened brute.

His lawyer claimed that this suicide vindicated White's trial plea of "diminished capacity." Yet maybe suicide was a reasoned response to reflection and dismay. Guilt is legitimate, long after legal proceedings.

White had provoked his fatal events by resigning as a city supervisor. Yet he had the support of the police union, and there were plenty who shared his disapproval of homosexuals gaining influence in San Francisco. Our city became a famous gay stronghold, where a majority supported gay rights, and where gay studs might walk naked in the sunshine in the Castro district. But as it became a "saved" city, a sanctuary, so it was easier to ignore a more reactionary America that began thirty miles inland and only a few miles to the south. The mindset of a split nation has grown and fostered horror and hatred on both sides.

The facts show astonishing changes in the mindset as well as a persistent conservatism in an allegedly liberal state. As recently as 2000, Californian citizens voted in favor of Proposition 22, which said that marriage was only for partners of opposite sexes. That measure passed by 61 percent to 39.

Then, in 2004, Gavin Newsom became mayor of San Francisco, succeeding Willie Brown and following in the line of Frank Jordan, Art Agnos, and Dianne Feinstein, who had herself succeeded George Moscone by virtue of being president of the board of supervisors. She had announced the murders of Moscone and Milk on national television moments after finding the bodies and feeling for a pulse.

Once in office, Newsom (aged thirty-seven, typecasting for handsome and promising) instructed the city clerks to issue marriage licenses to same-sex couples. These measures were then annulled by the state and by Governor Arnold Schwarzenegger as being illegal. Newsom heard the national criticism of his pioneering and said, "This door's wide open now. It's going to happen whether you like it or not." He was correct, but his action was provocative. Public ferment over its deliberate illegality weighed on the 2004 general election and was used by Republicans to undermine the candidacy of John Kerry. In November 2004, Kerry lost to George W. Bush in an election that split 50.7 percent to 48.3.

Then in 2008 the California Supreme Court declared gay marriage legal (banning it, they said, was against the state constitution). But that decision was immediately followed by Proposition 8 (an initiative put forward by conservative elements in the 2008 elections), which called for reaffirmation of the ban on gay marriage. That measure passed by 52.2 (just over seven million votes) to 47.7 percent. So new gay unions were put on hold until 2013 when the state court finally blocked efforts to impede the right to gay marriage. One may admire that decision, but a majority of Californians has never voted in favor of gay marriage.

This is all recent. We can rejoice in enlightenment while remembering how many are unpersuaded about the justice of gay rights. In many places in the nation, gay life is still under huge, unkind pressures. The same could be said for black liberty—or something like freedom and a pursuit of happiness for the poor. Some hate new possibilities in America to the point of vengeance. In the Alabama Senate contest of December 2017, Judge Roy Moore's defeat was taken as a breakthrough for liberalism though he lost by very few votes. A candidate less scarred by accusations of sexual misconduct but more circumspect, younger, more modern, and more gracefully bigoted would have won that election and been as hostile to sodomy as Moore. That biblical word was his.

Dan White's failure to apologize came from resolute antipathy, and such a certainty could kill again. It represents a primal horror over homosexuality wrapped up in "scripture." This cultural antagonism can take many forms, some foreboding, but some that are comic in retrospect. And comedy can be the best juice for compromise—and marriage.

In the spring of 1958, Gore Vidal was asked by MGM to work on the script for a remake of *Ben-Hur*. He groaned, even with William Wyler in line to direct and Vidal's friend Paul Newman willing to play Judah Ben-Hur. The studio was reckoning on a budget of $15 million, some of which could trickle down to Vidal. Still, he saw the project as deluded imitation of a religious belief that no longer prevailed. He read and disliked the first script (by Karl Tunberg).

Then he yielded, as writers often do in Hollywood. He signed his contract and gave it to a waiting studio messenger who happened to be the twenty-year-old Jack Nicholson trying to get ahead. When Newman and then Rock Hudson could not be secured for Ben-Hur, Charlton Heston came into view, no matter that Vidal felt he had "all the charm of a wooden Indian." And so a blond Episcopalian of Scots-English descent played a Jewish hero, and no one worried over the discrepancy.

As he wrote his script, Vidal could not understand how the characters Ben-Hur and Messala (friends since childhood) fell out. These old pals became bitter enemies, resolving their hostility in the famous chariot race. That needed a motivation, and Vidal had a subversive idea. He proposed to Wyler and the producer, Sam Zimbalist, "that Ben-Hur and Messala had been boyhood lovers. But Ben-Hur, under the fierce Palestinian sun and its jealous god, had turned straight as a die while Messala, the decadent Gentile, had remained in love with Ben and wanted to take up where they had left off. . . . When Ben-Hur rebuffs Messala's advances, a deep and abiding hatred fills Messala to the brim."

Wyler and Zimbalist flinched at this mischief. Don't tell Heston, they begged. That interplay now seems more entertaining than the film. But Vidal wrote his idea (he said) and then there were rewrites by Christopher Fry and others (only Tunberg got credit). Heston would say later that the Vidal interpretation was foolish. Vidal said Heston never knew about the gay subtext, but Stephen Boyd (Messala) enjoyed the innuendo. Later still, Heston insisted this approach was *not* employed. He felt Fry had clarified the key quarrel scene so that Messala the Roman tribune disapproves of Judah Ben-Hur's hopes for Jewish liberation.

So is Vidal's scene really "there" in the finished film? Is there a gay subtext in so many heroic movies? In 1959, audiences didn't notice it.

Ben-Hur was a triumph and one of the last movie testaments to our old-time faith: it won eleven Oscars and earned back ten times what it had cost. But it dated fast in the rush of the 1960s as *Jesus Christ Superstar* became a new spiritual model. Today, it is one of the more curiously enigmatic buddy films and a sign of how movies were turning to self-parody. The spectacle of the chariot race looks oddly pedestrian—or let's say equestrian—in an age of CGI. But Vidal's explanation lurks beneath the film's surface, and it helps us see that movies are only briefly owned by their makers before becoming public property, part of the waking dream about who we are or might be.

From time to time in this book, I have suggested subtexts half-hidden in famous movies (a cat in the bag)—and that may seem as mischievous as Vidal's reading of Messala. But humor can unlock meanings. In *Casablanca,* you recall, as Victor and Ilsa fly away from North Africa, Rick and Louis Renault (Bogart and Claude Rains) disappear into the fog on Rick's heard line, "This could be the start of a beautiful friendship."

Rick has elected to give up Ilsa—she really had no say in the matter—as a gesture of respect for Victor Laszlo and a feeling that personal lives count for very little in wartime. So Rick and Louis—cynics, gamblers, womanizers, and men of the world—are left to disappear into the hinterland of North Africa. What will "beautiful friendship" mean?

I'm teasing, but one can anticipate some gay potential in the male bonding of *The Sting, Red River, Casino,* the *Ocean's* films, *Fight Club,* Laurel and Hardy, Tom and Jerry . . . the list goes on. For decades, our elders thought it was grand to dwell on these eternal buddies. This could reach extraordinary raptures: Astaire and Rogers are less a heterosexual proposition than opposing atoms in a molecule called perfection. "He gave her class, she gave him sex." Does that mean the 1930s thought about Fred and Ginger "doing it"? I don't think so—just look at Fred with Cyd Charisse in *The Band Wagon* or *Silk Stockings* to feel how different the real thing might be.

Astaire (real name Austerlitz) was not gay, and on film he rose above notions of intercourse. I enjoy Astaire, because he is not entirely or merely human. He is made of light, music, and the sound of his heels on hard floors. Sometimes he feels more animated than carnal. Still, a lot of his admirers are unsettled by the idea of Fred as a gay icon. Some heavy Dan White instinct works against that. Is that business pressure and cultural habit, or is there dread involved?

I have argued that the arrival of movies coincided with and impelled our new hope for sexual pleasure—as a reward for true love and a comfort for people who had little else to look forward to. The structure of filmwatching (looking for enlightenment) encouraged the principle that desire was good. It let us look at both sexes at the same time, seeing that they were equally desirable. In voyeurism, so many impossible dreams were put in our laps that sex became cinematic. The engine of projection drove it. In the twentieth century—the movie era—that helped make sexual experiment more inviting. Weren't we sitting there like researchers (Kinsey researchers perhaps) sorting through human variety?

This was never organized, let alone conspiratorial. The first gay people at work in Hollywood may have been pleased with themselves and kept a few jobs for friends. But they no more intended that American movies be gay than they planned to make them Jewish, Communist, or multiracial. The power in movie was extraordinary and radical, but its owners and practitioners were anxious to keep the medium conservative or businesslike. The most productive gay directorial careers—George Cukor and James Ivory, say—stayed discreet, gentlemanly, and "inoffensive." They rarely touched gay material.

There was only one test in Hollywood: could you make money for the system? Even if Cukor had once offended Clark Gable, he was hired again on a string of profitable movies. So MGM revered *The Philadelphia Story, Gaslight,* and *Adam's Rib*—though now it has little idea how to make movies in which people talk together in fun, at cross-purposes, or near the end of their tether. Cukor was one of many effective gays in Hollywood who knew that you could have a career and do good work if you lived quietly. Nearly every active heterosexual I have ever known has had the same hopes. We most of us don't want to be noticed. The best Ivory-Merchant film may be *Remains of the Day,* which aches with feeling for a man so self-repressed that he cannot speak up for his own romantic feelings. That may be gayer than *Maurice,* the one Ivory film that addresses homosexuality directly and comes off rather awkward.

Gayness is ordinary; it need not be the crux of a story; it could be as incidental as having dark hair or being left-handed. Imagine *12 Angry Men* (1957) ending with juror no. 8 (Henry Fonda, calm, reasonable in his white suit but oddly cut off from the real, sweaty lives the other jurors lead; he is sort of saintly) leaving the court after those hectic jury room arguments and embracing his husband before disappearing into the city.

The real lives of gays are not melodramatically splendid or as lifted on the air of resistance that affected movies made during the struggle for gay liberation. Gays can be bored and boring. Yet we treasure characters like Andrew Beckett (Tom Hanks) in *Philadelphia* (1993) because they make heroic sacrifices, with a noble stance. Beckett was the first gay character to win an Oscar—presented to the Hanks who is often said to be as impeccably regular as James Stewart.

But there have been so many more gay people who had to accommodate anonymity and failure. If you now disapprove of Kevin Spacey (born in 1959) remember that he was a kid in love with acting who felt he had to bury his sexual identity to get work. He needed to chase that inner self out of sight. So some gays of his age went into hiding. For a time he was heroic, then he became powerful—a grave plight in America. Some had it much harder.

Portrait of Jason is a documentary shot in 1966. Jason Holliday was in his early forties, a black, gay hustler hoping to mount a nightclub act, an incorrigible pretender, a line-shooter, a liar, a vivid nobody. He was thrilled by the offer to be on film as himself. Shirley Clarke directed the simple, remorseless photography, with a crew that became Jason's audience for a day and a night at his Chelsea Hotel apartment.

Jason could be cool, dainty, and very funny: he says he fell in love as easily as turning on the light. He laughs at the disarray of his own life, but he is close to tears. He is defiant, drunk, desperate, and alone. The critic Richard Brody said of him, he is "the frustrated performer who performs everywhere but where he wants to." It is a haunting portrait of someone who sees the outlines of his own failure. You feel the crew watching him like interrogators or vultures. We marvel that Jason lived another twenty years. He had once studied with Charles Laughton, a victim of his own guilt who thought showing off could be his cover.

Portrait of Jason was well received when it opened at the New York Film Festival. Ingmar Bergman thought it "extraordinary." But a full portrait of a black, gay loser did not flourish. Most showbiz biopics celebrate success. Even if their subjects end up in the gutter, it's a movie gutter, with art direction and lighting. The film was believed to be lost until a print was found and it was restored. By the time of its re-release (2013), a gay loser was closer to being a cultural hero; and being black could be sustained.

Portrait of Jason is entrancing, and of great significance historically. For it is a glimpse into a wracked soul, a man who is not just gay and a pimp, not just black, but poor. He is a failure at something he loves to do: I mean acting, or pretending, or lying—at escaping himself. It is a regular part of movie culture that we cherish that pursuit and its dream of success. Weren't you tickled to hear that the kid Jack Nicholson was once doing humble messenger work on his way to being the Joker or Jake Gittes? Jason Holliday never made it, but there he is on screen for an hour and forty-five minutes illustrating that failure can be a natural American destination.

The reluctance of our movies to give credit to those ways of existing in America has been shaming and destructive. But it is not the entirety of our self-inflicted damage, for the cult of greatness, of winning, hangs over us. It is a thundercloud in which we find it hard to breathe. It wants to believe in Jack Nicholson instead of unknown New Jersey kids with few advantages who end up as vagrants. (The real Nicholson has a net worth of around $400 million.)

It has given us a tradition of films in which good-looking, strong, brave American men come through in the contests that require fortitude, righteousness, unshakable moral confidence, and force of arms, as opposed to the everyday discovery that our guys—us—are also inconsistent, afraid, weak, and fallible.

This movie code embraces filmmakers from John Ford and Howard Hawks to John Wayne, Errol Flynn, Gary Cooper, and Clint Eastwood. I am not attacking those people, or minimizing their capacity to see beyond heroes fit to be mesas in Monument Valley. For Hawks and Ford, Wayne played men who become tyrants and who need to be overthrown. Gary Cooper had an aplomb and a grin to die for in the 1930s, but he went on to play ruined figures in *Meet John Doe,* in *High Noon* even, and in *Man of the West.*

Another possibility exists of rounded Chekhovian male characters—brave cowards, unsteady leaders, anxious lovers (these are characters worthy of Renoir, Ozu, Ophüls, Mizoguchi, Buñuel, Bresson, Bergman, Fassbinder, Antonioni, and many others). That pantheon could include *The Devil Is a Woman, My Man Godfrey, The Awful Truth, Citizen Kane* (the story of a failure), *Bringing Up Baby, The Shop Around the Corner, The Lady Eve, Notorious, It's a Wonderful Life, A Place in the Sun, Vertigo,* and others that see the secure place of uncertainty and insecurity in America.

But there are so many films restricted by the stamp of male aplomb. And so many characters who have guns to back up that implacability. Decades of action-adventure movies carried admirable men forward to victory, the establishment of social order without debate or criticism, and an unswerving sense of these noblemen getting their women in a last triumphant close-up—so long as they didn't have to talk to them or ask for their ideas. These are not "bad" films: the generality of tales in which fine men save the world, their ladies, and our destiny could include *The Big Sleep* and *To Have and Have Not,* films I cherish.

The standard adventure films are in the mainstream assertion of moral prowess, male authorship and power, and gun rights. Even when a picture seems to have a critical or realistic edge, a secret glamorization is at work. The two parts of *The Godfather* are impeccable narratives in which the idea is proposed that America is an opportunity for organized crime where appealing people given power will turn lethal and corrupt. But that reading misses the ways male viewers want to be part of the Corleone family, because their company is close, loyal, and reliable, because it settles so many other distracting questions, and because it places women as subordinate figures who accept their role as weary, hushed trophies set to be betrayed, exploited, and shut out of the room.

Would you guess Dan White liked the *Godfather* films? They stroke so many immature male neuroses. Do you recognize how these subtexts are frequently perceived as reassuring gospel by the sections of

American society that most deplore gay life? And it's not just "them." So many of us want to be as brave as Michael in the Italian restaurant, executing Sollozzo and McCluskey.

The company of men in these pictures is a metaphor for male bonding that may exclude other levels of happiness or experience. The cultural civil war in America comes from male communion and its uneasiness with racial diversity, with female agency, and its fear and loathing of homosexuality. By a margin now, Americans may honor gay rights in many walks of life, and they will smile and be friendly with gay people, but for the rest there is an abiding hostility.

The grotesque rise of Donald Trump has helped harden it. And that disdain of gay life is as hostile as the attitude to people of color, foreign religions, and any other departures from white American norms. The rabid claims for American tribal supremacy are the fault lines of insecurity. That segment of society is also thoroughly armed and prepared to erase some of the niceties of civil rights. It is a height of irony that that mood clings to old movie values, like "Don't apologize!"—John Wayne says that in *The Searchers* as if it comes from the Bill of Rights.

Still, the breakdown of commercial or mass cinema has left room for modest, intelligent, and inquiring gay films, "independent" pictures offered in the way new novels about our emotional or inward experience are published.

We have had an amber era of such movies, and a pioneer in the movement came in 1992 with Neil Jordan's *The Crying Game,* where Jaye Davidson (a male) played a transgender woman and was nominated for a Supporting Actor Oscar. His character was incidental to the larger framework of a political thriller, but Jordan and Davidson handled the character without much melodramatic strain. So, you felt, life can turn out like this—though it was life in Ireland, not the United States. Seven years later, in Kimberly Peirce's *Boys Don't Cry,* Hilary Swank won the Oscar as Brandon Teena, who transitioned from Teena Brandon. It was a virtuoso performance, but the film lived beneath the burden of its agenda. It felt like a flag to be planted on the barricades, or something great actresses did.

I prefer the taken-for-granted attitude to the female alliance between Emily Blunt and Natalie Press in *My Summer of Love.* That is set in England, and it shows a love affair between women of different classes. Among others of note, besides *Brokeback Mountain,* is the work of Lisa Cholodenko, a very alert, considered, and benign realist, who made *High Art* (1998), *Laurel Canyon* (2002), and *The Kids Are All Right* (2010), in which gender choices are seen as open territory. In *High Art,* Radha Mitchell is a magazine intern who goes to write an article on a legendary but reclusive photographer, Lucy Berliner (Ally Sheedy), who hardly works any longer. They become romantically involved, and Mitchell and Sheedy are one of the most intriguing lesbian couples in American film. *High Art* is also lit up by Patricia Clarkson as Greta, a veteran from the club that made the films of Rainer Werner Fassbinder. *High Art* is alert to the flirtatious adventures among attractive or ambitious people around New York. By now, it is a subject of some wonder that those hideaway homes (sometimes in *Laurel Canyon*) may contain gendering experiments that seldom get into mainstream American films.

It was as part of that same interest in place (filming in Glendale) that Tom Ford made *A Single Man* (2009), adapted from a Christopher Isherwood novel first published in 1964. Isherwood is a valuable figure in this history. With his long-term lover, the artist Don Bachardy, Isherwood kept a house and a salon on Adelaide Drive in Santa Monica (from 1959 to 1986) that was a meeting place for locals and foreign visitors, literary folk and movie people of all sexual persuasions. Many film professionals went to the Isherwood house and some had sex there. Isherwood was also composing some of his best novels—*The World in the Evening* as well as *A Single Man.* And, to keep his hand in, with complete lack of shame, he sometimes worked on scripts for archaic, overblown movies: *The Great Sinner* (1949), adapted from a Dostoevsky novel, with Gregory Peck as a novelist who becomes a desperate gambler; *Diane* (1956), with Lana Turner as Diane de Poitiers, courtier and odalisque from the sixteenth century—a work of upholstered twaddle. Ish told a friend that his recipe on such scripts was simple: "I steal bits from Balzac, Dumas and history, and have lots of poignards, poison and purple velvet." Here was the arch irony of the queer spirit beholding the travesty of history à la Hollywood. It had a disregard for the culture of old movies not far from the parodies in *The Carol Burnett Show* or the pastiche movie reviews written by S. J. Perelman.

But Isherwood also did a script from an Evelyn Waugh novella for the film *The Loved One,* with Terry Southern as a later cowriter. More than that, his diaries—written in an intriguing third person—are reports on Hollywood's secret history. But in his lifetime, the revered Isherwood was only thought worthy of the biggest screens because of the showbiz update of *Cabaret,* taken from Isherwood's Berlin stories of the late 1920s and 1930s and famous now for the very cold, very hot, gay-going-on-trans master of ceremonies, a role that has been played by Joel Grey and Alan Cumming. (Isherwood refused to see the play or the film.)

For the film of *A Single Man,* Colin Firth played the gay professor, George, who has lost his devoted lover of many years and who is so alone he feels suicidal. It is a self-consciously elegant film—Ford was a fashion designer before he turned to movies—but one of the most earnest tributes to a sensitive, urbane, yet rather austere homosexual archetype. George is gay beyond a doubt, but like many heterosexuals in love he prefers not to draw attention to himself emotionally—he wants to be incidental.

Yet the real Isherwood was a rowdy laugher, inclined to drink and infidelity, and an uncontrollable or spontaneous man. He was forever curious. In 1951, he visited the set of John Huston's *The Red Badge of Courage.* MGM had had the publicity idea of casting Audie Murphy as the boy Henry in Stephen Crane's book about courage and its obstacles.

Murphy was a phenomenon. In 1951, he was twenty-seven, but could have passed as ten years younger. Born in Texas to Irish sharecroppers, he was known for his terrible temper and his baby face. He lied about his age to get into the war and he was a soldier for over two years in Europe, winning every available medal including the Medal of Honor, and killing more people than an ill-educated kid could remember.

He did not bother to act, but his screen legend grew on his temper and his kill count. He was inspired casting as Crane's boy. Isherwood watched the shooting and evolved a classic exercise in how the queer looks at Hollywood he-men:

> Christopher got to say only a few words to Murphy but watched him a lot of the time. Murphy fascinated Christopher, not only because he was still boyishly attractive but because he appeared to be such a mixed-up and potentially dangerous character. No doubt his buddies had kidded him about his baby face, and Murphy, being too small to lick them, had gone into action and killed every German within sight.

Putting the hollow classicism of Huston's film aside, wouldn't you rather see a black comedy written by Isherwood, about a soldier boy who goes into tantrums whenever he's called a sissy and kills everyone he can get his sights on? David Lynch might direct. And this kid ends with so many medals he can hardly stand up in his own uniform.

The very composed air of George in *A Single Man* wants to express unbearable anguish. It's a portrait of gayness smothering its own suffering or outcast state—yet you know it's there, along with the character's class and intellect. At the Venice Film Festival, *A Single Man* won the Queer Lion award (a prize begun in 2007). Firth also won the acting prize at Venice, the Volpi Cup, and later on he got an Oscar nomination (Jeff Bridges won for *Crazy Heart*).

A Single Man did well commercially: on a budget of $7 million, it earned $25 million—that is the kind of business life hoped for in small, independent movies. But the success had some doubters. As released by the Weinstein Company, *A Single Man* had posters and trailers that moderated the picture's gay content. Julianne Moore (who played a friend of the Firth character) was prominently displayed and in the trailer a gay kiss was lost for scenes that seemed to promise more heterosexual content. Ford himself was caught in the middle (it was his first film; Harvey Weinstein was always a very forceful distributor). Ford said, "I don't think the movie's been de-gayed. I have to say that we live in a society that's pretty weird. For example, you can have full-frontal male nudity on HBO, yet in cinema, you can't have naked buttocks. You can't have men kissing without it being considered adult content. So, in order to cut a trailer that can go into broad distribution in theaters, certain things had to be edited out."

Today it is still hard to present a candid film about gay life for a mainstream audience. *Moonlight* is a superb film, and it did win Best Picture (after hesitations), but it never reached a huge audience. It earned $65 million, whereas *La La Land,* the film it just beat at the Oscars and a pretty celebration of making it, grossed $446 million. At the same time, outlandish comic book heroes and perky robots were deemed fit for children. It is actually hard to make a valuable film about any kind of real sex. But sometimes a film helps us see and feel that sex is just part of an extensive ocean in which brave people try to swim. Luca Guadagnino's *Call Me by Your Name* (2017) is such a movie, so filled with tenderness and sensuality that our sense of desire is enriched.

The film is set in an appealing, old Italian villa near a small town (it was Crema, in Cremona). The time is summer; the colors and the pacing suggest heat and ease. We are observing a filmed place where we want to be while summer drifts by. The feeling of adolescence on the cusp is as well done as film has managed. The family that lives in the house includes a bright, uneasy seventeen-year-old son Elio (Timothée Chalamet). They have a lodger for the summer, Oliver (Armie Hammer), a postgraduate student from America.

Elio and Oliver fall into a deep friendship, playful and intellectual, that takes on hints of physical desire for Elio. The kid is the aggressor. At the same time, Elio has a girlfriend, and we see them have sex for the first time, in a touching, half-clumsy, but natural way. This seems good for them, even if the girl fears that Elio will hurt her one day.

This happens. Their romance is surpassed by the attraction between Elio and Oliver that overcomes the older man's reluctance. Few gay love affairs have been conveyed with such respect and warmth. The sex is important, it seems actual, but not as much as our feeling for two souls whose lives may be altered and improved. There is no prospect of them being married or living together. Oliver goes back to America where he finds a woman he wants to marry. Despite a full enactment of love, the two young men are not simply gay. They are growing up and learning.

So it's a film I wish America had made. While it was shot in Italy and financed largely by European money, it is in English because it wanted the American market. The two lead actors are American; the script was adapted from André Aciman's novel by James Ivory, the American director who often lived in Europe. Ivory had had a fruitful filmmaking partnership and a long marriage with his producer, Ismail Merchant. They did not draw attention to their bond, but Merchant-Ivory was the most fertile gay marriage in filmmaking history (enriched by the work of their screenwriter Ruth Prawer Jhabvala).

Despite all these credentials, it is hard to believe *Call Me by Your Name* could have been made as an American film. It was released in America by Sony Classics, with some controversy over Elio being only seventeen. Had he been raped? some asked. Not in Italy, where the age of consent is fourteen. But in subject, sensuality, and adult attitudes (and even with Elio being bumped up to eighteen), could it have been an American film set in Connecticut or on Long Island one idyllic summer? American audiences saw the film and some loved it. Some complained that it was too much about well-off people sitting around discussing their destiny. Fair enough, but the same could be said for *Hamlet, Don Giovanni,* and *The Portrait of a Lady.* The film's respect for the ordinary, carnal aspect of homosexuality, and its awareness of people finding love in different ways, still seemed a big reach for American money.

As a child, I was shaped by the wholesome desirability of movie marriage, so that I did not notice for a long time how my own parents were not exactly married. Every family I knew seemed to have a scheme for dodging searching questions about the members of a marriage. In the 1950s, I knew no one who was divorced—I did not realize that my father had another household and a second "wifelike" figure on the other side of London. When we played the card game Happy Families, there were four in every unit, Mr. and Mrs. and two little ones. This syndrome is still evident in the game known as the television commercial, where buying into the product apparatus of our economy hinges on carefree romance for model-like young people and settled home life even to the point of dealing with Alzheimer's, erectile dysfunction, and inadequate health insurance.

When I was moved at the movies in the 1950s, I was stirred by the wish to imagine some onscreen female as my real companion. I had grieved to think that Montgomery Clift and Donna Reed could not be together *From Here to Eternity*. I also nursed another urge. For in the scene at the end of that film, where Reed and Deborah Kerr meet for the first time on a ship taking them back to the U.S., I saw that both those sadly single ladies deserved rescuing, and that I might do bigamous double duty—like my father?

In the momentum of social change at the start of the twenty-first century, much emphasis was put on the right of gay marriage. That was justified because it turned on how partners in a gay union should have access to the legal and social security benefits that were due to people in "real" marital partnerships. In San Francisco and elsewhere, it was the issuing of marriage licenses to same-sex couples that proved so provocative. It was also a cover for undoubted anxieties over what same-sex people did together to achieve "sex."

The partnership in *A Single Man* had lasted sixteen years, and then Jim died. We are led to believe that the two men were faithful, and I think even enlightened heterosexuals are encouraged by that, no matter that a few infidelities may have occurred in their own "stable" marriages. One feels that George needed that stability—without it, he now contemplates suicide. In fact, he meets other men and is diverted by their charm and their kindness. One of them takes steps to prevent George's suicide. So George feels better—then he dies of a heart attack. And so his bond with Jim can last into eternity. Anyone hopeful about the enduring prospects for a gay marriage could leave the theater reassured.

But this ardent and reasoned defense of gay marriage has been taking place in a society increasingly skeptical about marriage itself. There could be an interesting smart comedy in which a married couple (they might be gay or straight) engage in this campaign. They are sincere and humane in their efforts, but at the same time they have grown children who are leading active sex lives and the parents are doing their best to talk them out of an early or misguided marriage. "After all," the parents say, "do you really need to get married yet?" Isn't marriage itself archaic? My excellent copyeditor points out this happens in *Mamma Mia*—I never saw it.

More marriages last than founder, but the increase in divorce in the last hundred years is inescapable—and no longer a sore point for moralists. The age of no-fault divorce has not erased all the stigma attached to the "failure," but it is a sign of intent, and it has been accompanied by more diligence in the matters of alimony and child support. We still try to believe in the moral necessity of marriage or the consequences of it that must be honored. More people live together without benefit of marriage; some couples will die after decades of companionship without a marriage certificate in a society that is flexible over the financial consequences of marital benefits. We are more sophisticated about recognizing the complicated ways in which people are "together." We are a good deal more suspicious about the condition advocated so long in the movies—that of a lasting but unexplored marriage.

Listen to the English actor Rupert Everett talking about this situation:

> I loathe heterosexual weddings. The wedding cake, the party, the champagne. The inevitable divorce two years later. It's just a waste of time in the heterosexual world, and in the homosexual world I find it personally beyond tragic that we want to ape the institution that is so clearly a disaster.

Everett shows the same wit when he's acting. He played the character who threatened to bring life, fun, and innovation to that limp romantic comedy *My Best Friend's Wedding* (1997). That film had a glimpse of what might be if Everett and Julia Roberts's straight character got married—because they had such a happy understanding of each other, and because they likely had the ingenuity to work something out in bed. That's what we all do, and it's one of the movies we're waiting for: the ordinary cohabitation of gay and straight, as if they were black and white.

The impact of these social shifts on film have been fascinating, not least because we are uncertain about how far film prompted some of the changes. I spoke just now about the chances of making a good comedy about confusions over marriage—I was thinking of Preston Sturges, Howard Hawks, George Cukor, or Ernst Lubitsch, directors no longer available. Our dilemma is graver still: our picture business (or our art of film) does not even want to make what once were known as "love stories."

This legacy is immense; it can overwhelm what we think some films do. There is still a sentimental orthodoxy that says Spencer Tracy and Katharine Hepburn must have been lovers, because didn't they seem like that on screen? Well, no, not really. They played people drawn to each other; they were married sometimes. But their characters bickered, squabbled, disagreed, and argued—that was their identity, and no one in the 1940s dreamed of their naked bodies doing it. It's actually hard to see those two naked. That was not a shortcoming; it was a glory in their work enough to demonstrate that we have lost the habit for showing people—even married people—in the kinds of friction that prevail in most marriages and constitute the "company" they swear by.

I have stressed how movies were an educational companion in the progress by which reasonably decent people discovered they could have sex without shame or compulsory marriage—and even with pleasure, despite the hangover of guilt that was attached to it. Once those movies got to sex itself (doing it), the romance of the action seemed to falter or dissolve, before being wiped away by the tsunami of pornography or simulated sex that inundated our old dry land. So maybe simulated sex became a way of life. Or was it just that we wised up to the degree of acting or performance in our sex lives? In our lives.

People do not seem as inclined now to go to the movies for the vicarious thrill of falling in love. It is as if the availability of sex—in bed or in the head—has diminished the romantic impulse in screen enactments. In turn that raises the question: did we only ever "fall in love" as a way of getting sex? That wondering is irresistibly comic, but that does not alleviate the damage in wishful thinking and dogged perseverance that has been done in its name. Are we a species that falls in love, or are we only really interested in having sex? Do we have an immense sense of our destiny, or are we digital identifiers, easily regarded as a mass in which identity loses currency? Can "desire" cover love and sex, as once it did in our history, or is the very word now drowned in "ambition"?

That hinges on our ability to distinguish life and the lifelike, and to see how the subject matter of movies has become the process of watching or being involved with them. So, more and more, movies are giving up the drama and conviction of stories for haunted wonderings over whether anything is quite real. This is natural in a medium where hidden meanings have often been more persuasive than those found in plot synopses. Think of *Dexter* as an oblique gay romance.

Dexter played on Showtime from 2006 to 2013. It had eight seasons, ninety-six episodes, so its total "movie" played around five thousand minutes or eighty hours. I stress this length to point out that the illusion of story was cover for something far larger and less organized: a mythic situation. In this case it was that Dexter killed people. There was a vestige of moral framework so that Dexter was "disturbed" and "brilliant." His killings were intertwined with his scholarly study of such events (and concentrated on deserving victims!). His profession was that of a blood-splatter expert helping the police. It was up to the viewer to determine how far he or she was waiting for the pleasure of murders that were done for us as entertainment. Is screened murder the new sex, trembling from our desire and more inventively depicted than sexual acts?

The series was drawn from the book *Darkly Dreaming Dexter* by Jeff Lindsay, and it was created for television by James Manos Jr. Dexter was played by Michael C. Hall, a good-looking actor, with a slightly aggrieved baby face. (There could be a book on baby-faced American actors.) Dexter had a foster sister, Debra (Jennifer Carpenter), and that relationship soon erased any need for Dexter to have significant girlfriends. The semi-siblings were held together in dread and fascination. The show became a study in suppressed incest; it implied that Dexter killed out of a kind of wounded sexuality. (Careful counters report that he had "at least 135 kills" by the end of the series.)

If you were a fan of *Dexter* (and about three million people watched its closing episodes, where Dexter sees Debra die and then commits her body to deep water) then you may say this reading is fanciful and inconsistent with certain episodes. But long-form TV series are made up as the show rolls along. They are not always sure where they are going, so inconsistency can be excused sometimes. But did you simply watch the ninety episodes for the suspense or the fun of getting off on all those killings? Or was there a mythic underpinning—natural and even comic, but also tragic and pregnant—that kept you in place? We do long for meaning. Actors feel that way, too: Hall and Carpenter were married during the show, and then divorced.

Dexter is trash, if you like, while George in *A Single Man* is resolutely tony or respectable, a touch too close to "Masterpiece Homosexual" or the more pretentious imagery in fashion magazines. But consider the two storylines as attempted responses to the modern question of what it is to be gay. George wants to be accepted in society. He is a teacher who takes his work very seriously; he believes in lasting and enriching relationships. Everything about him is pledged to a progressive society.

On the other hand, Dexter is not just disturbed but misshapen by life. He is solitary, an apologetic genius and a nihilist. He is doing what he does for the sake of being unique and an outsider. He has no hope for the progress of society. He believes death is the only destination for himself or his society so he is doing his best to make it available. Put like that, wouldn't this series be desperately anguished without his fateful relationship with Debra?

It's as if Dexter had looked at film history and summed it up: I see, around the late 1960s, the medium had the liberty to go with sex or violence—and it chose violence. Can you dispute that interpretation? So Dexter lives out orgies of murder. They are his satisfaction. And ours? Thus, his metaphorical gayness is a version of antisocial contempt and defiance. Incidentally, this permits an outlawry in describing a gay character that would not be permitted in our "correct" age.

Dexter is more resonant for me than George, the cowboys in *Brokeback Mountain,* or the victims in *Angels in America.* He lives in underground culture, like a Rock Hudson, so mortified by the lies he had to tell that he becomes an avenging and tarnished angel. These suppositions rest on this understanding of history: to be gay was to be opposed by your society, to be victimized and punished, to be deprived of rights and a chance at happiness. You were in a resistance movement or an outlaw. It remains to be seen if gay life can keep its integrity once the romance of resistance fades away.

Very broadly, this condition has lasted from Oscar Wilde to Caitlyn Jenner. Its courage often engendered witty defiance or a kind of carefree disdain. That's memorable in Wilde, some musicals by Stephen Sondheim, the splashy gaiety of David Hockney's L.A.-era artwork, and the essays of Gore Vidal. It's a tone that makes one wonder if Nabokov considered being gay but was too much of a snob to come out.

This also prompted wars in the courts of California and heroism in the scourge of AIDS. Those ordeals made many people brave enough to realize they were gay or to join the battle against hostility. So be ready for the chance that once the fight for gayness has been won, the brave identity of the condition may waver or recede. This will take time, and we may not have time. But surely some fruitful androgyny lies in our future, or a way in which different gender choices become just choices—like doing Hamlet with a mustache or a limp or playing him in a frock.

Are you still worrying that this book should stick to movies? Don't you see how movies, like mud, stick to everything? The compartmentalization of criticism and memoir is an error that allows us to dwell on technique or style while overlooking the meanings of films. Movies served as a prolonged dream, a transforming sleep, in which we nursed our longing and awoke to discover that we could be pleased with sex as it had been unfolded in a medium that tended toward a camp veneer on conventional romantic situations. The medium was altering us—and that drove Dan Whites everywhere so mad that they picked up their guns.

The guns are ready. Some have a mind and a certainty fit to use them. And all we have to oppose them is the realization that we need to think and feel and set aside the fools' safety net—that it will be enough to be manly or great.

Or yourself—that persona to which we are supposed to be "true," no matter the charm in suggestions that we are all acting and up for every role.

Dogged movie stories meant to move us may be gone forever—like Actors Studio sincerity in acting. Isn't it stupid to insist on single-mindedness in acting? Aren't we headed toward a numb climate of values in which humanism itself seems redundant? That's where Astaire comes into consideration as one of the first great asexual models in film. Buster Keaton was another: he seemed to be willing himself into a vacancy beyond ordinary human feelings because he felt he was hopeless at them.

I am not calling those men homosexuals: but I'm convinced that their meaning was, if not gay, then a step toward neutrality or the notion that being seen is the sexy thing in movies. So gay can refer to a style—just like feminine or masculine or childish. Some of the most interesting movie characters these days are such android or androgynous figures. It's as if in imagination, without admitting it, we foresee a culture in which personalities (and genders) will be interchangeable and something other than human. Artificial intelligence looms, but hasn't intelligence always been a mere construct, hopeful yet disappointing?

You can feel this in the monster and his bride, Karloff and Lanchester. More recently, we have had robots or replicants, in-betweeners, shining fakes (call them movie people). You can list Richard Gere's Julian Kaye; Sean Young's Rachael in *Blade Runner,* a film where nearly all the characters may be escaped mistakes; Ash (Ian Holm) in *Alien* and Bishop (Lance Henriksen) in *Aliens* and *Alien 3;* Alicia Vikander in *Ex Machina* (a skeletal form putting on a pretty face); the voice of Scarlett Johannson in *Her;* the becalmed Michael Fassbender, whether he's playing a robot or not. And why not Tilda Swinton, not just in acting jobs but in her gallery of arresting faces? Tilda was raised in the movie business as Girl Friday, cook, and bottle washer as well as iconic screen presence in the world of gay hero filmmaker Derek Jarman.

And then think of Kristen Stewart in *Personal Shopper,* a fashionista's factotum, drop-dead lovely (for she is not quite alive), leaning toward spiritualism and summoning up phantom elegance, and for a moment revealing her poignant breasts in a "medical examination" (movies really are too sly-cute to be respected), impassive and luminous, capable of anything and convinced about nothing. She had silent contempt for the film's story. She knew it was a séance with her presence, movement, and incident as the elements shining on the wall.

Sleeping with strangers? That's a fair description of the age of movie. Aren't we all strangers, finally, and isn't "sleeping" an expansive euphemism that begins to explore film's affinity with dreaming? So we gradually gave up the historic wish to gain an afterlife for the chance of getting a bit of fun here and now. And it was part of the ethos that the fun could be spread around to more or less everyone. Even poor and wretched people could get it.

I once saw a frail man, a wreck, masturbating furiously in a cancer ward, determined to come in his own last time and place before the chance was gone. He stared at me, watching him, and dared disapproval.

Not everyone was going to get happy, and it required a mass delusion to persuade everyone that the pursuit of happiness was a reasonable goal. Cinema was crucial in this con. As well as being an entertainment, an art, and a business it was an endless commercial for the pursuit, as great a plea for irrational trust as all our religious schemes had ever been. I think it worked, but I believe the trick is ending.

It's hardly enough to speak of it as a trick, for the effects were widespread and warping. That realization lay behind the fall of 2017 in which accusations began to be leveled at the predatoriness of men in the picture business. That anger was invariably justified: men had behaved badly in a licensed atmosphere. Exploitation was an engine in cinema. The owners and the practitioners of what we call the Golden Age behaved badly without thinking about it. If you want to come up to date, in the repudiation of Harvey Weinstein, Kevin Spacey, and Louis C.K., just wonder what you are going to do with Ingmar Bergman.

A lot of us regard Bergman as one of the great artists in the history of film. He died only in 2007. If you don't know all of his work, take a weekend and sample *Wild Strawberries, Persona, Cries and Whispers, Fanny and Alexander,* and even *Faithless* (a film by Liv Ullmann, one of his lovers, but written by Bergman). There's no need to go into detail, but Ingmar behaved appallingly with wives and children—he had five wives and at least nine children in addition to affairs with many of his stars. He took sexual advantage of actresses who longed to be in his films, because they believed he was so good. To read his autobiography, *The Magic Lantern,* is to meet a creep, a user, and a cold-blooded, self-pitying predator. He was awful, but fascinating. So will we ban his films now because of that?

I hope not, but I don't want a sophisticated finessing of the Bergman problem, like a tidy separation of his work from his life such as we often make with Picasso, Chaplin, or Wagner. The riddle is more complicated: the eye for women, the sexual curiosity, and the stress on desire in Bergman's films are inseparable from his biographical disorder. He gazed at women with conspiratorial longing, and some of those women featured in his private life as much as in his films. You can say that Bergman worshipped women in abstract, but so much of his best work puts them under cruel stress and keeps watching. He was as chronic a voyeur as Hitchcock. In *Persona,* the Liv Ullmann character sits back in silence, contemplating the Bibi Andersson character, in just the way we are allowed to watch both of them. The overlapping urges to adoration and predation remind me of Molly Haskell's pioneering book *From Reverence to Rape,* first published in 1974. Sometimes that is hailed as a feminist classic, but that label is belittling. Her book is about all of us—like Bergman's films.

Bergman behaved very badly; if he was working in our 2018, I suspect he would be closed down. He was at fault, but maybe cinema and even desire itself deserve some blame. In all the accusations leveled at men in the picture business there has been a sense of women deserving more power. Of course, occasionally that has worked: it reaches from June Mathis and Katharine Hepburn to Jane Campion and Isabelle Huppert. That includes *Four Horsemen of the Apocalypse, Adam's Rib, In the Cut,* and *The Piano Teacher.* But I'm not sure if that new outlook is compatible with voyeuristic desire.

The medium's arrow sharpness has been an expression of male arrogance and desire. That energy now seems deplorable enough to urge a civilized society to stop it. But the business is an actual profession, filled with creative and ambitious people. Sheila Nevins is one of its best success stories. Born in 1939, she became director of HBO Documentary Films in 1979. As such, she made and produced hundreds of award-winning documentaries and altered the place of that genre in American life. She won a Lifetime Achievement Emmy on top of her thirty-three personal Emmys. She was sometimes groped, and much more, by men in the course of her career. But, as she told Maureen Dowd, "I had no one to go to, and I didn't suffer. I just allowed it. Now I feel a little bit guilty for allowing it, but I have to say it's like a wound that healed, or a wound that never was. I'm not sure that I knew there was any other way. I had to have a job. I didn't have any money."

Nevins will be a marker in history as well as an essential figure in documentary and its attempt to dispel the overcast of fictional cinema. Still, she understands a culture of acceptance and emerging resistance.

But is it possible to reform fictional movie (everything from feature films to television commercials) or must its whole overcast be ended? Male desire on screen has given us masterpieces and a lot of fun, but it established a plan for male supremacy and female subordination that has brought us closer to the loss of liberalism. The special role of gay cinema has been its attempt to enlarge the possibilities of human experience and to encourage diversity. I'm not sure our existence can continue if male supremacy remains so domineering.

Still, I wonder, is cinema an inescapable expression of male desire and the aggressive ambition in seeing? Is that innate or is it something culturally acquired and capable of being reformed? I don't know the answer, but I think the doubt is observable in small moments of ordinary intimacy. So often, the male feels bound to take the initiating steps in sexual encounters, unbuttoning a shirt or turning out the light. Is that true desire or habit? And why does that male feel hesitant or inhibited? Is it fear of rejection, lack of confidence, or some sense that if sex is just a game why should he have to serve first?

Could desire be replaced by something less compulsive for an increasingly android, rationalized, and directed humanity? Think of it as a digital affinity. It's easy to be horrified by that prospect, as much as you know *you* would never have allowed slavery, the losses of the Great War, or delay in getting votes for women. But those "errors" lasted so long, and that teaches us to wonder what in the future will be seen as the unforgivable sources of damage today. Could it be the unheeded growth in loneliness despite the accumulation of social media and technologies that insist we are all together and in touch?

There are deeper possibilities that have to do with the overlap of technology and mythology. A lot of us noted in the revelations of 2017 how often the misbehaving men turned to masturbation in front of women. That sounded ugly, stupid, and inexcusable. But people do many things that bad, and often they have meanings worth exploring.

Despite every hope that movie sexuality was helping us to lead fuller, more pleasurable, sexy lives, there were warning signs. The managers of cinemas knew that some lone men would masturbate in their seats as they watched acts of seduction on screen. How horrible? Perhaps, but every survey of sexual habits has reported that masturbation is an ordinary and regular practice, even if it concentrates at either end of our lives when solitude is more prevalent. This is fact, no matter that he-man swagger says it is creepy and could make you go blind or have your hand fall off.

In 1948, Alfred Kinsey astonished the world, and himself, with reports that 92 percent of men masturbated, while 62 percent of women had done it at least once. The doctor was a pioneer, devoted to science, and a bisexual. His book *Sexual Behavior in the Human Male* was published by a medical textbook company with a printing of 5,000 copies, but it ended up selling 250,000 copies. There is a humane and compelling biopic, *Kinsey,* by Bill Condon, with Liam Neeson as the doctor, that used brief frontal male nudity, and there was a TV series, *Masters of Sex* (2013–16), with Michael Sheen as William Masters and Lizzy Caplan as his collaborator, Virginia Johnson, who seemed to be naked a good deal of the time, as if thorough sociology had had to make some concessions to Showtime and four seasons' life.

With the work of Kinsey, something rigid in American shame started to relax, but no one pointed out that just being at a movie and watching was a form of masturbation. You were taking in the bright fantasy to make your dream life more potent. You believed no one else knew. You were in control of your outburst. Two years after Kinsey, with Hedy Lamarr and Victor Mature in *Samson and Delilah,* it was clear that the Bible had inspiring stories in conflict with its moral lessons. A boy of ten could see that Delilah was wicked—still he wanted her, and became fearful of having a haircut when he had too little sense yet of what metaphor was.

That man in the cancer ward was one of the enduring brief encounters of my life. I wonder what he was thinking, and about the desperate contract he was making for a few moments. We are all going to be close to that man, or that woman, and I assert my loyalty to the vitality of his last spurt and the ability in movies to make us feel that life force. More than just natural behavior, masturbation may be a sign that people feel more alone or separate and more inclined to see that companions in love are strangers. Already, dismay is being voiced about the ways our technologies are usurping actual human touch or physical contact. Do we want our machines to do the touching? Is it science fiction to foresee an app that lets people "come" through their electronics with imaginary figures they don't know and will never meet? Or is that construct close to the way movies have always been? Science is fiction one day and habit the next.

George Balanchine was known as a seducer of ballerinas and a maker of dance. Maybe he had sex with his dancers (he married four of them and had relations with several others), but the true goal of the seduction was the creation of ballets in which anyone from Danilova to Suzanne Farrell embodied his vision. He held creative and career power over women who were begging for a sublime role more satisfying than nights in bed. Balanchine believed ecstasy was only reliable on stage, where it was transient.

Suppose the womanizer was intrinsically gay: he did not have enough faith in real life and was more drawn to the created life of bodies in the limelight and the music. That reminds me of Day-Lewis's Reynolds Woodcock in *Phantom Thread,* who wants to believe in women as clotheshorses. The memoir of Balanchine's wife no. 2, the dancer Vera Zorina, exults in his affection, his teaching, his obsession with dance discipline, and his cuisine. It's clear from the book what a lively friendship they had. They remained close after divorce and all through his later marriages and teamings. Zorina makes him sound like a lovely guy.

But did his appetite for primas mask an inner distancing? So many womanizers in the movie world only think they adore women, that "special" breed. So all those Mrs. Balanchines (without a single child) may have been a way of masking Mr. B's notion that sex in life was a pale version of dance. Passion's reputation is still pledged to sincerity, true love, and happy endings, but movie believes in worlds and lives that are open to pretending, the uncertainty of strangers, and our crossed fingers in sleep itself.

The movie screen is a window . . . and now there are screens like confetti. Are we still trying to get through these windows or will we ever learn that they are a trick and a diversion to confuse a more testing task—to see life and the ordinary?

Fantasy is our new religion, and it has been fun at the movies. A life of fun. But what has the fun done to life?

Acknowledgments

Kristen Stewart in *Personal Shopper* (2017)—the discreet charm
of a person and her clothes

OVER THE YEARS, I have talked to many people within the broad community of filmmaking. Those meetings covered many things, but some of those matters were enormously helpful in writing this book. So I am deeply grateful to the late Steven Bach, Michael Barker, Warren Beatty, Robert Benton, Dirk Bogarde, John Boorman, Ken Burns, Simon Callow, Alan Carr, Bill Condon, Fielder Cook, Francis Coppola, Mart Crowley, Michael Fitzgerald, James Fox, Stephen Frears, Cary Grant, Laura Harding, David Hare, Tippi Hedren, Katharine Hepburn, Patricia Highsmith, John Houseman, Anjelica Huston, Pauline Kael, Philip Kaufman, Elia Kazan, Klaus Kinski, Slim Keith, Gavin Lambert, Janet Leigh, Joseph Losey, Norman Mailer, Joseph L. Mankiewicz, Douglas McGrath, David McLeod, Daniel Melnick, Anthony Minghella, Ivan Moffat, Walter Murch, Jack Nicholson, Rudolph Nureyev, Arthur Penn, Sarah Polley, Michael Powell, Bob Rafelson, Nicholas Ray, Susan Ray, Ferdinando Scarfiotti, Paul Schrader, Martin Scorsese, Daniel Selznick, Irene Selznick, Jeffrey Selznick, Harry Dean Stanton, Tilda Swinton, Elizabeth Taylor, Robert Towne, Harry Ufland, Gore Vidal, Tuesday Weld, Billy Wilder, Debra Winger, Loretta Young, and Saul Zaentz.

Also in that category, but more important, are years of talk with Kieran Hickey and James Toback. My thanks to them are spelled out more fully—but inadequately—in the book.

That leads in to a list of friends, some of them enjoyed for decades, and some of the best conversationalists about the movies, romantic behavior, and so many other matters: Lili Anolik, Eleanor Bertino, Patricia Bosworth, Geoff Dyer, Elizabeth Farnsworth, Jean-Pierre Gorin, Sam Hamm, Molly Haskell (whose *From Reverence to Rape* is like a things-your-godmother-taught-you for this book), Dan Heaton, Mark Kidel, Philip Lopate, Patrick McGilligan, Julia McNeal, Chris Meledandri, Geoff Pevere, Antonia Quirke, Maurice Rapf, George Trescher, Jenny Turner, and Bernie Vyzga.

Then there are friends who amount to co-conspirators: Richard and Mary Corliss (always a pair), Mark Feeney, Greil Marcus, Doug "Rib"

McGuire, Laura Morris, Michael Ondaatje, Gary Rosen (always an Athenian), and Holly Goldberg Sloan (my Santa Monica).

A few people have been not just friends but patrons: Will Hearst; Tom Luddy (the third man to so many of us); the extraordinary David Packard; and a great editor and friend, Leon Wieseltier.

Steve Wasserman had the first idea for this book and was a constant source of encouragement and tempered incredulity.

At Knopf, for so long, I have enjoyed the friendship of Sonny Mehta (and Gita), Bob Gottlieb, Shelley Wanger, Kathy Hourigan, Kathy Zuckerman, and Carol Carson. But Jon Segal was both Bonaparte and citizen on this book (he has French connections). We have worked together a lot over the years, but he has never been a shrewder reader, a more inspired clarifier of what I wanted to say, and a more patient onlooker as I was lost over what to say. He is there on every page of this book, like a watermark. As is Kevin Bourke, my copyeditor, surgeon, and seer, and a brilliant companion on the text. Sam Aber was diligent, enthusiastic, and as quick as Tom Hagen.

Of course, the real inner circle is family—and this is a book about sex which can affect family life—so I am nowhere without Anne, Kate, Mathew, Rachel, Lucy Gray, Nicholas, and Zachary—plus Sean, Michelle, Steve, Grace, Joe, and Isaac. Above all, Lucy Gray, the stranger in my life.

Index

Page numbers in *italics* refer to illustrations.

A NOTE ABOUT THE AUTHOR

David Thomson was born in London in 1941 and educated at Dulwich College and the London School of Film Technique. He worked in publishing, at Penguin; he directed the film studies program at Dartmouth College; he did the series *Life at 24 Frames per Second* for BBC Radio; he scripted the film *The Making of a Legend: Gone With the Wind;* and he was on the selection committee for the New York Film Festival. He has written many books, including the pioneering novels *Suspects* and *Silver Light,* the biography *Showman: The Life of David O. Selznick,* and the *Biographical Dictionary of Film,* now in its sixth edition. He has been called the best or the most imaginative or reckless writer on film in English, but he presses on. His residence is in San Francisco, but he lives in his head.

A NOTE ON THE TYPE

This book was set in Adobe Garamond. Designed for the Adobe Corporation by Robert Slimbach, the fonts are based on types first cut by Claude Garamond (c. 1480–1561). Garamond was a pupil of Geoffroy Tory and is believed to have followed the Venetian models, although he introduced a number of important differences, and it is to him that we owe the letter we now know as "old style." He gave to his letters a certain elegance and feeling of movement that won their creator an immediate reputation and the patronage of Francis I of France.

Composed by North Market Street Graphics, Lancaster, Pennsylvania

Printed and bound by Berryville Graphics, Berryville, Virginia

Designed by Maggie Hinders